Praise for Working GlobeSmart

"Whether you are participating in a geo-dispersed team or leading a multinational organization, *Working GlobeSmart* provides pertinent information, tools, and techniques for successfully navigating new cultures and building global leadership skills."

—Sharon Richards, international trainer;
past president of Employee Relocation
Council and ERC International Committee

"There are many reasons to recommend *Working GlobeSmart:* you will like the content, the research methodology, the organization, the writing style, and the emphasis on practical application of intercultural competence. It is not often that such a serious and complex topic is made so interesting."

—Dave Potter, senior managing partner, The Global Guys;
former director, global account management,
Xerox Corporation

"As business relationships between customers and suppliers become increasingly global, the need for a culturally proficient work force has become urgent. This timely book teaches ways to achieve a fit in communication style, strategy, and organizational processes in order to work successfully together with global business counterparts."

—Lisa Napolitano, president & CEO,
Strategic Account Management Association

"Every chapter of this book verified my personal experience in building a worldwide intercultural management training business with offices in Asia, Australia, and Europe. I wish I had read it before we launched our international offices."

—Rita Bennett, managing director (retired),
Cendant Intercultural, The Bennett Group;
past president, Society for Human Resource
Management Global Forum

working GlobeSmart

working GlobeSmart

12

People Skills for Doing Business Across Borders

Ernest Gundling

NICHOLAS BREALEY PUBLISHING

BOSTON • LONDON

Paperback edition first published by Nicholas Brealey Publishing in 2010. Original hardcover edition first published by Davies-Black in 2003.

20 Park Plaza, Suite 610
Boston, MA 02116, USA
Tel: 617-523-3801
Fax: 617-523-3708

3-5 Spafield Street, Clerkenwell
London, EC1R, 4QB, UK
Tel: +44-(0)-207-239-0360
Fax: +44-(0)-207-239-0370

www.nicholasbrealey.com

Special discounts on bulk quantities of Nicholas Brealey books are available to corporations, professional associations, and other organizations. For details, contact us at 888-273-2539.

ISBN: 978-1-904838-25-8

Printed in the United States of America.
17 16 15 14 13 4 5 6 7 8

The Library of Congress has previously cataloged this edition as follows:
Gundling, Ernest
Working GlobeSmart : 12 people skills for doing business across borders / Ernest Gundling.
p. cm.
Includes bibliographical references and index.
ISBN 978-0-89106-177-9
1. Business communication—Cross-cultural studies. 2. International trade—Cross-cultural studies. 3. Businesspeople—Foreign language competency. 4. International business enterprises—Management—Cross-cultural studies. I. Title.

HF5718.G86 2003
658.4—dc21

2003046066

FIRST EDITION
First printing 2003

To Laurie, Chris, and Katherine.
Thanks for making the journey together.

Contents

Preface

The single greatest cause of difficulties in global business transactions is not a lack of technical expertise, hard work, or good intentions—it is a lack of "people skills" for relating successfully with counterparts from other countries and cultures. The number of people involved with global business has increased dramatically over the past decade, and now, with the advent of virtual teams, global people skills have become a daily necessity in many professions. There is a strong need for practical, skills-based advice that is neither overly academic nor overly technical; this book is intended to provide such advice.

Cross-border friction is generally shaped by underlying cultural differences, and the areas where it tends to emerge are relatively consistent and predictable. This book is structured around twelve critical people skills that often make the difference between success or failure in doing business across borders. Familiarity with these skills will help readers not only to accomplish business goals, but also to grow both professionally and personally. Each chapter is designed to

- Demonstrate one or more of the major stumbling blocks encountered by businesspeople who interact regularly with foreign counterparts
- Provide clear and practical recommendations for overcoming these problems through the application of knowledge and skills that enable us to get things done across cultural boundaries
- Illustrate this framework through examples and cases that make it concrete and readily applicable to new situations

Some of the best-known books about global business are based on interviews with current corporate leaders and attempt to identify characteristics that lead to success on the world stage.[1] Other works draw on survey data from corporate employees representing different nationalities, comparing their perspectives on various dimensions of thought and action.[2] The least-useful volumes provide laundry lists of do's and don'ts for country after country. It may be satisfying to memorize the list for a particular destination, but we quickly realize after arriving in the country that such a list only goes so far—there are many things that are not on the list at all or which even contradict it. Without a deeper understanding of the country and its culture, the list itself is likely to turn into an obstacle, encouraging a false sense of confidence and the illusion of knowing more than we actually do.

This book takes a different approach from any of those just described. It is based on the input of a group of more than two-dozen country and regional experts who were sought out for their experience in assisting global managers and for their collective knowledge of key business destinations on every major continent. Between them, these experts have worked with more than thirty thousand businesspeople doing business in multicultural environments. During the course of our interviews with each expert, we explored a pair of practical questions: "How do foreign businesspeople tend to go wrong in this location?" and, "What do they need to do to be successful?" We also asked them for specific "people skills" examples for their country of expertise. The answers they gave are a primary source of this volume's contents.

Utilizing the views of people who have "been there" and have long-standing ties to a different place offers a special advantage. These people can provide insights into cultural patterns that take us beyond the static and oddly truncated world of do's and don'ts. They have gone through the pain, embarrassment, and uncertainty of the adjustment phase that ultimately leads to real knowledge and competence. They have learned how to function effectively and how to "come back"—to straddle both worlds as a guide to others.

No better tool set exists for approaching an unfamiliar location than keen eyes, open ears, a flexible mind, and a willing heart. As we step into a new culture, learning ideally takes place through a gradual process of observation, imitation, comparison with one's own culture, and finally choosing to do things our way, their way, or through some new hybrid solution that we create together. In a business environment that demands ever-greater speed and effectiveness, accelerating this learning process without rendering it superficial is essential. Perhaps the wisest shortcut is to climb on the shoulders of an experienced "cultural guide" who can help us to learn rapidly—offering perceptions honed over many years—even as we still earn the benefits of our own hard-won experience.

Previous books have helped to put the intercultural and international management fields on the map, to provide a credible research foundation, and to demonstrate the relevance of this type of thinking to global businesspeople. Much of the writing done in the intercultural field, however, is still perceived as "soft and fuzzy" by business audiences. Many intercultural works are, in fact, written by academic authors with limited practical business experience—they often gravitate toward general cultural principles and communication skills without addressing the kinds of issues that are of greatest interest to contemporary leaders and managers: global teamwork, customer relations, change management, strategy, and innovation.

This book aims to achieve a new level of pragmatic value for the global businessperson. It focuses specifically on "how-to" skill areas that are at once practical, of broad cross-cultural interest, and of sufficient depth to be applicable in complex and changing business environments. Three different skill levels—interpersonal, group, and organizational—are addressed using a model that demonstrates the natural links that exist between communication and change, culture and commerce. Because the intended audience is Western readers and particularly businesspeople from the U.S., the cases and examples in the book emphasize situations that they are likely to encounter. However, non-Western perspectives are included; the text highlights the views of counterparts from other countries to encourage readers to take these into consideration as well.

Ultimately, this is a book about global leadership. The essence of leadership is often described as the creation of good vision and strategy and their dissemination throughout the organization, culminating in successful implementation. But, it is essential to bring these things to life in a global context, creating a corporate culture of engagement with customers and employees from around the world. By *engagement* we mean an ongoing, profound, multidirectional conversation with every part of the global organization. In this sense, intercultural skills and strategy go together. Developing good strategy without the intercultural skills that enable us to engage others is almost impossible. At the same time, intercultural skills are only meaningful if they are deployed for a strategic purpose.

Acknowledgments

It is a privilege to have been touched by many wonderful teachers, some living and some already gone. My thanks to Pat Mantle, who had the rare wisdom to let a curious young person read about things in class other than the subject she was teaching. Robert McGinn, Lee Yearly, and Al Hastorf helped an eager but raw young mind to find direction and grow. Frank Reynolds gave freely to a generation of students his wise guidance, hearty laugh, and warm faith in their work.

Hideo Tanaka took a kind interest in my research in its early stages and gave me a window of understanding into the practices of his organization. Priscilla Storandt provided crucial introductions and deep insight into a world I knew little about. Mika and Kazuo Tagawa have made ties of goodwill last across generations and showed me Japan through their eyes.

Jack May introduced me to the business of assisting companies to work more successfully across borders and taught me how to tie a necktie properly after too many years in graduate school. Clifford Clarke offered the first chance to work with a set of pioneering global enterprises, a glimpse of how to connect with a client's own dreams for the future, and the freedom to generate new ideas—he taught me a number of worthwhile lessons. Laurie Mack, Brett Fenwick, Dave Dickey, Bob Wright, John Gillespie, Noriko Ogami, Kay Jones, Tony Pan, Chris Jay, Hiroshi Kagawa, Pamela Leri, Lynn Witham, Mitch Hammer, Yoichi Shimakawa, and others from those days were, and continue to be, valued colleagues and advisors.

George Renwick has been astonishingly generous with us at Aperian Global over the past ten years, appearing in several of our video series and providing many hours of welcome advice and input on this volume. Ted Dale, a friend and business partner for more than a decade, has contributed his thoughts, energy, and never-say-die attitude. He read the initial draft and had the good sense to suggest numerous cuts. Some of the most concise and reader-friendly portions of the text are his. Lisa Spivey has been an enthusiastic supporter and astute strategic voice through many moments of self-doubt.

Another colleague, Charlie Bergman, has been my mentor in learning about China and was the primary author of the chapter on negotiating with Chinese. Julia Sloan's work with the U.N. has taken her to parts of the world I have never seen and has been another source of extremely valuable input. Jim Latimer provided an eye-opening introduction to the *maquiladora* world and contributed to those segments of the text. Yukiko Kuroda has helped me to believe that cross-border partnerships can actually be successful. Molly Lewis provided timely and welcome assistance during the editing process.

Clients have been great teachers as well, bringing with them a refreshing sense of what is important and what is not. My heartfelt appreciation goes to Stan Durda, David Wilson, Margaret Alldredge, Kay Grenz, Masayuki Ichikawa, Tak Kaneko, Ron Baukol, David Adams, Lou Golm, Michiko Achilles, Jim Adams, John Solberg, Hector Rualo, Yayoi Masuda, Bob Gargani, Mercy Corrales, Kathleen Torres, Tom Grant, Judy Lessin, Lawrence Yeh, Bill Buckley, Miho Ebata, Sharon Richards, Mary Eckenrod, Tracy Ann Curtis, Wendy Wisniewski, John Weaver, Eric Lindner, Karen Nee, Jim Mackin, Kozo Ohashi, Kenji Wada, and many others not mentioned here for the opportunities to work with them over the years.

The overall framework of the book and a number of the Asian examples were created on the basis of my own work as a business consultant and the experience of other colleagues at Aperian Global. Its contents also incorporate materials from a course called Global Management Skills that I have taught for the past eight years at the Haas School of Business at the University of California, Berkeley. I am grateful for the challenging questions and enthusiasm of Haas School students from over fifteen different countries, plus the different ethnic groups, cultural perspectives, and mixed heritages that they represent. These students have pushed me to think about the prospects for a new generation of global citizens. Thanks to Ramesh Dewangen in particular for his insights on the relationship between U.S. and Indian software engineers.

Lastly, the bulk of the practical examples and observations in the pages to follow are drawn from research conducted in the creation of GlobeSmart (www.globesmart.com), Aperian Global's online reference tool, which is currently in use at numerous Fortune 500 companies. A wide variety of country and regional experts, writers, editors, advisors, and technical assistants have contributed to GlobeSmart. I would like to extend my deep appreciation to each of them, as well as to everyone else mentioned above, while taking full responsibility for any errors or omissions.

GlobeSmart contributors include Irene Anderson, Judith Ashley, Glen Bautistas, Cathy Benton, Vincent Bianco, Betty Chung, Sylvia Cowan, Tony Cox, Miguel Daud, Rick Elinski, Daniel Farias, Luis Fernando, David Forkey, Kitty Fung, Eric Girard, Luis Guisasola, David Hahn, Heather Hinrichs, Kay Jones, Jong-Min, Joo-Yon, Stephania Wong Kaneda, Christine Knudsen, Vivian Kroner, Ajit Kumar, Sandra Lehman, Pamela Leri, Tracy Lewellen, David Lin, Gladys Liu, Winifred Loh, Laurie Mack, Keith Maher, Kate Mailfert, Igor Malanchuk, Rossana Miranda-Johnston, Amra Montri , Katie Muldoon, Misa Ono, Krittika Onsanit, Tony Pan, Sue Petty, Lisa Pollman, Jaime Quiros, Linda Rebenstorf, Sunit Rikhib, Susan Rinderle, Enrique Rueda, Luis Sanchez, Richard Sanderson, Ruth Sasaki, Kris Schorno, Suresh Seshadri, Geraldine Shearan, Jeremy Solomons, Lisa Spivey, Rick Tette, Hitomi Togashi, Roberto Vega, Pat and Scott Watkins, Maria Wayne, Dennis Whitney, Bob Wright, Christine Wu, Anita Zanchettin, and William Zhuang.

About the Author

Ernest Gundling, Ph.D., is a founder and co-president of Aperian Global. He currently serves on the board of directors and heads the company's Global Leadership Practice Group. His job is to assist clients in developing strategic approaches to leadership development, innovation, and change management in a cross-border context as well as relationships with key global business partners. He often works with multicultural management teams to help them formulate business plans based on strong mutual understanding and a joint commitment to execution.

Gundling received his doctorate from the University of Chicago. He wrote his dissertation on Japanese management training programs; his field research was funded by a U.S. Department of Education Fulbright Fellowship. He received a master's degree from the University of Chicago and a bachelor's degree from Stanford University.

Gundling has been involved with Japanese language, culture, and business for over twenty years, including six years' residence in Japan. He has worked and traveled extensively elsewhere in Asia, and lived for extended periods in Germany and Mexico. Gundling has also been a lecturer at the Haas School of Business at the University of California, Berkeley, for more than ten years, where he currently teaches a course called Global Management Skills. He formerly worked as director of consulting and organization development at Clarke Consulting Group.

A partial list of clients Gundling has served includes ACCO, AT&T, Canon Information Systems, Chevron, Cisco Systems, Deutsche Bank, Ford Motor Company, Fujitsu, Hewlett-Packard, Honda, Intel, Intuit, KAIST (Korea Advanced Institute of Science and Technology), KLA-Tencor, Kodak, Levi Strauss, Lucent Technologies, Mazda, Morgan Stanley, Mitsui Bussan, Motorola, Procter & Gamble, Qualcomm, Saudi Aramco, Texas Instruments, and 3M. He is also a member of the organization development panel of the Society for Human Resource Management (SHRM).

Gundling is the author of numerous publications, including two other books: *The 3M Way to Innovation: Balancing People and Profits* and *Global Diversity: Winning Customers and Engaging Employees Within World Markets.* He has been a contributor to Aperian Global's pioneering Web tools, *GlobeSmart* and *Global Teams Online.*

The Global People Skills Model

If you observe the obstacles that global businesspeople encounter in their work, after a while clear patterns begin to emerge. Not unlike mythical heroes setting out on a journey, almost all those who cross a national or cultural boundary face a common set of hazards.

The hazards outlined here represent not only a source of hardship, but also the doorway to success for aspiring global leaders. Those who learn to overcome them and acquire new skills will find that subsequent projects go more smoothly—the challenges involved in adjusting to each particular foreign setting are related to the ones encountered in the next. Every destination presents fresh issues and the opportunity to make serious blunders, but deep knowledge of the most common skills required to work effectively across borders becomes a valuable resource for future journeys. Why make the most predictable and costly mistakes when you can learn from others' experience before setting out on your own?

Figure 1. **Global People Skills**

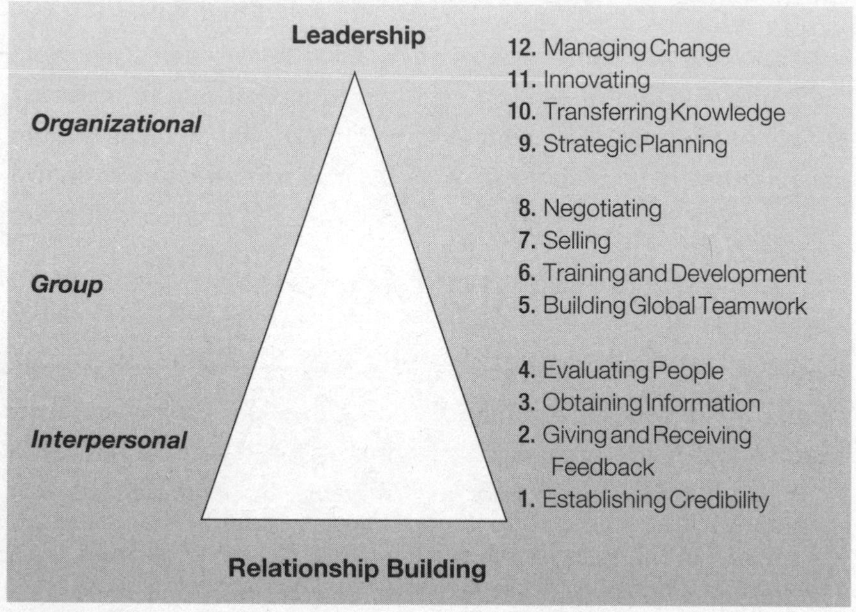

The Model: An Introduction

The twelve skills, or competencies,[1] that form the basis for this book are divided into three levels—interpersonal, group, and organizational—as shown in figure 1. Each skill area has been selected because it emerges repeatedly as a cross-border flash point. The terms are familiar enough that more precise definitions are unnecessary here. Business issues associated with each skill are taken up one by one in subsequent chapters and explored in detail.

This framework of twelve skills on three levels is not exhaustive. There are other worthwhile skill areas such as conflict resolution or motivating employees that deserve attention elsewhere. Nor are people skills everything. Those who are involved in global business transactions need to work from a broader model that takes into account issues such as political climate, trade laws, labor relations, physical and social infrastructure, and the presence of local suppliers or competitors. Nevertheless, by embracing these skills early and often in their global careers, managers and executives can avoid rivers of frustration and wasted effort while realizing important business opportunities that would otherwise be missed.

People Skills and Global Leadership

Global leadership can be defined in numerous ways. A frequently underestimated part of the global leadership craft is full mastery of the people skills addressed in this book. This includes the ability to disseminate all twelve skills throughout an organization. Beyond the capabilities of any particular individual, creating an institutional culture that sponsors and cultivates people skills on a broad scale is essential.

Each level of people skills builds on the prior one. Proficiency at the level of interpersonal skills enables one to function better in diverse groups; interpersonal and group skills are essential building blocks for success at the organizational level. Some of the most spectacular failures of global leaders can be traced to organizational change efforts that never took hold among working groups or in everyday interactions between individual employees. Success, on the other hand, is achieved through sustained, effective efforts at every skill level.

Global People Skills: The Business Case

People skills are a particularly challenging element of global business because behaviors and assumptions that have been functional in a domestic context can be dysfunctional elsewhere. Of course, people skills are important in domestic business contexts as well. Leading companies are paying increasing attention, for example, to the link between high-involvement management practices and profitability.[2] Yet, competent, mature professionals with a track record of success in familiar business settings regularly encounter difficulties when they apply the practices they have learned to a new environment without modification.

Indeed, given the growing diversity and need for virtual teamwork in the domestic workplace, previously accepted methods of getting things done at the home office are becoming more problematic as well. People skills for global business may be equally helpful in a meeting with a guest from another country, a videoconference with a diverse group of co-workers, or a conversation across the hall with a foreign software engineer.

By addressing the topic of global people skills in a comprehensive way, both organizations and individuals can build a significant source of sustained competitive advantage. It is important to offer distinctive, high-quality products or services that customers are ready to buy. At the same time, providing real value to those customers over time also requires an organization with the people skills to match the products. This dual strategy—which makes products and people skills two wheels of the same vehicle—needs to be more than an accident or an afterthought when an organization is operating in multiple regions and time zones.

The best way to begin to gauge the magnitude of the risk as well as the potential benefits associated with the people skills factor is to consider some examples, such as the three cases that follow.

The Whirlwind Tour

A U.S. executive, newly appointed as the head of International for his company, made his first trip to the European region. He carefully analyzed the state of the company's operations in each subsidiary location, listening to presentations and recommendations by the country management teams. He then instructed the top leadership of each subsidiary on strategic positioning of the company's products in local markets and on next steps to address key issues and generate more revenue.

After a rugged two-week trip to six countries, the Western executive returned home tired but satisfied. Based on his own extensive experience and strategic savvy, he was confident that the business was on the right track. Other pressing matters at headquarters and with different regions quickly began to demand his attention, although he continued to track the progress of initiatives in the European countries through periodic conference calls and e-mail. Six months passed before he was able to return to the region. There he was surprised and concerned to find that, upbeat reports to the contrary, no real progress had been made on any of the instructions he had left.

Analysis

The U.S. executive in this example of *strategy without engagement* did not succeed in transmitting his strategic intent. However incisive his views may have been, they were not well integrated with those of the European subsidiary managers he visited. His subsidiary counterparts were doubtless asking themselves a host of questions such as

- "Who is this new executive?"
- "How often will he come here?"
- "Should we take his views seriously and act on them, or listen respectfully to his position and then do what we think is best?"
- "What is his relationship with his predecessor who worked with us for the last several years?"
- "Why did his predecessor leave? Why has the strategy changed?"
- "If we disagree with his opinions, how can we make him understand?"

With questions like these yet unanswered, it would be hard for the European managers to move effectively in any direction at all.

Missing global people skills:

- ***Establishing credibility***
- ***Building global teamwork***
- ***Strategic planning***

Organizing for Innovation

A Korean electronics enterprise was determined to grow beyond its traditional status as a "fast follower," or copier of other companies' innovations, and become a breakthrough innovator itself. It engaged expensive foreign consulting firms and examined overseas benchmark organizations. Based on this input, the company created a new organizational structure that modified its existing pyramid-shaped hierarchy to focus more on flexible, egalitarian project teams. Former divisional heads were freshly anointed as team leaders, and all managers were encouraged to lead teams and work with their employees in a way that enabled innovative ideas to "bubble up" from the lower levels of the organization.

Entrenched management habits, however, refuse to die easily. Team leaders did not change their stripes overnight and still frequently resorted to a top-down, command-and-control style of leadership focused on short-term results. The new "coaching" practices that the company had encouraged managers to adopt to help elicit more active employee participation did not take root immediately either. Managers were accustomed to telling employees what to do and found it difficult to draw out employee thinking and encourage subordinates to make their own choices.

The more fluid organizational structure envisioned by the company turned out to be very difficult to put into practice. A number of people, both at headquarters and overseas, began to take a skeptical view of the commitment of top leadership to the new structure, calling the supposed transformation a change in name only.

Analysis

This is an example of *structure without enablement.* The Asian firm that aspires to become a breakthrough innovator installs a novel management structure (partly on the advice of Western consultants) but does not enable either the managers or employees within it to make the structure work. Old authoritarian habits of both managing and following undermine the innovative intent of the new structure, making it appear to be a cosmetic and superficial adjustment. The participants need to acquire fresh competencies and to redistribute real control and authority. Only in this way will an individual employee with a bright idea become able to gain the support and take the risks necessary to bring it from the desktop or laboratory bench to commercialization. Such a deep-seated change cannot be accomplished through a structural shift alone.

Missing global people skills:

- *Evaluating people*

- *Training and development*
- *Transferring knowledge*
- *Managing change*
- *Innovating*

Cross-Border Knowledge Transfer

"Joaquin, why is this machine still running?" the foreign manager asked the senior shift mechanic during his regular rounds to monitor the process. "This process measurement recorded by Hernando is far below what it should be!" "I have been too busy to check up on it," Joaquin replied. Next, the manager called over to the machine operator who recorded the measurement. "Hernando, do you know that this measurement is out of tolerance?" "No," Hernando replied. "No one told me what the spec was." In reality, the specification was clearly posted on the wall over his machine.

A maquiladora operation in Mexico sought to install a quality system that would allow factory workers to make continuous improvements in the manufacturing process. The new system generated a constant stream of precise data about whether or not each piece of factory machinery was operating within acceptable tolerances. Using the new system, workers had the capability to monitor product quality and take corrective action. The next stage planned for the Mexican factory, beyond simply running the manufacturing process it received, was to use the accumulated data and improvements to take the operation to higher levels of quality and productivity. But the key hurdle, as it turned out, was to persuade the Mexican factory workers to actually use the system. Considerable time was lost while the factory struggled to put a team of people in place that was both able and willing to develop along with the manufacturing process itself; high rates of maquiladora employee turnover made it difficult to establish lasting solutions.

Analysis

Here in this example of a *system without execution,* a quality system installed with expensive, first-rate technology and good intentions is held back for many months by managers and workers who are not committed to its implementation. A long and unanticipated series of hands-on measures will be necessary to begin to move the system from documents on the wall to a fully functioning process integrated with daily factory activities. What the factory needs to make the quality system fully functional is a shift in organizational culture toward values and work habits that support and enhance quality practices. The organization needs to encourage employees to move away from more hierarchical and passive behaviors to ones that entail greater individual accountability and to cultivate managers who have the confidence and technical skills to take the lead in linking testing to production.

Missing global people skills:

- *Evaluating people*
- *Training and development*
- *Selling*
- *Transferring knowledge*
- *Managing change*

Lost Opportunities: The Common Denominator

None of the three examples provided above amounted to a high-profile disaster that would necessarily draw the attention of top corporate management. Failures in global business are most often insidious rather than acute—they take the form of death by a thousand cuts. Chronic problems have a lethal cumulative effect: wasted energy and effort, delays in project implementation, unsteady progress toward shared goals, a residue of misunderstandings and negative judgments between people in different locations. The common denominator is lost opportunities, which are hard to measure because they are never realized. The total opportunity cost may nevertheless be enormous: six months of unaligned operating strategies; an innovation drive begun with much fanfare and considerable expense that fails to produce results; an expensive quality improvement system that does not actually lead to better-quality products.

Experienced managers will observe that such problems can occur in domestic as well as global business ventures and that some of the behaviors described in these examples would not lead to success anywhere. This observation is absolutely true: such overlap does exist—the differences between domestic and global business issues are normally ones of degree rather than kind. At the same time, there are common ingredients to each of the scenarios described here that make them more complex and troublesome when they occur in a cross-border context:

- Open communication is more difficult due to language and cultural barriers
- Gaps between the expectations and assumptions of participants are harder to discern
- Feedback may be delayed or indirect
- Lack of physical proximity makes it harder to accurately track progress and results
- Normally surefooted managers are thrown off balance by the reality or perception of unfamiliar ways of doing business
- Underlying differences between organizations or business practices are not immediately visible
- Cultural differences may actually be real or used as a ruse to disguise poor performance
- Misunderstandings fester between key players and become a source of further problems
- Risks and penalties increase as problems remain unresolved
- The cost of lost opportunities is muted by distance from the corporate center

The "3 S's" and the "3 E's"

The management levers that Western-trained businesspeople still customarily reach for when they encounter problems doing business abroad are those that McKinsey consultants coined long ago as the hard S's: strategy, structure, and systems.[3] In the three scenarios above, these levers by themselves were insufficient—in fact, the bias toward "3S" solutions is in itself a major source of problems in global business settings. The 3 S's tend to work well only when accompanied by a parallel set of factors that are grounded in people skills, the 3 E's: engagement, enablement, and execution (see figure 2).

People skills are the best way to bring the 3 E's to bear in a global business context. The negative outcomes in each of the three scenarios presented were due first and foremost to a deficit of people skills at all three levels: interpersonal, group, and organizational.

People Skills and Mistaken Assumptions

So why aren't global people skills more widely understood and applied? Even managers who acknowledge the importance of both the 3 E's and people skills in cross-border transactions still tend to underestimate the challenge due to several comforting but misleading half-truths:

"Everybody speaks English."
"They are eager to adopt our way of doing things."
"Our corporate culture is the same everywhere."

At least a thin layer of elite English-speaking inhabitants does exist in most countries. Many people in these countries are genuinely eager to emulate Western business practices. A strong corporate culture can provide common ground for employees of the same country to work together. However, when such half-truths become fixed assumptions that justify minimal effort or adjustment, they take on a tone of arrogance and complacency that colleagues abroad find irksome.

Expecting others to speak one's own language may lead to isolation from key customers or employees and drastically limit the quality of information that is available. Emulation is often accompanied by strident criticism or perhaps loathing for Western and particularly American

Figure 2. **Global Organization Development: The 3 S's and the 3 E's**

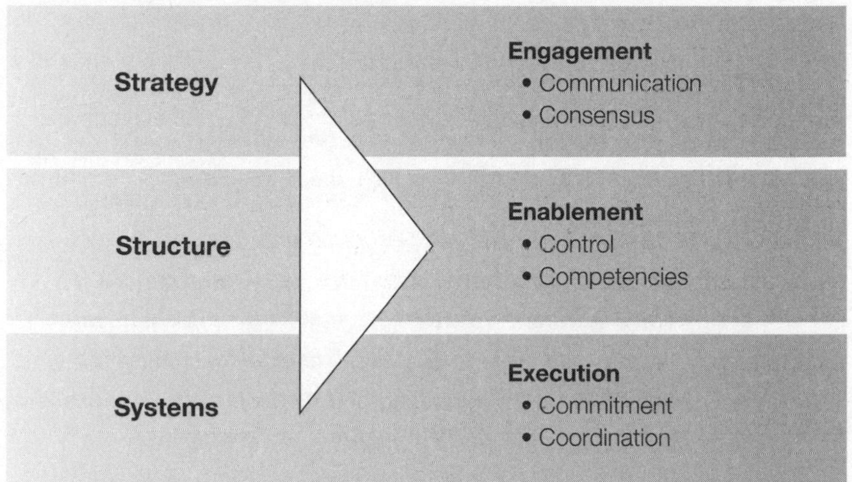

practices. "Corporate culture" usually refers to a set of beliefs and practices defined by headquarters that embody values of the firm's home country; employees in other countries do not automatically buy into these values.

A substantial body of research suggests that we assume others to be more similar to us than they actually are. "Projected similarity" is the first hurdle to overcome in taking global people skills seriously because it causes us to labor under an illusion of mutual understanding without even perceiving the need to adjust.[4] Unexamined assumptions that paper over real differences and convey a not-so-subtle message of superiority and self-satisfaction are the perfect recipe for disaster.

Relationships: The Starting Point for People Skills

Global people skills are built on a foundation of strong personal relationships. Before addressing each of the various layers of the people skills model, it is worth examining this foundation, as fatally flawed assumptions or illusions often begin with misconceptions about relationships.

U.S. managers—particularly driven, individualistic, technically minded personnel—seem to have trouble establishing effective relationships with colleagues abroad. Many quickly conclude that they understand the meaning and significance of relationships and check this subject off their list, but in fact they are neither fully aware of its implications nor committed to investing the time and personal sacrifices that will be required. If you speak to this kind of manager about his or her counterparts abroad, you will frequently hear something like, "Oh, Sanjay and I have a great relationship." This first-name shorthand accommodates the manager's taste for familiar speech, even when nobody would use this label for the person locally. And if you go speak to "Sanjay," he will say something like this:

> *Ah, Mr. Stevens. He always has such a full agenda and is in such a hurry when he comes here that we hardly have time to get together. We do our best to make him comfortable as our guest and cooperate with his initiatives, but there are many things that we just can't explain and that he wouldn't want to hear even if we told him. Perhaps he feels that he knows us, but I don't think that he really knows us at all.*

The sarcastic or bitter undertone that commonly accompanies such comments reveals as much as the words themselves. In short, the idea that a bona fide "relationship" exists is another one-sided assumption based on a lack of true understanding, and what passes for a personal connection is a stunted, limited bond of convenience that does not offer either partner the full picture of the other.

Defining Relationships

Task-driven managers who are anxious to get on with the business at hand may define relationship building as preliminary chitchat about weather, hobbies, and other "getting to know you" questions—an obligatory waste of time that one has to endure before moving on to matters of greater significance. Or, relationships are dreaded because they mean very long days with too many dinners out (the current term in China is "death by banquet") and an unnecessarily roundabout way of getting things done. At best, these people slog forward dutifully in a systematic networking mode, shaking hands and collecting business cards from others who could be of practical use. But these views are all beside the point.

Relationships are important anywhere, but they are indispensable in many foreign contexts. Business tools taken for granted in countries such as the U.S. or in parts of Europe are simply unavailable in other places where a free-market infrastructure either does not exist or has evolved in a different form. Standard characteristics of numerous fast-growing world markets include

- A legal environment that is ambiguous or unfavorable to foreign interests
- Different ethical assumptions with regard to intellectual property or trade secrets
- Lack of objective market research tools
- Opaque government and industry relations
- A social structure that favors those with "insider" status
- Family or quasi-family business practices with little separation between personal and company life
- Relatively permanent social ties, with severe penalties for mistakes that embarrass partners

Under these circumstances, strong relationships with local industry and government counterparts become the only reliable means for ensuring legal protection, exploring market potential, gaining market access for new products, learning about upcoming changes in regulations, and obtaining the other strategic advantages of insider status. A critical ingredient to success is who we know and how well we know them. Yet, business relationships are established gradually because the societies themselves are more compact and less mobile (the business of even some very large countries is concentrated in the capital city and dominated by an elite who attended the same schools together). Failed partnerships can have serious negative consequences for all concerned, and there may be no second chance in a country for the foreign firm that enters into an agreement and then elects to withdraw from it.

What Overseas Partners Want

One key to building successful relationships is to be aware of what your potential partners are looking for. A busy, task-focused approach to relationship building in such an environment seldom leads to positive results. It is this very impatience that often leaves potential business partners feeling that their guests are too pushy or moving too fast. Counterparts in more traditional environments are certainly interested in relatively objective factors such as technical competence, design, quality, and price—but these are seldom the only elements that shape the decision about whether or not to embark on a long-term business relationship.

Time and commitment count: Are you, the foreign partner, going to be around long enough to follow through on promises and make a mutual investment of time and energy worthwhile? Local contacts will be trying to figure out how much substance and staying power you have. They will also show a strong interest in more subjective factors such as your background or pedigree, business track record, and work ethic. Another variable is the "loose cannon" factor, or the possibility that you might bring unpleasant surprises along the way. You must create a sense of reliability, stability, comfort, and fit. An atmosphere of mutuality is crucial as well—a feeling on the part of local counterparts that you are going to accommodate their agenda and not simply impose your agenda on them. Careful handling of the relationship-building process and an understanding of the local partner's broader agenda will actually open more doors and make for better business in the long term.

George Renwick is a veteran China hand and one of the most respected thought leaders in the intercultural field. Based on his long experience in Asia, he mentions a list of desirable capabilities that are both familiar and surprising:

> *Like westerners, I find that Asians do look very closely for competence, but they are looking for a wider range of competencies than we normally do—certainly technical competence, management competence, yes. But another area is organizational competence. An Asian will respect us if we are able to mobilize different parts of the organization in order to get things done. A lot*

here depends, of course, not only on our position within the organization, but people's respect for us. So, if we can work our own system, then we're going to receive a lot more respect from them.

In addition to technical and management competence and organizational competence is interpersonal competence. First, and we often don't anticipate this, Asians are watching and assessing our competence with our own people—other westerners on the negotiation team, on the senior management team, people from the home office—when they visit. What is the quality of our relationships with our own people? If we haven't gotten that right, if there isn't trust amongst us, Asians will know that the chance of us establishing really trusting, productive relationships with them are few. Also, I find that Asians want to see us be competent with groups. We tend to manage one-on-one, but the highly effective leader in Asia is able to mobilize the energies, the talent, the intelligence, and the potential of the whole group.[5]

The assessment of these qualities in a potential partner, often a silent process, is a major component of the relationship-building phase in most parts of the world. It occurs through a variety of different means, depending on the country and its customs. Typically, an elaborate courtship begins even before the first face-to-face encounter. A series of structured, ritualistic events gives potential business partners a window through which to see each other's qualities and enables everyone to judge whether there is a mutual fit. Much of the initial chitchat that some westerners find so exasperating is part of a preliminary screening process that utilizes a series of coded messages or symbolic exchanges. By anticipating this process and the mode in which it will occur, participants who are less accustomed to it will have a better chance of ensuring that they convey the right messages. See table 1 for a list of typical relationship-building activities, accompanied by the questions and concerns that are likely to be in the minds of foreign counterparts.

So relationships must normally be established before tasks are undertaken in earnest, in contrast with the typical approach in the U.S.

Table 1. **Relationship Building: Common Behaviors and Their Meaning**

Relationship-Building Behaviors	**Symbolic Significance to Potential Partner**
Preparation: introductions, pre-contacts, information exchange, meeting arrangements	"Who do you know already that is willing to vouch for you? How much effort are you willing to put into preparing to work with us?"
Initial greetings: handshake, name card exchange, giftgiving, serving of refreshments	"Are you aware of local protocol? Can you pronounce and remember our names? Will you accept the drinks that we offer in hospitality?"
Small talk: the trip, impressions of the country, accommodations, length of stay	"How much have you tried to learn about us and about our country? What is your approach to learning more? Do you have the good sense to know what topics not to raise at this stage?"
Personal and professional background: self-description, questions for hosts, presentation on company	"Do we have common interests outside of business? Are you interested in us for short-term deals or as long-term partners? What is your status within your own company, and how long will you be around?"
Language use: Do you learn the local language?	"How important is it for you to do business in our country? Do you expect us to operate on your terms?"
Transition to business topics: Initiated by guest or host?	"Are you willing to work at our pace, or will you impose yours?"
Foods: What dishes are you willing to try?	"Are you willing to step out of your comfort zone and sample things that we like? Are you open to different ways of doing things?"
Singing: Will you take the stage for karaoke?	"How much of your character are you willing to reveal to us? Do you have to be smart and in control all the time? What do you look like when you're playing and not working?"
Follow-up: subsequent contacts, project updates, completion of action items, respectful use of network	"Do you follow up on your commitments, or do you forget about us? Will you leverage our business network with care?"

that puts tasks first. Plus, relationship building is not a phase that one simply completes and then moves on. Relationships ideally continue to deepen and expand over time as the business grows—this subject will be revisited in later chapters on selling and strategizing. But having some kind of relationship in place is a prerequisite for getting started. Managers with experience in business locations as varied as Europe, Asia, Latin America, and the Middle East counsel patient, consistent efforts to cultivate local contacts while testifying that the benefits are enormous:[6]

- "For me the difference between having a strong relationship and not having one is like the difference between day and night. Cold calls are almost impossible in this country, and relationships take a long time to establish, but it's well worth the effort."
- "The typical perception of the foreign company is that you're here to make a quick profit and then you will be gone. You need to show that you care about the people here and that you are committed to being around for some time. If you let them know how much you appreciate them, it makes a difference."
- "The U.S. tendency seems to be to act in a casual and familiar way right from the beginning. People here dislike this and regard it as being shallow and superficial. They say that Americans are easy to talk to initially but avoid deeper relationships after that. We think that we can learn a lot about another person in a few minutes, but they have a very different view."
- "Your customers are your friends, but this takes a long time. There will be chances to eat together or just have coffee or a couple of beers. It's important to value these invitations and to offer them in return."
- "Personal contacts are absolutely essential for foreign managers here. You have to keep in touch with people no matter how long you stay in the country. It's worthwhile to invest a lot of time and energy into building strong personal contacts."

Only when there is a fit in the relationship and a complementary rhythm has been established does the business really take off. The process is like a dance where the partners need to discover the same rhythm and learn how to move smoothly together without stepping on each other's toes. This dance could lead one to places that might be considered exotic: a tent in the Saudi Arabian desert, a banquet complete with sheep's head in Kazakhstan, or the steaming hot water of a public bath with a Korean customer. But the aim is the same: to establish common ground on a human level that allows mutual trust and respect to take root, setting the stage for a successful transaction of the business yet to come.

The Global People Skills Model

SUMMARY AND REVIEW QUESTIONS

1. How would you describe the qualities that global leaders need to be successful? Do these include people skills in some form?
2. Have you seen instances where directives issued by a manager from another country were ignored by local employees? Why did this occur?
3. In your own experience, what is the difference between domestic business challenges and those that occur in multicultural or cross-border settings?
4. Do you agree that engagement, enablement, and execution are as important to global business success as organizational strategy, structure, and systems? Why or why not?
5. Can you think of any way in which you might be assuming that your foreign counterparts are more similar to you than they actually are? In what ways are others either trying to become more like you or to preserve their own distinct cultural values, business practices, or life-style?
6. How would you define a good business relationship? How do you best become acquainted with people—through socializing or through working together? In your relationships with people from other cultures, what do you find works in favor of the relationship? What seems to work against it?
7. How do you think your foreign counterparts view their relationships with you?
8. What do you think your overseas business partners want? How can you confirm that they want what you think they want?

CHAPTER TWO

Global People Skills and Culture

People skills are related to culture because they address the functional areas where national cultures tend to diverge most drastically. Whether we are giving feedback, conducting a negotiation, or initiating a change process, chances are good that a cross-border transaction will be more complex and demanding than one conducted strictly in a domestic context. Learning about people skills and their varying applications across cultures is a bit like learning the pressure points on the human body used for centuries in Chinese medicine—applying just the right amount of pressure in the right spot works wonders, while inappropriate or misplaced pressure produces either great pain or no effect. Before moving on to a discussion of each of the people skills, however, we must first provide a working definition of *culture.*

Concepts of Culture

Recent decades of experience and research have produced a rich array of materials with increasing sophistication and practical business value. Pioneers in the intercultural field—Nancy Adler, Clifford Clarke, Jack Condon, Edward Hall, Charles Hampden-Turner, Geert Hofstede, Robert Moran, George Renwick, Steven Rhinesmith, Fons Trompenaars, and others—have provided us with important concepts while offering new models for multicultural or transcultural effectiveness. The definition of culture that businesspeople tend to find most useful is that it consists of a way of solving problems in a particular environment. Human groups have organized themselves over time to become more effective in dealing with the challenges of the desert, mountains, prairie, or sea—whatever nature has in store—using the resources they have available.[1] Different environments have given rise to different solutions and hence contrasting cultures. Common forms of thought and action in any culture reflect a problem-solving style that is specific to that place and the struggle of its people for survival.

Of course culture has broader significance: the renowned anthropologist Clifford Geertz defined culture as a "historically transmitted pattern of meanings embodied in symbols." Culture in this sense provides both a conceptual framework for understanding the world and a template for shaping human conduct within any cultural group.[2] Culture can also be more or less accessible depending on how it is manifested. Many people are by now familiar with the distinction between readily visible artifacts, such as buildings or cars, and aspects of culture that are less visible or explicit, such as customs, attitudes, beliefs, or assumptions. This is the significance of the so-called iceberg model, which depicts physical objects and behavior as being above the water's surface and the rest as part of the invisible bulk that lies beneath.

Questions About Culture

Global leaders and managers tend to ask a number of questions about culture that are worth addressing before we move on:

- "How important is culture?"

- "Isn't there considerable variation within each culture that contradicts the stereotypes?"
- "Do cultures change over time?"
- "Can we create confusion by adjusting too far in another culture's direction just as they're adjusting to accommodate us?"
- "How is cultural understanding going to benefit me?"

Culture's Importance

Considerable nonsense is expressed regarding the question of culture's significance for business. Some hold the self-congratulatory view that others are striving to become "more like us." They argue that culture makes no difference at all, or that it is only a matter of time before cultural differences are erased. This perspective is far too simplistic. In relation to the U.S., for example, many people, including millions of immigrants, are seeking to adopt our values and behaviors. However, there are those who appear westernized in some ways while actually holding quite different assumptions, others who seek to import U.S. technology while rejecting this country's values, and still others who reject Western civilization altogether while struggling mightily to sustain their own independent culture.

From a practical standpoint, key workplace behaviors do vary considerably from country to country, and culture appears to play a crucial role in shaping them (see table 2). For example, anyone who has been involved with customer/vendor relations in places such as the U.S., Russia, Mexico, and Japan is acutely aware that different practices exist and that one had better be aware of them to be successful. The partnership of semi-equals that can be established between customer and vendor in one environment may not be transferable to different locations where the customer is either in a position of great power or subject to the whims of more powerful government authorities. There are in fact a number of readily identifiable differences in business customs.

Yet, it would be equally misguided to regard culture as the only, or even the most significant, variable in every cross-border business

Table 2. **Workplace Behaviors Shaped by Culture**

- Customer/vendor relations
- Criteria for selecting new business partners
- Negotiation and meeting styles
- Ideal images of leader and subordinate
- Concepts of career path
- Ways of handling problems or disagreements
- Views of gender-appropriate behaviors
- Standards of ethical behavior
- After-work socialization

problem. This is an error committed on occasion by interculturalists who lack substantial business experience. There are multiple factors involved in most scenarios, and cultural differences are likely to surface as one element in a complex mix.

Thus, in addition to the influence of national culture, the issues present in a given environment could be shaped by other factors: individual personalities, professional specialties, levels of career development or experience, or the distinctive culture of an organization, as shown in figure 3. A global team, for instance, might experience communication issues that are shaped by differences in national culture: some team members typically have a direct and vocal style of presenting their views, while others feel that their views are not being heard. But the team's difficulties could easily stem from other factors such as personality conflicts or divergent opinions held by engineers and salespeople. There could also be disagreement between more- or less-experienced team members or difficulties that arise from the fact that the team comprises representatives from two separate company divisions. Further variables such as gender, age, and the expertise of the team leader could have an influence in shaping teamwork issues as well. Knowledge of culture in this kind of complex situation is important for discerning not only when national culture is a key causal variable, but also when it is not.[3]

Figure 3. **Culture and Behavior: Key Factors**

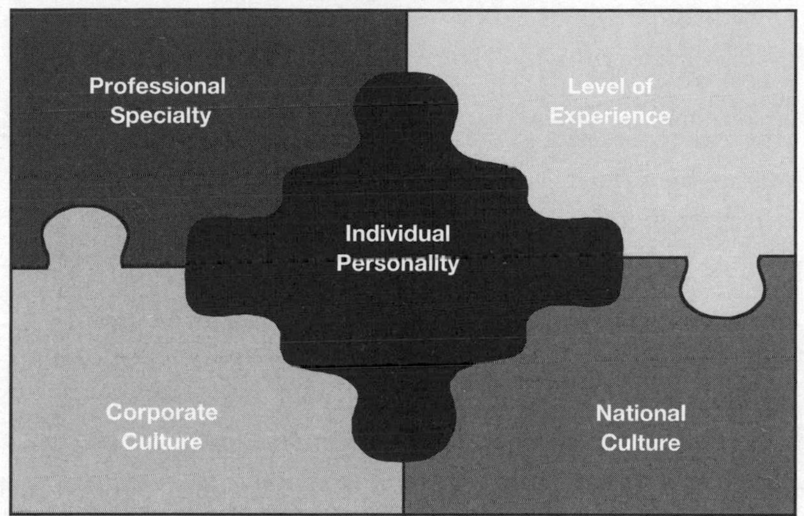

Variation Within Cultures

Stereotypes about a particular nationality can be both inaccurate and dangerous. Many question whether it is a good idea to apply simple labels to the rich variety that exists within any country. The tremendous diversity present in the U.S., with nearly every national and ethnic group on the globe represented among its residents, is a case in point. What sense does it make to generalize about "Americans," "Chinese," or "Brazilians"?

On the other hand, generalizations about national culture can be genuinely valuable in helping us to anticipate how people in unfamiliar settings will act. A generalization that describes the peak of the statistical U-curve for a given culture provides an initial guide regarding local behaviors. However, such generalizations must be consciously held, tested against the facts, and modified based on real experience.[4] Unlike rigid stereotypes, generalizations are modified based on new information, as depicted in figure 4.

Variation around a norm is part of the standard distribution of behavior in any cultural setting. The individuals whom we encounter may or may not represent established norms. But even though considerable variation is present within a country, regular and predictable differences

Figure 4. **Stereotypes vs. Generalizations**

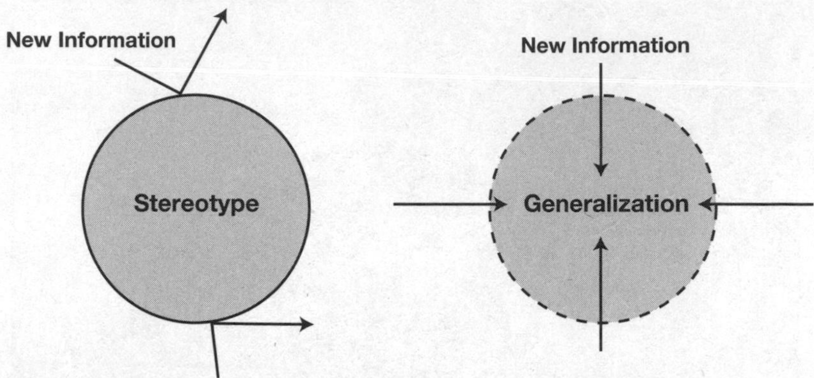

between national norms do exist that make it easier to understand how and why everyday workplace behaviors differ. Moreover, cultures tend to organize themselves around core themes, and the variation itself is often a variation on a theme: U.S. citizens with their myriad expressions of "freedom," or Mexicans with their rich sense of "family." The highest ideals and the greatest shortcomings of any society often represent extreme versions of values shared by the general population.

One practical means for reconciling undeniable variety with sometimes useful generalizations is to develop better tools for describing the complex situations that businesspeople encounter. In this way one can keep in mind basic cultural differences while also considering multiple strategies for coping with diverse counterparts. The example displayed in figure 5 sets up possible contrasts between workers from several age groups who have differing types of organizational affiliations. However, comparisons like these, while they represent an improvement over the broadest kind of cultural generalizations, still need to be more finely drawn. Not every senior member of a state-owned enterprise is likely to hold more traditional attitudes, and not every young employee who has entered a foreign-owned firm will be an eager advocate for change.

Cultural Change

Cultures do indeed change over time. Alterations in culturally based values and behaviors often take place in tandem with economic, religious, or

Figure 5. **National Diversity by Age and Employer Type**

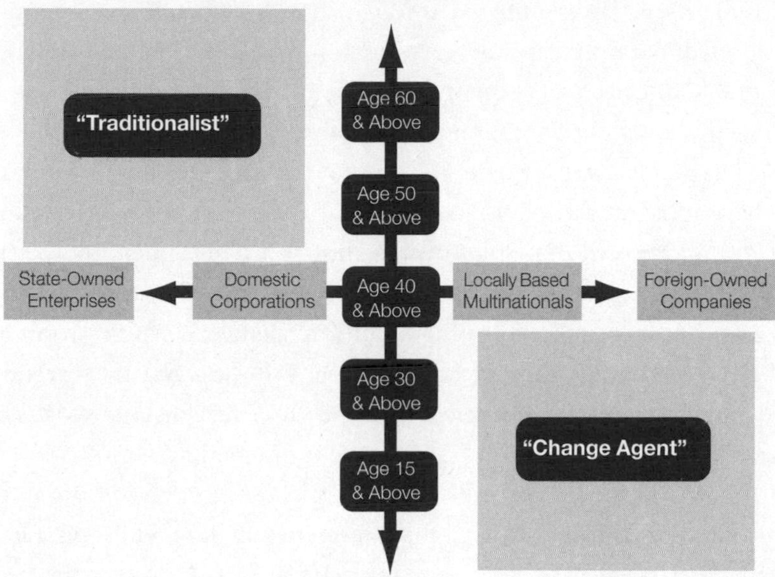

political shifts. A new technology such as mechanized agriculture or electricity can fundamentally transform the conditions for survival that are the crucible from which any culture is formed. At the same time, the introduction of a new religious belief system may bring with it new cultural values that either encourage or obstruct the dissemination of technology. Major political events and wars between nations have their own impact on culture: Japanese social institutions were radically altered under the U.S. occupation after World War II; the withdrawal of the European colonial powers from Africa and the emergence of independent nations there precipitated enormous changes that are still under way today.

Cultural transformation normally occurs slowly and almost imperceptibly but may speed up under duress as the conditions for survival are modified. It is not necessarily unidirectional—a society might embrace a brand-new way of doing things or, just as readily, seize upon the vision of a past golden age or a set of traditional practices to which it seeks to return. Splinter groups often set off in different directions from the mainstream. Furthermore, change is seldom total; a new value is typically integrated with other preexisting ones to create fresh patterns that are nonetheless continuous with what came before. Workplace practices common elsewhere are filtered through local systems of meaning and interpreted in a different way—a "reduction in force" could be seen as a regrettable but necessary response to difficult economic times, or as an outrageous violation of the company's obligations to its employees.

The good news for would-be corporate change agents is that they do not have to affect the whole social fabric of a nation. They belong to a cultural microcosm that is influenced, but not determined, by the national ethos. Companies also have the advantage that they can exert control over a number of levers to shape cultural change: recruiting, training and development, performance management, reward systems, executive modeling. Long-term employers tend to produce very distinctive subcultures within the larger cultural environment of a nation.

Yet, employment comes last in a long succession of cultural influences that begins from birth. Companies generally hire adults who have already been shaped by their families, schools, communities, the mass media, and so on. Changes in organizational practices that cut against the grain in a particular cultural environment eventually must be reconciled in some way with preexisting values. Lasting cultural changes are achieved when there is a fit between the new values and the old. For example, a new emphasis placed on "individual accountability" may have to be reconciled with more traditional cultural values such as respect for hierarchy and the corresponding expectation that subordinates will be taken care of, along with a focus on the group or team.

While it is possible to make changes in a corporate setting, the challenges involved in introducing new cultural elements should not be underestimated. Simple-minded global "cultural assimilation" programs hatched at headquarters have little chance of success without ongoing dialogue with locations around the world and a willingness to adapt to local circumstances. (The topic of cross-border change management will be dealt with in more detail in chapter 12.)

Mutual Overreaction?

There is almost always someone in the most introductory workshop on global business who slyly asks, "Isn't there a danger that we will adjust to them too much just as they are adjusting to us and that we will end up confusing each other?" For the vast majority of people working across borders this is a false issue. Worse, it can be a red herring that conceals an all-too-common attitude, seldom voiced directly, which is, "Why should we bother to adjust to them when they need to learn how we do things anyway?"

So long as we are operating in our own language with limited experience living elsewhere, there is little danger of knowing or adjusting too much—the dangers more commonly lie in a conspiracy of ignorance and arrogance that puts our own values and behaviors at the center of the universe. If we do our best to accommodate our counterparts, and they strive to adjust to us as well, we might just find common ground in between.

Overadjustment is a concern primarily for expatriates rather than for business travelers. It is sometimes referred to as "going native" and takes at least two forms: (1) walking on eggshells to avoid even minor violations of host-country sensibilities, or (2) rejecting home-office or home-country values while embracing local customs even more avidly than the local residents. The caricature of this extreme is the foreigner who dresses up in traditional local garb that the natives themselves would be embarrassed to wear. A serious consequence of either manifestation of "going native" is that such people may become ineffective in introducing new ways of thinking into the host environment.

The term *style switching* is used to suggest that we can alter conduct to accommodate business partners abroad while retaining the skills required to function in our home-country environment. Some also claim that changing styles enables us to keep our fundamental cultural identity intact, but this is more problematic. Long-time residents abroad will attest that the more they act in the manner prescribed by another culture, the more it seeps into their minds and hearts and begins to unsettle the assumptions that they brought from home. People can respond to the challenges of a different cultural environment by integrating new viewpoints into their existing values or by swinging to extremes of nationalism or nativism. Figure 6 illustrates the contrast between style switching and a flexible embrace of new ideas, with the polarized alternatives of going native or retreating into a defensive posture.

Figure 6. **The Pendulum Phenomenon: Adjusting and Overadjusting**

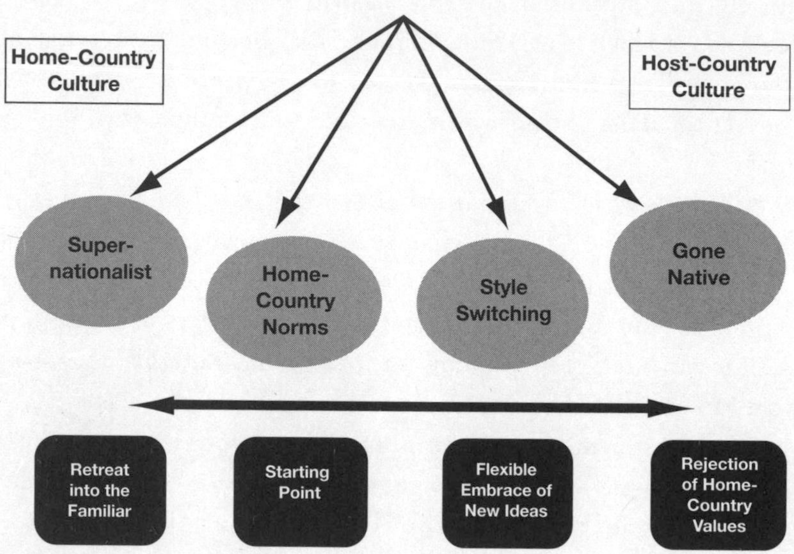

Benefits of Understanding Culture

Knowledge of culture is essential to sorting out almost any cross-border problem. Because most global business problems involve the complex mixture of factors portrayed in the diagram in figure 3 (p. 25), identifying the contribution made by national culture enables us to distinguish more effectively between this and other potential causal factors. If culture is ignored or treated as a black box, its role—major or minor—will never be clear. A jigsaw puzzle is easier to fill in if you know the places of some of the parts.

Beyond helping us get to the bottom of complex problems, cultural knowledge also enables us to pinpoint our own fundamental assumptions and how they are similar to, or different from, the assumptions of other cultures. Knowing what gaps exist between ourselves and the average profile of another culture provides clues about possible areas of friction or misunderstanding. (We can also discover how we measure up vis-à-vis the norms of our own country!)

A number of survey tools are available for generating a self-profile. The Peterson Cultural Style Indicator™, for example, analyzes responses based on dimensions of national culture defined over many years of research.* Figure 7 shows one way to display the results—focusing on the dimensions of individual/group, task/relationship, direct/indirect, and equality/hierarchy—depicting not an individual profile but the U.S. norm versus the norm for Saudi Arabia. Not surprisingly, a large gap exists in every dimension.

Each of these gaps has workplace implications. Taking the score disparity on the first line, the individual/group dimension, as an example, the U.S. score is weighted heavily toward the "individual" side while the Saudi score is more to the "group" side of the scale. This means that Saudi counterparts will be more likely to emphasize

- Cooperation and group goals
- Loyalty to friends
- Group affiliation as a way of determining identity
- Group decision-making processes
- Placing the team before individuals
- Conformity to social norms
- Lifetime membership in a group

By learning in advance what the potential gaps are between our norms and the norms of another culture, it is possible to predict areas of potential conflict, handle them more objectively, and draw upon model solutions developed through the hard-won experience of others. Returning again to the individual/group dimension, by almost any measure the U.S. is among a handful of the most individualistic countries in the world. This means that the minute U.S. managers step beyond their own national borders, they are going to encounter people who are more group oriented and will need to find ways to cope with this difference. If we are aware of this fact, certain differences with Saudi counterparts need not be taken personally but can be attributed to divergent cultural back-

*See appendix A to examine the Peterson Cultural Style Indicator. To create a personal profile, access an online version of the survey at www.globesmart.net.

Figure 7. **Cultural Dimensions: A U.S.–Saudia Arabia Comparison**

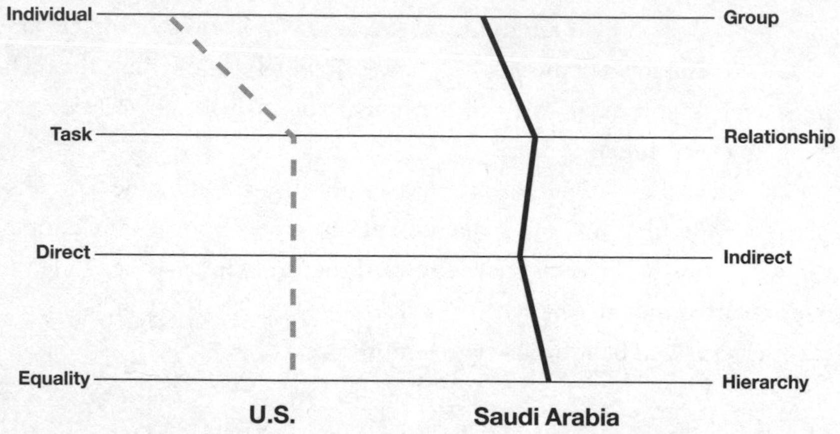

Individual — Group
Task — Relationship
Direct — Indirect
Equality — Hierarchy
U.S.
Saudi Arabia

grounds. Both sides can also consider potential solutions to clashes between individual and group-based values that draw upon best-practice models: individuals might be rewarded for behavior that benefits the team, or a team could be asked to set and enforce criteria for judging individual accountability.

Awareness of our own cultural profile also makes it easier to define personal limits. The deeper our involvement in a foreign environment becomes, the greater the likelihood of an experience that tests our most basic assumptions.[5] Ultimately, when differences emerge and have been analyzed and understood, it is necessary to choose: our way, their way, or a hybrid that incorporates contributions from both. How much can we handle before we lose our moorings and drop off the edge of our own mental world? Cultural knowledge enables us to make choices with greater clarity about who we are and what the alternatives will mean for us and for others.

Doing Business Across Borders: Other Approaches

The global people skills framework used in this book is complementary with other approaches such as the national/cultural dimensions compared above or the lists of personal characteristics or values stressed elsewhere. Indeed, the three approaches depicted in figure 8 are all useful and should be viewed in relation to one another.

Figure 8. **Approaches to Culture: A Three-Part Model**

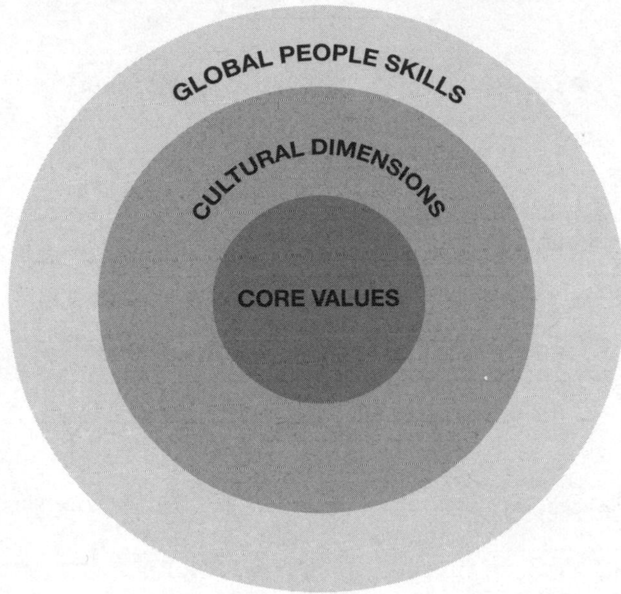

Core Values

At the center of this three-part model is a set of core values, characteristics, or abilities—they are described in different ways depending on the source. Although genetics and learning both play a role in their development, terms such as *values* or *abilities* are preferable because they suggest greater room for learning. Research going back several decades has identified common predictors of effectiveness for managers on foreign assignments or working in multicultural environments. More recent studies have established common features of global leaders—these have considerable overlap with the earlier research.[6]

The core values displayed in figure 9 are particularly challenging in a cross-border context because the behaviors associated with each tend to vary across cultures. We can utilize and disseminate these core values in a multicultural setting by stressing their importance, forging common definitions, and setting a personal example. The values enumerated here are best viewed not only as personal or individual assets, but also as the foundation for multicultural teamwork and positive team discipline. Can we as a team arrive at a common language for practicing these values together?

Figure 9. **Core Values**

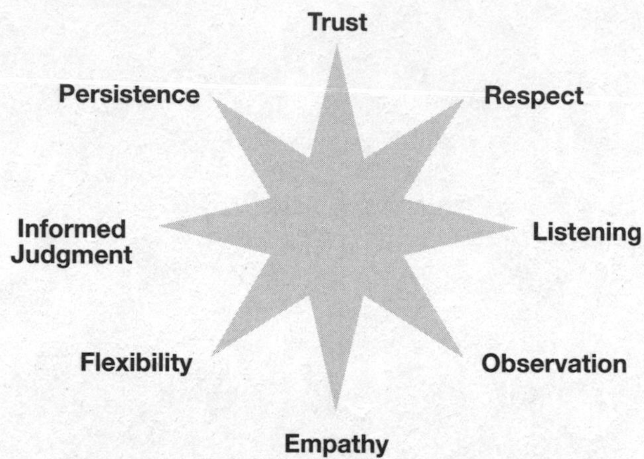

Here are more specific examples related to each of the core values:

- **Trust.** The ability to build trust across cultural barriers is vital, especially when some of the behaviors that we regard as evidence of trustworthiness may be interpreted as signs of unreliability in another environment.

  Example: Adjusting our description of past achievements so that it is not interpreted as intolerable boasting in an environment where qualifications are normally communicated by other means.

- **Respect.** The members of a multicultural group must develop behaviorally encoded forms of respect that are practiced by each participant.

  Example: Asking for input from each participant; waiting for others to finish their thoughts.

- **Listening.** The challenge for managers in a multicultural environment is to listen for what they do not expect to hear. Can we deal with new information that is beyond the range of our normal, commonsense assumptions?

  Example: Learning about markets where advertising is a new concept and "customers" are actually not so important.

- **Observation.** In certain cultural contexts, what is not said is more important than the literal content of the discussion.

  Example: Discovering how important points are communicated through rituals and forms, such as who comes or does not come to a meeting and where they sit; silence also has many shades and qualities.

- **Empathy.** Being able to sense and respond to the feelings of our foreign counterparts, while vitally important, can also be very difficult because the cues are unfamiliar.

  Example: Decoding the smile that could signal embarrassment, or emotional demonstrations that are calculated to probe for concessions.

- **Flexibility.** Can we adapt to what we have heard with new ears, seen with new eyes, and felt with a new emotional register, transforming our management style in a way that makes it more locally effective?

  Example: Learning to solve a problem by offering indirect feedback instead of tackling it directly.

- **Informed judgment.** The finely honed ability to quickly read and assess business counterparts may go terribly awry when we are outside our cultural familiarity zone. Cues that we normally rely on as windows into another's soul turn out to be false leads or dead ends; meanwhile we miss what is locally obvious. Judgments are best made when we are fully informed by guides who know the local business territory.

  Example: Asking for a local manager's assessment of an employee who seems competent but modestly denies his or her abilities.

- **Persistence.** People who give up the first time something goes wrong will not last long abroad. Individuals and groups who face adversity by coming back and trying again and again to create solutions—this doesn't mean repeating the same mistake—are the ones who will prevail.

  Example: Making a comeback from an embarrassingly poor first attempt at addressing a group of employees in the local language and getting steadily better at it.

Dimensions of Culture

Any manager in a global enterprise is confronted with the fact that people approach their work differently, with their thoughts and actions shaped in part by culture. It is helpful for those who work across borders to carry in their mind a map, or grid, of these varying perspectives. These dimensions of cultural difference have been expressed in various ways by a succession of writers (Parsons, Kluckhohn and Strodtbeck, Hofstede, Trompenaars, Walker et al.). A summary version is offered in figure 10, which includes the four dimensions used previously in the cultural comparison of the U.S. and Saudi Arabia: individual/group, task/relationship, direct/indirect, and equality/hierarchy (see p. 32).

Global managers or executives must first of all be able to recognize these dimensions to comprehend why a foreign counterpart would propose a different solution to the same work issue. They should also be prepared to advocate solutions based on either pole of a given dimension or to create a fresh, combined approach as appropriate for a particular environment. To take the well-known task/relationship dimension as an example, it might be in the best interests of a global organization to evaluate employees based on task performance, to sell by building deep customer relationships, and to negotiate joint venture partnerships that balance a task focus with trusting personal relationships.

Rather than regarding their own customary patterns of action as fixed, the most effective employees in global enterprises find that learning and exploring the full range of each cultural dimension offers a significant growth opportunity for both themselves and their colleagues abroad. If our natural inclination is more individualistic, there may be profound lessons to be gleaned from increasing our capability to work with a group or team; meanwhile, group-oriented colleagues could benefit from learning how to demonstrate more individual accountability. Those accustomed to focusing on the future can discover critical insights into themselves and their counterparts by exploring the past; people who draw their national pride and sense of hope from the past also need to focus on how to create a better future.[7]

Figure 10. **Dimensions of National Culture**

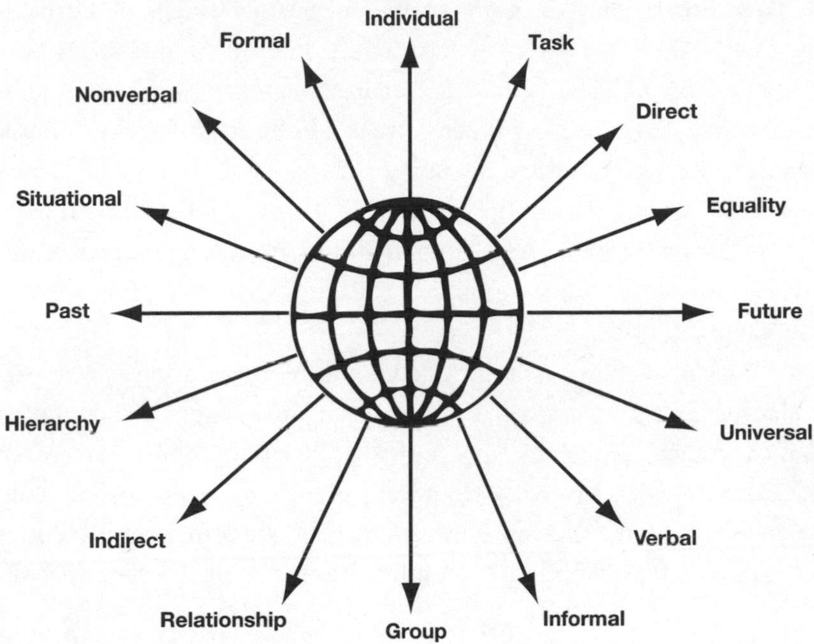

Global People Skills: The "How-to"

Few would disagree with the importance of core values such as trust, respect, or empathy. And the notion of cultural dimensions has largely carried the day as the dominant model in the intercultural world over the past twenty years. Yet, these concepts still leave practical businesspeople looking for something more. "Great, but now what?" is a common reaction to the first two rings of the three-part model in figure 8.

The global people skills that are the theme of this book form the third layer—the pragmatic, "how-to" interface with common global business tasks. Core values are the basis for each of the twelve global people skills, and the cultural dimensions provide a conceptual framework for understanding why they are required and how each skill set bridges a chasm between different cultural practices. Global people skills are where the rubber meets the road, where cultural or transcultural competence adds value to everyday transactions.

Admittedly, it is somewhat arbitrary to confine the "skills" label to the twelve areas I have selected. There are certainly other skill elements involved in the inner layers of the circle. Some of the qualities I have labeled as core values—"listening," for instance—can also of course be seen as skills. As for cultural dimensions, to adjudicate differences in business behaviors, we must first develop the cognitive skills required to recognize the various dimensions in action. Other skills linked with these dimensions include establishing a shared understanding of areas of difference with a multicultural group of colleagues and developing mutually acceptable solutions.

The global people skills included in this book were selected for particular qualities: they are specific rather than abstract, operational rather than theoretical, and primarily acquired rather than inborn. Moreover, they have not been treated systematically elsewhere. Global people skills are, in fact, a key missing link between the good work that has been done in the intercultural field and the best intentions of global businesspeople.

Global People Skills and Culture

SUMMARY AND REVIEW QUESTIONS

1. What is your own cultural heritage? How was it transmitted to you? As a young person, what exposure did you have to other cultures? What attitudes or beliefs concerning these differences were part of your environment?

2. How would you define culture? Are there any cultural differences between people from different ethnic or national backgrounds that have had a significant impact on your work?

3. Can you think of people you have met who either fit or did not fit the stereotypes regarding their culture? In what ways were they similar or different from the stereotypes?

4. Have you seen examples of cultural change over time within a country or a large organization? How did the change occur?

5. Do you know anyone who has swung from one extreme to another in adjusting to a different country environment—retreating into familiar behaviors and criticizing the host culture, or rejecting the values of their own home country?

6. How aware do you think you are of your own cultural assumptions? Think of a situation, either in your personal life or at work, that led you to rethink assumptions that you had taken for granted. In what ways was this a negative experience? In what ways was it positive?

7. Compared to people who you know well, do you consider yourself more individualistic or more group oriented in your communication style? To what extent is your focus on tasks, and to what extent on relationships? Are you more egalitarian or more hierarchical in your approach to work than others?

8. Which of the core values described in this chapter (trust, respect, flexibility, persistence, etc.) are you able to demonstrate readily in a multicultural group? Which are more difficult to practice?

Part I

Interpersonal Skills

CHAPTER THREE

Establishing Credibility and Feedback

Establishing credibility and giving and receiving feedback are two foundation skills on the interpersonal level that often pose significant obstacles for managers who have limited cross-border experience. Both are vital for gaining effective traction in the new environment.

Global People Skill #1: Establishing Credibility

Managers who launch into joint tasks without establishing credibility may find that their presence in the host country is regarded as the proverbial typhoon: the wind blows very hard and considerable damage may be done, but after a time it will blow over and go away; then the local residents come out and look around, clean up, and begin to go back to business as usual.

Experienced managers tend to take their own credibility for granted. They have long since learned how to establish their credentials easily when meeting new business contacts. Under normal circumstances they can accomplish this quickly before proceeding with the business at hand.

In cross-border settings, however, the code for establishing our value in the eyes of new colleagues and customers may differ from what we are accustomed to, and even this seemingly rudimentary step in creating business relationships can become a major stumbling block.

Introductory Speech

Here is a partial text of a speech planned by a U.S. executive newly assigned to head up an Asia-Pacific sales operation:

> *I'm very pleased to have the opportunity to work with all of you in our Asian organization. Although I have worked with many Asian companies in the past, it is an exciting opportunity to now become a part of the APAC sales force with you. While I was director of sales for the Western region in the U.S., we made a strong contribution to the company's earnings. I believe that we now have a great opportunity to build a strong and profitable business together in Asia that will yield outstanding returns for the parent company and our shareholders. My wife and I look forward to living out here and getting to know you better.*

Possible Interpretations by Local Employees

This may sound like a perfectly good set of comments to those who share the background and expectations of the U.S. executive, but the audience of Asian employees he will be addressing is unlikely to respond to it favorably. While their thoughts are often not voiced in public, and certainly not directly to a foreign manager, the local employees may have these kinds of interpretations:

- "He sounds very proud of his accomplishments."

- "It seems like he doesn't recognize all the efforts we have been making here."
- "Why does he have to talk about profit on a formal occasion like this? Of course we recognize that profit is necessary, and we're all working hard to make that happen. But he makes it sound like we are only concerned about our stockholders."
- "Does he think that Asia is one place?"
- "Why did he mention his wife?"

Having a group of colleagues who are thinking about a new manager in this way just after his introductory remarks is not an ideal start in a new environment. Already, in the very initial phase of this manager's presence abroad, an image of boastfulness, arrogance, and shortsightedness is being shaped that could require considerable time, energy, and goodwill to erase. Even worse, local employees are naturally reluctant to cooperate with a leader who is labeled in this way—at times they display passive or even active resistance to the leader's directives. Good intentions and a formula for self-presentation learned in one's home-market setting can actually become a recipe for trouble elsewhere.

Cultural Comparisons

Why do such misunderstandings occur? Nearly every cross-border business relationship begins with a mutual description of identities, backgrounds, roles, and current work, and yet the manner in which this is accomplished varies significantly from culture to culture. Nonverbal forms of communication such as body language and gestures make this kind of preliminary exchange still more complex.

Negative stereotypes are shaped in part by different assumptions about how we should present ourselves during these initial contacts. Different business environments require a different pace or style of leadership. Managers can more quickly establish their credibility and begin to work productively with foreign counterparts by presenting their qualifications and business priorities in a way that takes local perspectives into account.

My Mistake:* Establishing Credibility

There had just been a change in top management at a U.S. health care firm. A new CEO had been brought in from outside to take the company in a new direction. The firm's Japanese customers were uncomfortable with this sudden change, expressing concern over the shifts in both personnel and policy. I advised the U.S. company that it would be a good idea for the new CEO to go to Japan, meet with key customers, and reinforce relationships that would be very important for the future.

The U.S. firm responded that this was an excellent idea, and the new CEO was pleased to schedule a trip. He was known within the company as a real people person—everyone, even lower-level employees, called him by his first name. The firm's Japanese subsidiary worked cheerfully for several months to prepare for a big event, to which they invited a number of health care executives and physicians. They rented a large banquet room in one of the best Tokyo hotels and made meticulous preparations of transportation, lodging, food, drink, and entertainment for this prestigious gathering.

Finally the big evening arrived. The guests had gathered, and the U.S. CEO swept breezily into the room with an entourage of Japanese and American aides. He was wearing a brightly colored suit that stood out among the very conservatively clad Japanese medical professionals. Not deterred by this difference in dress, the CEO began to work the crowd, steered toward key individuals by his assistants. He greeted each person with a booming voice, shook hands, grabbed arms, and even gave some key customers a pat on the back or a warm hug.

The Japanese staff members who had arranged the event began to shrink back and look smaller—the body language of some seemed to indicate they would have preferred to be under a table. Soon the CEO had only other American company members and expatriate customers around him, and the center of the room had gone from a happy buzz to a strained murmur, with a few people bravely maintaining their conver-

*This and other "My Mistake" examples describe actual errors committed by the author or close colleagues.

sations around the edges. Then, two senior members of the Japanese subsidiary stepped forward and physically steered the CEO toward the edge of the room, suggesting that it was time for a break. The event broke up earlier than planned. Later, when I eagerly asked one of my contacts in the Japanese subsidiary how it had gone, he reminded me that the president's visit had been my idea.

Some relevant cultural dimensions, along with their implications for how to establish credibility in an unfamiliar environment, are presented in table 3.

Recommendations for Establishing Credibility

While it is easy to single out establishing credibility as a common flash point where many first efforts go awry, it is impossible to provide a single prescription or a list of do's and don'ts. The best approach to take truly varies according to the situation we face, including the host of variables indicated by the diagram on page 25: national culture, corporate culture, professional specialty, experience level of our colleagues, individual personalities present, and so on. George Renwick provides what is perhaps the best general advice to foreign managers going into a new environment:

> *Many managers go into an overseas assignment asking the question, "How much can I change, how fast?" Big mistake. Let me suggest a better question: "What can I change, when?" Still better is, "What can we change, when?"*
>
> *But the very best question is, "What must I not change?" What is going on here, in this organization, that deserves to be preserved? The local employees have been here, many of them, for years. They've been doing some good work. What is going extremely well? So I start, not with alteration, but with affirmation.*[1]

For the newly appointed manager in the example provided at the beginning of this chapter, an approach such as the following would probably be more successful with an Asia-Pacific team:

Table 3. **Establishing Credibility: Comparative Styles**

Cultural Orientation	← Expectations and Behaviors for Establishing Credibility	→	Cultural Orientation
Individual	Emphasize our own past history, accomplishments, vision for the future	Focus on the team and its past accomplishments, mutual cooperation, and our desire to work together in the future	**Group**
Task	Talk about what needs to be done and how to do it	Discuss the need to get to know each other well and our eagerness to do so	**Relationship**
Direct	Mention specific accomplishments; clearly outline strengths and weaknesses of the organization	Ask a third party to circulate biographical information in advance; praise the prior accomplishments of the team; modestly deflect compliments	**Indirect**
Equality	Present ourself as an eager colleague and co-worker; openly admit lack of knowledge or expertise	Have a more senior manager make the initial introduction in which he or she properly "positions" the new person; do not readily acknowledge lack of knowledge or expertise	**Hierarchy**
Verbal	Say what is on our mind; speak frankly with colleagues to establish a tone of mutual openness; expect issues to be voiced explicitly	Use formulaic expressions and watch carefully for nonverbal signals; use multiple occasions and listening techniques to draw out underlying messages	**Nonverbal**
Achievement	Emphasize track record of achievements and accomplishments relevant to tasks in new job	Rely on factors such as education, age, title/rank, tenure within organization, and gender to convince others of our potential to contribute	**Ascription***

*Achievement/ascription is a further cultural dimension used by Fons Trompenaars and Charles Hampden-Turner to compare environments where qualifications are based on a track record of accomplishments versus those where social credentials matter most. See *Riding the Waves of Culture: Understanding Diversity in Global Business*, 2d ed. (New York: McGraw-Hill, 1998), chap. 8.

> *It's a pleasure to meet with you today and to have the chance to work together with you over the next several years. As you all know so well, this is an exciting and competitive part of the world, and we have many opportunities to become an even more vital contributor to our worldwide organization. There is much that I need to learn about doing business here and about each country and culture in the region. I look forward to getting to know each of you and the people in your sales organizations much better.*

If this example is analyzed in light of the cultural dimensions outlined in figure 10 (p. 37), the cultural factors that come into play include preferences for a more group-based, indirect, and relationship-oriented approach rather than one that is individualistic, direct, and task-focused. As for the equality/hierarchy dimension, although the countries involved in this example—Taiwan, Singapore, Malaysia—are all more hierarchical than the U.S., modesty on the part of top leaders is usually interpreted as an indirect statement of confidence and sophistication. A capable leader need not blow his own horn because others will do it for him. Compliments and flattery are typically met with a polite attempt to deflect them, even if everyone present knows that they are true.

Ascriptive qualities such as education, age, title or rank, years of tenure in the organization, gender, and so on may be just as vital to establishing credibility in these countries as a specific track record of achievements. Such qualities need not be stated verbally because they are obvious to everyone without explanation—it is more important to demonstrate that we are receptive and aware of the behavior appropriate to the situation than to provide a laundry list of accomplishments. Finally, the reference to the spouse is omitted because, with the possible exception of Malaysia, spouses are typically not involved in business dealings or business socializing.

While in general it is best to adjust in the direction of accommodating host-culture norms, credibility in the new environment may derive from the very fact that one is different. Take the case of a CFO who has been sent to work in a subsidiary environment to ensure that financial statements are accurate and that the organization is in full compliance with corporate practices. This person is likely to have as part of his or her job description asking tough questions and educating local finance personnel in headquarters practices. Initial attempts to establish credibility on local terms will probably be helpful in building valuable relationships; at the same time, it is necessary for someone in this role to strike a balance over the long run that does not mean setting aside specific functional expertise, professional standards, and business objectives.

Global People Skill #2: Giving and Receiving Feedback

Different feedback styles can easily lead to misunderstandings. It is common for people from cultures that favor relatively direct and verbal forms of communication to misinterpret or miss entirely messages that come in more inexplicit and nonverbal ways. Meanwhile, very direct messages may cause offense or have unintended meanings read into them by those who are commonly more circumspect about delivering sensitive ideas or impressions.

Feedback in Turkey

Margaret Bealby has been working in Turkey for the past several months in her role as director of information technology for a global company. Her transition to working in Turkey has gone relatively smoothly except for one problematic relationship she is having with a subordinate.

Margaret was personally involved in hiring Mehmet Savasan. His academic credentials were very impressive, with multiple advanced degrees from prestigious universities in Turkey and London. His work experience was a bit more difficult to determine. During his initial interview, Mehmet provided limited examples of the types of IT projects he had worked on previously and seemed evasive when Margaret asked him to discuss his strengths on the job. Yet, a colleague of Margaret's who provided a job referral on behalf of this new employee was so effusive in praising his skills and expertise that Margaret decided to hire him. This colleague had in fact worked together with Mehmet previously and, based on that experience, assured Margaret that he would be an excellent addition to her staff.

The problem Margaret is now having with Mehmet is his continued pattern of evasiveness. During group meetings, when she asks him for input on project updates, he answers in vague terms and seems reluctant to provide the necessary details. Several times during the weekly team meetings, he has appeared to agree to her requests but then failed to deliver on time. From a technical point of view, his work is excellent, yet she is concerned about a hit-or-miss pattern of work and wondering whether Mehmet is really the right person for the job.

Possible Interpretations by the Foreign Manager

Margaret could easily reach several different conclusions about Mehmet based on their interactions, such as the following:

- He does not have the experience required to do the job effectively; her colleague "oversold" his skills to help out his friend
- He does not trust her yet as a manager; he is not being direct with her because foreigners are regarded with suspicion
- He is not trustworthy; he is lying to her by promising to do something and failing to deliver

Although plausible from Margaret's perspective, these conclusions are all incorrect in this case. Mehmet is in fact a gifted employee who has undersold his work experience because in Turkish business culture it is normally inappropriate to appear boastful about one's achievements.[2] The real problem is that Margaret is missing his tactful attempts to give her feedback. The situation described here is a good illustration of how global people skills are embedded in reciprocal relationships and quickly build on one another. Margaret may not have established strong enough relationships in the local environment for her Turkish colleagues to be open in providing feedback. Mehmet as well lacks the style-switching ability to fully establish his own credibility on the assertive terms that would make sense to Margaret. Her lack of certainty about his capabilities and her tendency to form mistaken interpretations of his signals are a consequence of a mutual lack of knowledge and key people skills. Under such circumstances, giving and receiving accurate feedback is difficult.

Cultural Comparisons

In the U.S. and parts of Europe, employees are often trained to give feedback directly—in a style that is verbal or explicit; immediate, right here and right now; and given to an individual, to a particular person. People who have received such training generally find it helpful to consider an additional range of options, including feedback that may be indirect—nonverbal or implicit; periodic or delivered over time on a number of different occasions; given in a different place; or offered to a group even if the target is one or more particular individuals.

By being aware of this full range of feedback styles and feedback options, not only are we able to give feedback in a form that is culturally appropriate in any location, but we are also better able to recognize it when we are on the receiving end. Table 4 contrasts alternative methods of delivering feedback in terms of the various cultural dimensions introduced in chapter 2.

Recommendations for Giving and Receiving Feedback

The most likely interpretation of Mehmet's case is that Margaret has been missing distress signals from him that are clear to everyone else who has been attending the same meetings. She is asking him directly in front of fellow team members to accept tasks that he does not support or for which he feels there would be significant barriers to implementation. Yet, because saving face and preserving personal dignity are important in Turkey, Mehmet does not want to embarrass himself or his superior by refusing her requests directly. His indirect answers and evasiveness stem from his desire to save face—both for his boss and for himself—and not from competence issues. He is reluctant to say no to Margaret and risk an open disagreement with her in front of the other team members.

Table 4. **Giving and Receiving Feedback: Comparative Styles**

Cultural Orientation	← Expectations and Behaviors for Giving and Receiving Feedback →		Cultural Orientation
Individual	Individuals who have feedback to offer should provide it to other individuals using the appropriate techniques	Feedback is commonly provided on a group basis and may be provided to a group even when it is intended for an individual	**Group**
Task	The person and the task are separated; the focus is on how to do the task well	Person and task are not separated; feelings and facts are both important when giving critical feedback	**Relationship**
Equality	Feedback can be given both ways between a superior and a subordinate	Feedback is given—and expected—primarily from the superior to the subordinate	**Hierarchy**
Universal	Work-related feedback is usually provided at work; it is important to follow the proper procedure and make it concrete, objective, and constructive	Informal get-togethers outside of work may provide a setting where feedback can be given and received more freely, even between managers and subordinates	**Situational**
Verbal	Feedback is explicit to prevent misunderstandings	Feedback is not given explicitly to avoid confrontation and damaged relationships	**Nonverbal**

Mehmet is providing ample feedback to Margaret in his own terms through his vague answers and visibly reluctant assent to her requests. Margaret is the person who is missing the point. It would be better for her to discuss project requests with him one-on-one, explore potential barriers to completing these requests, and solicit his input on the tasks he is being asked to do. Margaret is far more likely to get clear and informative feedback in this setting, where face and personal dignity are not at risk in front of the group. She could later announce what was agreed to during the team meeting.

Following are other techniques for giving and receiving feedback that are usually effective in cultural settings where more indirect practices are the norm.

Maintaining frequent informal communication.

Feedback exchanges may be more effective when there is a regular, casual exchange of information between manager and subordinate or between colleagues. The standard practice of many Western managers is described as "delegate and disappear," and feedback under these circumstances becomes a formalized exercise where large doses of positive and/or critical information are delivered through a performance evaluation. More frequent contact makes it easier to insert critical points into the ebb and flow of daily interactions. Albert Sui, a human resources vice president for AT&T based in Hong Kong, recommends conversations that refer to strengths and weaknesses in a holistic manner:

> *In the Western sense, we always like to say, "Well, let me share with you some positive feedback, and then I'll share with you some 'developmental' areas." It is not necessary to say this. As we describe the strengths, we can also describe some areas for improvement, but we don't have to catalog them in two separate categories and present these to the person. Because by doing that we already cause the person to lose face by nailing down a category called "areas for improvement." But if we can build that into the whole dialogue, where we can address it in the entire conversation, the same objective will get accomplished.*[3]

Asking third parties to convey information.

A time-honored means of resolving difficult situations in Turkey and many other countries is to call upon a trusted third party. It is best to select an individual who knows the people involved and is respected by everyone. Such a go-between is normally senior in age or rank. However, the third party could also be a junior engineer, for example, who serves as a mutual feedback channel between protagonists at odds over a business issue. This kind of back channel can often open up a mutually acceptable solution that would not have been possible had both sides burned the bridges between them through more direct forms of feedback.

Anticipating problem areas and providing specific models.

A clever alternative to potentially awkward feedback is to offer "feedforward":

> *I suggest we give "feedforward." We anticipate those places where local employees may make mistakes, walk them through them, and describe the appropriate way of handling those situations so they are not going to make the mistakes for which we might have to criticize them. The second suggestion is that we give them a model, a specific example of what we would like them to do. For example, take the format for a report that we want them to complete. They study it, we walk through the format with them, and then they write their own report. Then we, together with them, compare what they've done with the excellent example.*[4]

Some managers might protest that part of their job in the foreign environment is to teach others how to provide feedback in accordance with the direct and task-focused norms of the parent organization—and that they don't have the time or the mandate to model different types of practices. Yet, the introduction of unfamiliar feedback practices is most likely to be successful when local counterparts are aware that these new practices are being imported and are eager and willing to learn.

Their best efforts notwithstanding, foreign managers need to be aware that the style of providing feedback they consider to be "normal" can have unforeseen impacts. For example:

> **Local manager:** *Mr. X came to me and said that he wanted to transfer to another division.*
>
> **Foreign manager:** *Why? He is one of our best salespeople.*
>
> **Local manager:** *He thinks you are not happy with his work.*

Foreign manager: *But I told him I think he is doing a great job. I just mentioned that he ought to come talk to me about pricing next time before he talks to the customer.*

Local manager: *Many of our joint venture employees like Mr. X come from very traditional companies. For them, you are the big boss from headquarters. If Mr. X thinks you are unhappy with his work, he may feel that he has no future with the company.*

Foreign manager: *But how do I give feedback then to somebody like Mr. X?*

Local manager: *Let me talk to him. I might speak to the group as a whole and mention some points about pricing that would be useful for Mr. X. Later, once he knows you better, you can speak with him more directly.*

Foreign manager: *This is feedback?*

Local manager: *Or I might tell him a story about one time when I gave pricing information to a customer without consulting with the right people, and the result was a big discount for the customer.*

Foreign manager: *You did that?*

Local manager: *I told you. It's just a story…*

Indirect Feedback Styles

Employees who are accustomed to indirect feedback are seldom able to quickly transform behaviors that they have learned in their own culture from birth. They may instead begin with relatively oblique messages and move gradually toward more straightforward approaches.

As in the case of Margaret Bealby and her Turkish subordinate, Mehmet Savasan, it is essential that foreign managers be able to perceive and then further draw out the messages behind these less obvious forms of feedback so as not to be left in the dark about what their colleagues are thinking. Indirect feedback tends to emerge through a sequence of interlinking techniques such as the following:

- **Open questions.** "So, what did you think about yesterday's customer meeting?"

  The acute listener will take this as a sign that there is something about the meeting that the questioner would like to communicate and will begin to draw him or her out: "It seemed okay to me. But I'm very interested to know what you think…"

- **Selective praise.** "Your description of our factory expansion plans was great. The customer was really impressed with those plans."

  Ah, yes, but this could be like telling the waiter at a restaurant that the egg rolls were delicious because that is the only nice thing you can find to say about the meal. You need to provide the speaker with a clear indication that you are receptive, ready, and willing to hear what comes next. Agreeing that the presentation went well without providing a further invitation for comment would be like the waiter agreeing with you that the egg rolls are indeed delicious.

- **Incomplete sentences.** "I thought that the meeting went well overall…"

  This type of statement is usually just the introduction to the real message that comes next. However, it is made while gauging the reaction of the listener, and the train of thought that is leading toward a more critical remark could be halted at any point if the listener appears to have a substantially different opinion.

- **Multiple related hints.** "Have you had any message from the customer since our meeting?"

  There are those words *meeting* and *customer* again! This is an even clearer signal that the other party has something in mind. Your counterpart may be beginning to feel a bit desperate at this point because you are just not getting the message or providing an opening for deeper dialogue. Try asking a question such as, "Do you have a concern about how the customer is going to respond?"

- **Specific questions.** "How did you think the discussion about product specifications went?"

Here is an indication that product specifications are at the heart of the issue. Sensitive listeners will quickly ask themselves what about that discussion could have been problematic. A good conversation tactic for getting more explicit feedback here is again to give a brief, noncommittal answer and then redirect the question to the speaker.

- **Personal stories/self-critique.** "One time with your predecessor, Mr. Y, I did not have time to have a complete discussion with him before our meeting with the customer, and I said something during the meeting that contradicted what he had told the customer. I felt very sorry about this."

  This is your last golden opportunity to read into the message and realize what you are expected to derive from it. You can provide the speaker with a mutually face-saving way to proceed by responding with a statement such as, "You know, I've done that kind of thing before myself. Was there anything I did in this case that made the meeting difficult for you?"

- **Pained agreement.** "Yes, sir. You are probably right. The customer was happy at the end of the meeting."

  Such statements should never be taken at face value when they are accompanied by nonverbal gestures that convey embarrassment, hesitation, reluctance, or resentment. The nonverbal emphasis here is still on what is unstated.

- **Direct feedback.** "To tell the truth, I didn't think that the final result of the meeting was so good for us. The customer was happy, but we gave them different information."

  While more direct, the message here may still be incomplete.

- **Explosion.** "You embarrassed me in front of the customer! When they pushed you, suddenly you promised that we could provide new product features that I previously told them were impossible at the current price. Now the customer thinks that I am just a yes-man and that you have all the authority. Why don't you just take care of this account yourself?"

> Real direct feedback often flows only from managers to subordinates, except perhaps under the influence of alcohol. An alternative pattern when frustration mounts is that indirectness is abandoned, giving way to an explosion, negative comments laced with emotion, or personal attack. A more open and responsive approach at an earlier phase in the conversation could prevent this.

Useful feedback can be delivered either directly or indirectly. There is no one feedback style that is necessarily more effective than all the others so long as the partners are consciously employing the same pattern. Even hard-bitten U.S. managers who have been introduced to indirect feedback practices sometimes say things such as, "It will be good to have a wider set of options in my home-country workplace as well," or, "Now I realize what so-and-so [a work colleague, friend, or spouse] has been trying to tell me!" Attempts to enforce a single set of feedback practices as the corporate standard based on home-country norms are commonly ineffective unless accompanied by adequate explanation, training, and mutual flexibility in their application.

Establishing Credibility and Feedback

SUMMARY AND REVIEW QUESTIONS

1. How do you normally go about establishing your credibility in a new situation?
2. In what ways, if any, would you personally be challenged to establish your credibility in a cultural setting that placed high value on hierarchy and personal relationships?
3. What part of your background would you emphasize in your self-presentation if you felt that ascriptive factors such as age, title, rank, organizational tenure, or gender were important to your counterparts?
4. What is your preferred method of providing feedback to a counterpart or subordinate at work? To a group?
5. Can you think of a time in your own work experience when cultural differences contributed to difficulties in giving or receiving feedback? How did the experience lead you to modify your approach in such cases?
6. In a setting where an indirect style of giving and receiving feedback is the norm, some of the following techniques might be typical ways to invite a more detailed and useful exchange of information. Which of these techniques would you be likely to try yourself, and why? Would you be able to perceive the underlying meaning if such techniques were used to convey a message to you?

- Open-ended questions
- Selective praise
- Incomplete sentences
- Multiple related hints
- Specific questions asking for evaluation of a situation
- Personal stories/self-critique
- Pained agreement

CHAPTER FOUR

Obtaining Information and Evaluating People

The baseline interpersonal skills of establishing credibility and giving and receiving feedback continue to provide challenges as we make new contacts and expand existing relationships. At the same time, they become the foundation for further key people skills such as obtaining information and evaluating people.

Global People Skill #3: Obtaining Information

Often it is necessary to go beyond feedback regarding our own ideas, behavior, or management style and probe additional questions that are vital for the success of a cross-border project or business venture. The skill of obtaining information can help us to better grasp organizational capabilities, project management issues, or market opportunities. Most important, it enables foreign managers to understand what the employees working for them have to contribute.

Software Development in Bangalore

Allen Dykstra is a senior software engineer. Several months ago he was assigned to manage a software development project. As part of his responsibilities as project manager, he was asked to take over the management of a team of off-site Indian software developers from their previous manager, Mr. Prasad, who had been reassigned to another project. Allen made a short initial trip to Bangalore to meet the Indian engineering team. The supervisor of the team on the Indian side is Atul Nettar, a talented design engineer who previously spent six weeks in the U.S.—his first trip abroad—as part of a personnel exchange program with the Bangalore subsidiary. The Indian team was well prepared and seemed agreeable to Allen's directions. They were also hospitable to the point where every day and evening was full of activities. Allen was impressed by the team's technical skills and got the impression that they appreciated his technical expertise as well. He felt that their work together was off to a good start.

Since returning to the U.S., however, Allen has begun to feel some frustration with his Indian counterparts. The project is proceeding satisfactorily overall, but there has been a reluctance to make changes from the original software design plan, even when these changes are verbally agreed to during regular conference calls in which all the key players participate. Allen would also like to have a freer exchange of ideas and information, and he feels that the team's attitude toward him is too deferential. "Yes, sir," is a common response from Atul, but that statement sometimes seems to have a slightly sarcastic edge to it, and then plan changes are not always implemented. Recently Atul joined a phone conference with Allen and a customer for this new set of software tools. Although Atul's words were very polite, Allen perceived his tone toward the customer as being a bit condescending, as if Atul had a better solution in mind.

This is a relatively straightforward development project, and Allen wants to complete it without any major problems. He is under pressure from his own management to meet project deadlines and deliver a timely solution to a satisfied customer. The Indian team is a good, low-cost resource for the company. Allen would like to find out more about what is going on in Bangalore so that the work can move ahead on schedule.

Possible Interpretations by Foreign Counterparts

There are several reasons why Allen has not been able to achieve a satisfactory two-way flow of information.

Status gap.

One issue overlaps with the case of Mehmet Savasan presented in chapter 3: Allen is asking Atul to provide opinions during a conference call, while Atul is reluctant to contradict his manager in front of junior colleagues. This may be what Atul is thinking:

> *It is not my role to tell my boss in front of others what I think about what he's saying. If Allen really expects us to make sudden changes in the project plan, he should bring it up in a better manner. He should approach me one-on-one rather than in front of other people, especially if he wants to hear my thoughts on changes from what our previous boss, Mr. Prasad, had asked us to do.*

From an early age in India, people are taught to respect persons of age and authority, and a formal, polite distance is usually maintained between people on different organizational levels. Scenarios may arise in which a more junior person would like to pass on some information but is unsure how to bridge the status gap. Given the proper opportunity, junior people will often share what they know, but Allen and Atul have not yet been able to create a mutually satisfactory process. A contributing factor to the limited information flow is that Atul is still not clear why his previous boss was transferred to another project and feels conflicting loyalties.

Positioning and motivation of the Indian team.

Part of the tone expressed by the Indian team may also stem from a motivational issue. This talented engineering group is being asked to carry out a relatively simple project because they are regarded as a low-cost design resource. As gifted engineers, they would like to take on more challenging work but do not see any immediate prospects for doing so. Headquarters does not seem inclined to really develop them or treat them as full-fledged company members. Moreover, when the firm is in a cost-cutting mode, they do not feel that they can easily say no to any requests.

Atul's U.S. experience.

The attitude of the team has also been influenced by Atul's six-week experience in the U.S., which unfortunately reinforced the perception that the contributions of Indian team members are undervalued. After his return to India, Atul reported to them with sadness:

> *I arrived in the U.S. proud to be an employee of this fine company. But when I arrived at the office, I was met by a human resources manager who simply gave me a brief explanation and took me to my workstation; she was not aware of the schedule for my visit. She gave me a piece of paper telling me where to go to lunch. There was an e-mail from my host manager saying he would meet me later. When we were finally able to meet, he only had a few minutes before rushing out, and he introduced me to his colleague as a "contractor from India."*
>
> *It was only thanks to Mr. Prasad, who was not my direct manager at the time, that I eventually figured out how to adjust and began to meet other people. He took me to his home to meet his family and served an Indian supper.*
>
> *Toward the end of my stay, there was a speech by the company president. He described our Indian design center as a low-cost solution but said nothing about our capabilities or the contribution we have already made to the company. This made me think that our technical expertise is not fully understood or respected.*

Cultural Comparisons

Information may not be shared readily for a variety of reasons that include but go beyond the circumstances of the Indian case mentioned above. As usual, many of these factors would be present in a domestic context as well, but they become particularly acute in cross-border relationships. Here are some thoughts that can become obstacles to free information exchange:

- "I don't trust you."
- "I'm not confident in my ability to express thoughts and feelings in your language."
- "I'm not sure whether the information I have is important—or whether you would think it is important."
- "I don't know what you are going to do with what I tell you."
- "I don't want you meeting with my customers because you may upset them or undermine me."
- "I am afraid that sharing information will get me in trouble (e.g., my immediate boss would be upset)."
- "I'm afraid of what your reaction would be if I told you."
- "You wouldn't listen even if I told you."
- "You don't ask, so you must not be interested."

In general, concerns about sharing information directly are more pronounced in hierarchical, group-oriented cultures where enduring relationships are a key personal asset. To place in jeopardy your relationship with a senior member of the hierarchy or a key network member could have dire long-term consequences. A frontal approach to either obtaining or providing information will probably be a less effective strategy in such environments. It is important to keep in mind an array of different possible attitudes and approaches as outlined in table 5.

Table 5. **Obtaining Information: Comparative Styles**

Cultural Orientation	**Expectations and Behaviors for ← Obtaining Information →**		**Cultural Orientation**
Task	Information is an objective resource obtained by password as needed or through technical skill; access is determined on a functional basis—hazards arise from "hacking," or unauthorized system access	Information is embedded in relationships and context; it is only safe to speak freely with close friends, family, or other trusted partners; information is obtained through exchange or quid pro quo; hazards arise from the betrayal of personal trust	**Relationship**
Direct	Controversial viewpoints should be stated as clearly and directly as possible; constructive confrontation is desirable	A difference of opinion is likely to be understated, conveyed through nonverbal means, or voiced only if the counterpart appears receptive	**Indirect**
Equality	Active exchanges of opinions occur even when people of different ranks are present; information sharing is encouraged between all organizational levels	When people of different ranks are present, more junior members will avoid stating opinions; information may not flow freely upward within the organization unless proper channels are in place	**Hierarchy**
Universal	Ideas and opinions should be expressed freely regardless of context; information can be shared via technology—anytime, anywhere—and needs to be captured and distributed as fully as possible	There is a time and place to share information—what is shared depends on who is present and what they are ready to hear; access is determined by who you know and how well you know them	**Situational**

More country-specific factors can influence the flow of information as well. Protocol such as whether or at what point one discusses business on social occasions will influence the behavior of foreign counterparts (according to French dining etiquette, for instance, business topics are customarily taken up toward the end of the meal). And, as in the case of feedback, there may also be a roundabout process where one is first treated to a small glimpse of the subject so that the narrator can gauge the reaction before gradually expanding the scope of the conversation.

In a more serious vein, the legacy of repressive political regimes makes even corporate sector employees very cautious about sharing information beyond the boundaries of their most trusted inner circle of friends and family.[1] An active mafia that preys upon a country's business enterprises could also dampen the willingness of employees to say anything about profits, goals, or customer relationships that would make their company a target.

The problem in some countries may not be too little information but the objectivity or quality of the information one receives. In Brazil, for example, subjective perceptions are in many cases given equal or greater importance than objective "facts," and the line distinguishing fact from fiction tends to be less well defined than in many other cultures. Information in Russia is often poorly collected and inefficiently organized (and sometimes simply not released), either due to lack of access or methods to process it or the belief that the public does not need to know. Company information that is standard in many other countries, such as annual reports and marketing brochures, is not always available. Connections and relationships can provide useful information, but it is generally a good idea to employ a cross-checking process in order to verify the information provided by different sources and look for common threads.

Recommendations for Obtaining Information

Returning to the case outlined at the beginning of the chapter, how would a manager like Allen get to the bottom of what is going on with his Indian colleagues and take the appropriate actions? He has walked into the middle of a complex situation, with attitudes and perceptions that have been formed by a wider set of factors before he arrived on the scene. What follows are some strategies and tactics for obtaining accurate and complete information that could be employed under such circumstances.

Ask via a third party.

This is sometimes called "triangulating," or clarifying through other parties. It would definitely be wise for Allen to seek out Mr. Prasad, Atul's former manager, for example, to ask him for his insights and advice. Assuming that Mr. Prasad himself had a solid relationship with the Indian development team during the time that he managed it, he could also provide assistance in getting them to open up and exchange views with Allen more freely. AT&T VP Albert Sui puts the concept of triangulating this way:

> *When we try to ascertain whether the important issues have been heard, there are ways we can do that without trying to ask directly. We can, for example, get other parties involved who have the information, knowledge, and a stake in the project. And we can get their perspective as to whether the critical issues are being acknowledged and will be attended to.*[2]

Change the setting.

The degree of openness in communication is often based on the context, and an informal setting will usually allow for a more direct and open exchange of information. In the case of Allen and his Indian IT team, informal face-to-face contacts would be difficult and expensive to arrange because they are not co-located. However, Allen could easily schedule a weekly one-on-one check-in call with team supervisor Atul to create a more private venue for the exchange of views. They could use this informal setting to continue building their relationship and to work through difficult problems together before they are addressed by the full team. Periodic videoconferences with the team would also give Allen more visual cues. By trying to obtain information in multiple settings, he would have a better chance of finding out what they are really thinking.

Explain background and context.

People who place a high value on hierarchy and group relationships often find it difficult to open up about what they are thinking unless a string of green lights is in place. They may hold back out of concern about the impact that sharing a particular piece of information will have on their relationships with others.

Allen could anticipate this need and provide more background to the requests that he is making. This, in turn, would make it easier for his Indian counterparts to be forthcoming.

> *We need to change our design plan to accommodate a change in the customer's own IT environment. Let me provide you the details... I'm aware that this may cause a delay in the completion of the project and would like to get an estimate from you on how much extra time you think it will take. I've gone back and spoken with Mr. Prasad about this as well, and his advice was that we go ahead and make the changes that the customer was requesting even if there is a delay involved.*

Show genuine interest.

At times it is necessary to demonstrate very clearly the level of your interest or depth of your concern about an issue before you will be taken seriously. Given the chip that Atul has on his shoulder after what he perceives to be second-class treatment in the U.S., Allen may have to approach him more than once and appeal to his wounded pride.

> *I appreciate that you are willing to do what I ask for, Atul, but I also really want to hear your views. You and your team have technical skills that will add even more value to the project if we have an open exchange of ideas.*

Show precedent.

The past is as important as the future in many countries, and explaining how something has been done similarly in previous situations, or how other organizations have handled a similar issue, is helpful in encouraging others to speak up. Allen actually has Indian business culture on his side in this situation. If he can get beyond the Indian team's deference to him as a superior in the corporate hierarchy, he may find that they are very good at discussing an issue from various perspectives to determine the merits of one course of action over another. In India, informally discussing and rethinking issues through intense and ongoing group dialogue is a very familiar way to engage with one another. In fact, it would be useful to refer to company precedents for this.

> *You know, I worked on the Project 21 design team together with Indian members last year, and they contributed lots of good ideas. I would like to have that same kind of exchange of information between us. Mr. Prasad also told me that sometimes you all had some very lively and productive debates that helped to create the current project design.*

Probe politely but persistently.

Persistent repetition of a question or similar type of questions is often seen as a sign of seriousness of intent—not as a rude intrusion. It can be taken as a cue for providing another layer of information that was not offered in the first response.

> **Initially:** *Atul, how could you and your team contribute more of your own ideas to this project?*
>
> **Then later:** *I'd really appreciate it if you could help me understand if there is anything holding you back from contributing more of your ideas.*
>
> **Again at a later point:** *Is there something I could do to make it easier for your group to freely contribute ideas?*

Rephrase the request.

Rephrasing a request into a statement that assumes it will be difficult for the other party to honor your request can often help you to find out if you will get what you are asking for.

> *My sense is that you do not think it is a good idea to change the design plan at this point. Is this true?*

Clarify and confirm.

A good way to ensure that both sides come away from a conversation with the same understanding is to ask the other party to confirm what they will do. This makes it easier to recognize remaining areas where expectations differ and to avoid so-called agreement that is merely a signal of good intentions and a desire to please. Sending follow-up confirmation in writing helps to establish that a shared understanding has indeed been reached.

> *So Atul, could you confirm what your team will do over the next week?*

Over the long run, it is feasible for Allen to develop a richly informative relationship with his Indian colleagues if he can become a part of their informal communication loop. Indeed, even secret information rarely remains so for very long in many Indian settings. People love to exchange information and to discuss the problems and issues involved with it. They are very closely networked by means of family connections, business interactions, school ties, neighborhood gatherings, and other associations. It is quite customary to engage in giving and receiving information among all these groups.

Gathering more sensitive information—such as learning about a person's character or about the reputation of a supplier—is possible through building ties or staying in contact with colleagues at other companies and government agencies. In India, people who meet one another in the same social circles or belong to the same business organizations will readily exchange information and experiences in informal settings such as lunches and dinners. They often do favors for one another and, in return, expect help when they need it. This atmosphere is more difficult to create in a "virtual" relationship with only occasional face-to-face meetings, but it can be approximated with patient efforts to listen and build trust.

Global People Skill #4: Evaluating People

Once the process of relationship building has begun and credibility has been established, we must also try to make a fair and accurate assessment of employees in the new location, however strange their business practices might seem at first. The skill of evaluating people naturally draws on other skills such as giving and receiving feedback or obtaining information on sensitive topics. Who can you depend on for market intelligence? Who is really getting things done for the customer? Who can give you valuable advice and insight into organizational issues? Longer term, another critical task for leaders is to select and develop successors for themselves and other members of the leadership team. Who are the right individuals to lead the company into the future?

Evaluating a Russian Executive

Your company is involved in a joint venture with a Russian company. You are not Russian, but you have been residing in Russia and directing the venture for the past year. Although there have certainly been many difficult challenges, overall you are pleased with the progress that has been made in reaching business goals. You have, for example, been able to implement most of the financial tracking and reporting systems that you feel are crucial in laying the groundwork for a successful long-term venture.

At the beginning of the joint venture, both companies agreed that the top position would be turned over to a Russian director after one year. Ivan Petrovich was the agreed-upon successor for many reasons: he is the most senior, experienced, and respected member of the Russian company; he is well educated and fluent in several languages; and he understands the financial focus and requirements of your company, which has 51 percent control of the joint venture.

After working together and observing Ivan Petrovich for the past year, however, you have some concerns about his style and ability to manage the venture. His leadership style is authoritarian and direct. He seems to order his subordinates around quite a bit, criticizes them publicly for their mistakes, and sometimes yells at them. You have observed that his employees only do exactly what they are told, and it is not unusual to see one employee doing nothing right next to another employee who is working hard to complete a project. Ivan Petrovich seems to tolerate this behavior. These are not the leadership qualities you had hoped for in your successor.

Possible Actions and Consequences

Here are several possible courses of action and how they might be interpreted by local partners and by Ivan Petrovich himself:

- **Take up your concerns directly with Ivan Petrovich.** It would be very difficult to talk with Ivan Petrovich without him feeling that you are questioning his abilities and doubting his leadership effectiveness (which is exactly what you are doing). Furthermore, Ivan Petrovich will probably doubt your effectiveness if you begin to criticize qualities he views as being culturally appropriate and most effective for this organization in Russia.
- **Remain in your position and manage the joint venture for another year while working with him on his leadership style.** This is a risky strategy that could become an affront to the Russian partners' strong sense of pride. You need to make sure that there is no indication of a patronizing "we know what's best" attitude toward the Russian company. If you stay in your position for another year, it may well seem like you don't trust their abilities.
- **Find another successor because Ivan Petrovich does not have the leadership qualities required to manage the joint venture.** The Russian employees in the joint venture may regard an authoritarian

style as being quite natural and effective in their environment. Moreover, in joint ventures with Russian companies, certain qualities and skills are required at the early stages—such as a focus on financial controls and establishing systems and processes—while a different set of qualities and skills is required at a later stage. Ivan Petrovich probably has what is needed at this stage of the venture.

This situation with Ivan Petrovich is potentially an explosive one, and if it is mishandled, it could place the joint venture itself in jeopardy. It is not uncommon for Russian partners to ask or even force their counterparts to leave the country—they may not "own" a controlling share of the joint venture, but they control the physical infrastructure, the security, the work force, the surrounding community, the banking system, and so on.

Aside from judging this Russian executive's capabilities, there are a number of additional pitfalls involved in evaluating personnel in other parts of an organization. These, too, could lead to significant rifts with local employees. Here are several of these hazards as they appear from the local perspective:

- **Information about individual performance is limited or distorted by people in key roles.** Foreign managers who do not speak the host-country language are particularly vulnerable to this problem. They are dependent on the people immediately around them to interface with the rest of the organization, to obtain accurate information, and to form judgments about others. These "gatekeepers" can abuse their position by skewing information in a way that supports their personal agenda or advances the fortunes of their own political favorites within the organization.

- **Poor business results are attributed to the wrong causes.** It is fine to introduce the notion of accountability but only if this is coupled with the understanding that market circumstances could have unexpected effects on results. Even competent, hardworking employees may be frustrated in achieving their objectives by infrastructure deficiencies, supplier errors, or government restrictions that are beyond their control. If employees feel that they have been criticized without sufficient justification, they will begin to harbor open or silent resentment.

- **Consistent evaluation criteria are lacking.** Employees may feel whipsawed between one set of evaluation criteria set by a foreign manager and other, perhaps less visible, criteria expressed by local managers. For example, the foreign manager might ask them to complete a project requested by headquarters in time to meet an upcoming deadline, while a local manager—even one with whom there is no direct reporting relationship—is urging them to solve a separate customer issue. It is difficult for employees to serve more than one master and particularly awkward when the tenure of the foreign manager is known to be limited while the demanding local manager will be around for many years to come.
- **Development opportunities are inadequate.** Junior employees in growing but still immature subsidiary organizations often do not have the benefit of a strong middle-management cadre to facilitate their development. Middle managers may not have key skills themselves or are simply too busy with their own jobs to focus on training and developing their subordinates. Therefore, bright young people are thrown into difficult situations with minimal preparation and sometimes fall flat due to sheer inexperience. It is important in that case to render judgments about these individuals based on a realistic assessment of the organizational context and the strengths and weaknesses of the managers for whom they are working.

Unfortunately, some leaders with very solid people instincts back home make the wrong choices in a more diverse environment. The most common trap of all is to evaluate people positively on the basis of their language skills and communication style even when their skills in crucial areas such as managing subordinates or working with customers are deficient. This error sometimes takes on almost ludicrous proportions, with foreign managers attempting to promote individuals who are clearly unqualified in the eyes of local colleagues—to the point where the people being promoted are embarrassed at being singled out. Lee Ting, former head of the Asia-Pacific region for Hewlett-Packard, recommends that we keep our eyes open for indications of leadership potential other than those we find to be most familiar:

> *In looking for the qualities of a leader…, I think you need to go beyond the outward qualities of a leader in a Western context, which is often somebody that is outwardly aggressive, somebody who speaks good English, for instance, or someone who is socially active. Obviously, for an Asian, unless he is brought up in the U.S., English is not his primary language, and his communication might not come across as being very effective sometimes. People may mistakenly judge the quality of this person's communication as a sign of the quality of this person's leadership.*[3]

Cultural Comparisons

So, conduct that would signal competence in one's own environment—assertiveness, for example—could have an entirely different significance elsewhere. It is important to learn local standards for evaluating people and to cultivate broad sources of information so that you can arrive at balanced assessments. Table 6 lists possible differences in evaluation criteria that lead to misperceptions and mistaken evaluations on the part of managers who move from one environment to another.

Recommendations for Evaluating People

The best solution in the case of Ivan Petrovich is probably to turn the direction of the joint venture over to him as planned. At this stage of the project, he may well be the right person to take over leadership. His leadership style is more culturally appropriate for Russia than someone unfamiliar with the country may realize. A legacy of thousands of years of authoritarian rule and decades of communism has created a work force that often expects to be told what to do and is very cautious about taking initiative. Admired leaders in Russia tend to be tough, direct, and demanding. Publicly criticizing an employee is not uncommon and can be more effective than private one-on-one feedback because it indicates to the other employees that the leader is in charge. Although Russian

Table 6. **Evaluating People: Comparative Styles**

Cultural Orientation	← Expectations and Behaviors for	Evaluating People →	Cultural Orientation
Individual	People who are willing to take responsibility and get things done are evaluated positively	People who are adaptable and willing to do what is necessary for the good of the team are evaluated positively	**Group**
Direct	Candidates for promotion are expected to be open about their qualifications and ambitions; assertiveness is valued	"Silent virtue" is valued and recognized; outward displays of modesty and humility are the norm and seen as preferable to aggressive self-promotion	**Indirect**
Equality	Mature managers treat capable employees as peers; 360-degree evaluation that includes the views of subordinates is standard practice	A tough, authoritative management style is admired; subordinates may not have the experience to render a correct judgment of their boss	**Hierarchy**
Universal	Performance evaluation criteria should be objective and applied to everyone to ensure fairness	Flexibility is necessary to make an accurate evaluation; unique talents and special circumstances must be taken into account	**Situational**
Achievement	Employees are evaluated on the basis of their performance records	Employees are evaluated based on both performance and other factors such as education, age, gender, and years of loyal service to the organization	**Ascription**

business practices are changing, a leader who is more egalitarian and provides "suggestions" instead of directions might find that these practices are disrespected by Russian employees.

Observers from more egalitarian cultures are likely to miss the fact that leaders who appear to be authoritarian also maintain very close

My Mistake: Evaluating People

Some years ago, a scientist from India became part of our work group. I found myself to be uncomfortable with him from the beginning. He dressed in fancy, expensive clothes and was meticulous about his appearance and keeping his carefully oiled hair tidy; I preferred a more plain and "natural" look. He was talkative and gregarious—happy to theorize and debate at great length about almost anything; I felt it was a virtue to stay quiet if I had nothing important to say. He spent a lot of time in the cafeteria chatting with acquaintances; I spent the bulk of my working hours in a cubicle churning out the action items that I had committed to completing.

At one point I shared with another U.S. participant my view that the Indian member of the project was not adding a lot of value and looked like kind of a slick operator. My U.S. colleague took issue with this view, pointing out that there were various angles to the project and that our Indian member had made important contributions in generating new ideas and building wider support with others in the organization for the next implementation steps.

My remarks eventually found their way back to the Indian scientist himself. He confronted me with them, and I had to sheepishly admit to making such statements. He rebuked me for my bad manners and pointed out that there were many different ways of getting things done. I was embarrassed both for evaluating him incorrectly and for passing on that mistaken view without verifying it.

touch with their employees and are well aware of their needs and aspirations. Highly effective leaders of this kind have the trust of the people who work for them because they have their best interests at heart and are willing to represent these interests—they provide counsel, assistance, protection, and opportunities at the same time that they exercise their power. For example, a Russian management practice in some industries that foreign managers find strange is holding "personal office hours" during which individual employees can come to discuss home- or family-related issues. The ties between leaders and subordinates built through these contacts or through after-hours socializing can be as strong and enduring as those created by any enlightened egalitarian.

The best recipe for evaluating people in a multicultural setting is to constantly look through others' eyes as well as our own. If we are looking primarily through the lenses of our own assumptions and expectations, the probability that a poor decision will result is high. Knowing how employees or customers from another culture would regard the same person is a vital step in making an informed choice—even if we do not ultimately agree with their views or choose to make evaluations based on a blend of their views and our own.

Western businesspeople working with Japanese colleagues find it helpful to compare the concepts of the "stand-out" and the "stand-in" leader.[4] They could search endlessly without success to find a Western-style "stand-out" leader who forges ahead with a vision and mission for the organization and orchestrates a team of specialized individuals. Meanwhile, they would be missing solid leadership candidates who are striving to achieve a different sort of leadership ideal based on indigenous traditions. Characteristically the "stand-in" leader

- Is senior, experienced—knows every job
- Is always there for people—sits with the team; arrives first and leaves last
- Assumes full responsibility for subordinates' actions; expects quick notice when problems arise and consults with employees to generate solutions
- Understands subordinates better than they understand themselves; acts as a career mentor as well as a manager
- Demonstrates a strong dedication to quality, reliability, and customer service
- Has a broad network of human connections that helps to get things done

- Knows how to use either discipline or positive motivation, as appropriate
- Rarely gives verbal compliments; may direct public criticism at promising subordinates in order to stimulate others
- Socializes after hours to draw out and solve problems
- Teaches more by implicit example than by explicit explanation

Another way of seeing through the eyes of others is to understand the labels that local employees themselves use in evaluating people within the organization. Table 7 gives examples of four employee types commonly found in foreign capital companies in Japan. "Traditionalists" can become a source of frustration for foreign executives who seek to introduce new ideas or business practices. When there are conflicts over the change agenda, it is difficult to perceive or effectively utilize the loyalty and steady effort invested by employees who value consistency with the past. The next two labels, "Lone Wolf" and "English Store," are direct translations from Japanese expressions (*ippiki ookami* and *eigoya*). Foreign managers often diverge widely from their Japanese colleagues in evaluating these two types. They tend to overestimate the capabilities of the Lone Wolf based on his or her assertive self-presentation, failing to see problems with teamwork and management. The English Store is the Japanese version of the glib and self-confident speaker who leads a foreign executive astray with strong communication skills that mask deficiencies in other areas. Finally, true "Internationalists"—whom everybody wants—are not always easy to spot because they may lack those strong communication skills; when promoted ahead of others without proper positioning they also become a target of envy and political infighting.

A typology such as this one is easily misunderstood and misused. It is not intended to reduce complex individual personalities to broad and simple types. The purpose is rather to assist a foreign manager in beginning to view his or her people through local perspectives instead of just through imported lenses, expanding the range of vision while promoting constructive dialogue and inquiry into further variety.

Any one of these categories could be elaborated into additional subcategories. For instance, variations of the English Store include good

Table 7. **Common Employee Types: Foreign Capital Companies in Japan**

Factor	Type 1: Traditionalist	Type 2: Lone Wolf	Type 3: English Store	Type 4: Internationalist
Reason for joining	Only viable option; seconded by joint venture	Personal challenge; limited career prospects in local enterprises	To use English language and cultural skills	Broad perspective; interest in new ideas and practices
Work style	Relationship-oriented; interdependent	Task-oriented; independent	Prefers Western company salary, perks	Open, flexible, assertive; appropriate style switching
Communication style	Indirect	More direct	Direct	More direct
Self-perception	Loyal, hardworking	More individualistic; puts self and family first	Hopeful but lacking in real confidence	Adventurous; curious
Appearance to westerners	Faithful but lacking initiative, creativity	Capable; results-oriented	Very capable; knowledgeable; easy to work with	Capable; a winner; still young
Appearance to local colleagues	One of us; trustworthy but mediocre	Competent in specialty; divisive; poor at managing people	Flatterer, fawner; can't do real work; misleads foreign management	High potential; admired, envied; good with customers

employees who have the potential to develop other capabilities but are simply inexperienced, those who are already stretched in their current role, "Smokescreen" types who point to false cultural differences as a way to mask poor results, and manipulators who abuse their privileged intermediary position to further personal or political ends. But the ultimate point is to get beyond types altogether and to evaluate each employee accurately based on assumptions that are both flexible and regularly reexamined.

Obtaining Information and Evaluating People

SUMMARY AND REVIEW QUESTIONS

1. How do you usually go about obtaining sensitive or time-dependent information? What part do your established relationships with people play in this process?

2. What particular strategies would you use to obtain information in a cultural setting where objective data are hard to find?

3. The following are sample means of obtaining information in an environment where group ties, indirectness, and past examples are valued. Have you used these techniques, or would you be comfortable using them?

   - Ask through a third party
   - Change the setting
   - Explain background and context
   - Show precedent

4. When you evaluate a colleague's leadership abilities, what emphasis do you usually place on a vocal and assertive communication style? What are some other leadership qualities that are important to you?

5. When assessing the performance of an employee in a foreign setting, how would you gather information on which to base your evaluation?

6. Do you personally have any of the characteristics of a "stand-in" leader? What might be the appeal of such a leadership style to workers in another country? Should this type of leadership be recognized and/or cultivated?

7. Do the four types of employees identified within foreign capital companies in Japan seem familiar to you? Are there different cultural settings in which some of these same types might be found? What other general types would local workers identify in a culture that you know about? Can you think of employees you know in that same culture who do not fit these types? If so, why don't they fit?

Part II

Group Skills

CHAPTER FIVE

Working on a Global Team

Multicultural teams present a critical challenge for global organizations. Although such teams play an increasingly vital role in accomplishing corporate business objectives, teamwork is not easy for a diverse group whose members may bring with them very different viewpoints and assumptions.

Without special attention, the performance of such teams often falls short of company and team member expectations. On the other hand, when multicultural teamwork is cultivated in a conscious way that balances both performance outcomes and team member relationships, the creative potential exists for results that far exceed those of a single-culture group.

Global People Skill #5: Building Global Teamwork

There are a variety of different types of global teams: top management teams, project teams, cross-functional teams, joint venture teams, and so on. One of the most common is a globally dispersed functional unit—for example, Marketing, IT, Purchasing—that must rely heavily on virtual forms of communication to coordinate its activities.

The Global Purchasing Team

The following scene re-creates a conference call connecting Global Purchasing Department members in the Netherlands, Germany, the U.S., Thailand, and Australia.

The conference call participants include:

Mirjam Wouters	The Netherlands/team leader
Gerhardt Krause	Germany/Dresden factory purchasing manager
Teresa Wilson	United States/manager of global supply partners (GSPs)
Sombat Nasuwan	Thailand/Bangkok factory purchasing manager
Adam Clark	Australia/Asia-Pacific purchasing manager

Mirjam (team leader): *How's everybody today?* [Greetings from others on the line.] *Khun Sombat and Adam, thanks for making yourselves available so late in the evening.*

Sombat: *No problem.*

Adam: *Right.*

Mirjam: *Okay, let me summarize. We are making good progress toward our 20 percent cost reduction goal for components in the new product cycle, but there are still a couple of problem areas. One is the question Gerhardt has raised about the flexibility of some of our global supply partners. The other is the yield issue in Thailand, where we're meeting the cost goals but still have some problems to resolve before we can certify several key suppliers. We also need to discuss the executive visits to Europe and Asia next month. Gerhardt, could* *you please start by describing the GSP issue and giving us your recommendations?*

Gerhardt: *Well, the simple fact is that we need greater flexibility from some of the GSPs, particularly the two largest suppliers from North America and the U.K. They are not very flexible when our team needs to request minor design alterations, and our early test results indicate that there may be some serious quality issues with certain components. Frankly, we think that we would be better off in the long run if we could keep some of our previous arrangements with local German suppliers.*

Mirjam: *That would make it a lot more difficult to achieve our cost-reduction objectives.*

Gerhardt: *Sometimes these corporate initiatives don't make any sense. If we have quality issues with the new product cycle and have to recall products once they are out in the marketplace, this will be much more costly in the long run. I would suggest that you speak with your division head there in Amsterdam and ask him whether he thinks the aggressive cost savings are worth the risk of recalls. I think a 10 percent cost reduction target would be more reasonable than 20 percent.*

Mirjam: *It is up to us to work with each supplier to meet the quality goals.*

Gerhardt: *Yes, of course, but our quality engineers tell me that they are really concerned about the test data.*

Teresa: *We have also gone through a lengthy certification process with each of the GSPs. Our certification process did include a full range of quality tests, particularly for the electronics components.*

Gerhardt: *Process or no process, I'm telling you about the data we are seeing. Our factory has the highest quality of any of our facilities in the world. How can we work with suppliers who think that they can tell our engineers what to do? They have even questioned our quality* *test results. And we still need these GSPs to make minor changes to accommodate our product design modifications. The engineers in our Dresden factory are complaining that the GSP personnel have the attitude that they are in charge because of their relationship with our corporate headquarters.*

Teresa: *They give us volume discounts based on the contractual understanding that they can offer us standardized components. They're just pushing back to see if they can accommodate your needs without adding costs.*

Gerhardt: *This situation is unacceptable if we intend to meet the scheduled product launch date with the optimum design and proper quality levels. And I haven't even mentioned the fact that our lead times for component deliveries will increase because the nearest GSP warehouses are in Düsseldorf...*

Mirjam: *Teresa, could you please stay on the line with Gerhardt after the conference call and get some more detail from him? Then perhaps you can talk to the GSPs to see if we can resolve this.*

Teresa: *Okay, but they are probably going to come back to us to try to negotiate price increases for any design modifications that are outside of our existing agreements.*

Mirjam: *I understand. Let's move on to the next topic. Khun Sombat, please tell us about the yield issue you discovered with the supplier in Ban Pong.*

Sombat: *Overall, the certification process for local sources of supply is going well. We found a small problem with one supplier.*

Adam: *You're bloody right we found a problem. We went to the supplier, and they told us they were meeting our targets for eliminating defects and getting high-enough yield rates of products to meet our quality standards. The data looked okay, but when we asked to tour the plant, I went around the back and found a huge pile of defective parts. I think they were taking these out of the equation in order to meet our yield targets.*

Mirjam: *Khun Sombat, what do you think about this?*

Sombat: *Well, they were anxious to meet our targets. I will speak with them about how they collect the data.*

Adam: *After what we saw, I don't have a lot of confidence in this supplier. And they still don't seem to be up to speed with our Web-based order system. Our IT people have been getting lots of calls from them...*

Mirjam: *Do either of you think there could be similar issues with our other Thai suppliers?*

Adam: *Probably. But we also don't have the luxury of continuing to import high-cost components from Japan and Korea. China is our only alternative from a cost standpoint.*

Mirjam: *What is the next step? We've got to make sure that each supplier really meets our targets.*

Adam: *I plan to be rather severe about our data and reporting requirements. If the Ban Pong fellows don't give us what we need, then we'll have to find someone else. Right, Sombat?*

Sombat: *Yes.*

Mirjam: *Could you provide us with a further update on this during our next call?*

Adam: *Sure.*

Mirjam: *We need to move on now to discuss the executive visits to each region...*

Views of Team Members

During a team meeting such as this one, each participant naturally has his or her own private thoughts. Here is a sampling of what each of the participants could be thinking:

Mirjam: *It is hard to pull this group together. Gerhardt thinks he is the expert on everything but doesn't really understand our global cost pressures. He's also very protective of his German supply base and not very trusting of data that do not come from his own factory engineers. Adam has plenty to say—maybe too much—but I can't really read what Sombat is thinking.*

Gerhardt: *Dealing with amateurs is frustrating. I don't know why they appointed Mirjam as head of this group—she has only a few years of experience and lacks detailed knowledge of either the Dresden or the Bangkok factories. I feel that Purchasing has an important responsibility for the quality of the product that comes out of the manufacturing process, but the others are so focused on meeting near-term targets for cost reduction that they are taking dangerous shortcuts.*

Teresa: *I agree that there are problems with the global supply partners, but Gerhardt is not going about it in the right way. He's alienating other team members with his confrontational style, and the GSPs say he is a pain to work with.*

Sombat: *Adam doesn't realize that the Ban Pong supplier is our best alternative in Thailand for the hi-tech components we're trying to source from them. If we cannot work with them, we will have to look at higher-cost sources in Japan or Korea. He thinks he can get the best results by crashing around like an angry elephant, but all he is doing is making enemies and pressuring suppliers so much that they alter their data to make him happy. They are trying very hard to improve their quality and are making real progress. We've got to work with them as friends to help them to improve their capabilities.*

Adam: *Sombat needs more backbone. He won't stand up to suppliers he knows well and demand that they perform. A lot of the suppliers here in Thailand will smile and blow smoke at you unless you ask the tough questions. I've got to get into that country and dig around some more to make sure that they're not pulling the wool over our eyes.*

Analyzing Global Team Issues

There are many different levels or layers to the problems commonly experienced by global teams. Indeed, in the scenario depicted above there are at least six interrelated factors that make the team's mission difficult to accomplish. The form that each of them takes is shaped, though not determined, by its cultural context.

- **Individual personalities.** Gerhardt is seen by Mirjam and Teresa as being abrasive, pedantic, and somewhat narrow-minded, while he questions their competence (there may be a gender issue here as well). Sombat harbors a quiet dislike for Adam and is withholding feedback that Adam needs to hear.

- **Mutual trust.** Team members in this case evidently do not trust one another fully. Gerhardt is critical of the global supply partners and does not trust their product quality or Teresa's ability to assess it. Adam does not trust the ability of Sombat, his Thai colleague, to ferret out the shoddy production or data collection practices of local suppliers.

- **Communication styles.** Several of the meeting participants—Adam, for instance—are very direct and verbal. Sombat hardly participates in the meeting in spite of his valuable inside knowledge; he is more reticent about voicing his real thoughts or confronting other members of the team. The fact that this meeting is taking place over the telephone, without the opportunity to study nonverbal cues or to readily clarify points outside of the meeting, could be contributing to his reluctance to speak up as well.

- **Team systems.** The decision-making process that set a 20 percent cost reduction goal does not appear to have the unanimous support of team members. Gerhardt, for example, representing the German factory, questions whether such an aggressive short-term target could lead to expensive recalls of defective products in the long run. Team members are also taking very different approaches to problem solving: Gerhardt is confrontational and analytical, Sombat will contribute only if others carefully draw out his views, and Mirjam is attempting to integrate different points of view.

- **National interests.** There is a natural tendency for members of the team to defend the interests of their own particular location. Gerhardt and Sombat have close ties to local suppliers. Teresa represents the company's major "global" suppliers, some of which are located in the U.S., where she lives. Mirjam is linked to the parent company through her nationality and her location at corporate headquarters in Amsterdam. For the team to be successful, its members will have to build greater collective commitment to goals and practices that transcend national interests.
- **Global business challenges.** Global purchasing operations in most manufacturing firms must increasingly struggle to meet cost-cutting objectives through a combination of global agreements with major suppliers and the cultivation of local sources of supply in low-cost manufacturing locations. In this case, global supply partners are being introduced to the Dresden factory, a relatively high-cost location, in place of local German suppliers who offer flexibility and high quality but at a higher cost. Thailand, on the other hand, is a lower-cost manufacturing location where the challenge is to cultivate suppliers who can meet not only cost but also quality goals.

A number of other differences that are not prominent in the case cited above but which nonetheless occur frequently could arise between multicultural team members. Basic contrasts in values and assumptions regarding the role of the team leader or meeting styles, for instance, make it difficult to establish and work toward shared goals and commitments. What good teamwork looks like often varies from culture to culture. Here are some areas of contention and questions that are worth asking to draw out divergent points of view:

- **Leadership.** Is the group more hierarchically structured, or is everyone on equal footing? What is the role of the team leader? How is he or she selected?

- **Team member relations.** Is the team temporary or permanent? Do the team members know each other well? How often do they meet? To what extent do their personal and private lives overlap?

- **Role definition.** Are the roles defined more by professional specialty, or is everyone expected to contribute whatever they have to offer on any subject? How broad is each person's area of responsibility?

- **Meeting practices.** What is the preferred method of exchanging ideas and information—in a group or in a one-on-one setting, spontaneously or in more structured forms? Are meetings used to make decisions and resolve conflicts or to announce conclusions that have been reached in a more private forum?

- **Motivation.** What motivates team members to perform? Is it the possibility of personal advancement or to gain greater "face" within the company? Is it the importance of not letting one's colleagues down? Do team members see themselves as individuals or as part of a kind of family? Are there collective ideals?

- **Commitments and accountability.** What does it mean to commit to perform a certain action? Is this a way of making others feel good, a sign of positive intentions, an indication that one will make a strong effort, or a guarantee to deliver results? Should accountability focus on team or individual performance, and what are acceptable sanctions or rewards?

- **Internal diversity.** How homogeneous or heterogeneous are the team members, even those from the same country?

The more diverse a team is, the more information and perspectives there are available and the more alternative solutions the team can generate. This is extremely valuable in complex, rapidly changing business environments. But, that same diversity also makes it more difficult for the team to chart a common direction and to keep the team on course. Basic differences in assumptions such as those listed above make it difficult to establish and work toward shared goals and commitments. Table 8 lists possible differences in attitudes toward building global teamwork.

Table 8. **Building Global Teamwork: Comparative Styles**

Cultural Orientation	Expectations and Behaviors for ← Building Global Teamwork →		Cultural Orientation
Individual	Team members are individual contributors who have joined forces for this particular team effort; they either pursue their own jobs concurrently or will return to them once the team effort is complete; each person is still accountable for achieving specific goals	The identity of team members is defined through their presence on the team; team priorities take precedence over individual job descriptions; the team as a whole is accountable for achieving its goals	**Group**
Task	Team members are present primarily to get the job done; they may or may not develop close friendships with others on the team; workplace contacts need not affect the private lives of team members	Effective team functioning begins with strong relationships; team members know each other well; professional and private relationships overlap, with frequent after-hours socializing among team members	**Relationship**
Direct	Team meetings are for direct discussion and resolution of key issues; anyone with an opinion is expected to speak up at the meeting; problems are analyzed openly, and constructive disagreement or conflict is expected	One-on-one contacts outside of team meetings are used to draw out the opinions of others on key issues and to reach agreement prior to meetings; more junior meeting participants may refrain from expressing opinions directly	**Indirect**
Equality	Decisions are made through consultation or by consensus; team members consider themselves to be partners in the team effort and expect to take part in defining objectives and planning strategy	Decisions are made by the team leader, who has clear authority to set the direction of the group; team members consider themselves to be subordinates of the leader and expect explicit instructions	**Hierarchy**

Table 8. **Building Global Teamwork: Comparative Styles (continued)**

Cultural Orientation	Expectations and Behaviors for ← Building Global Teamwork →		Cultural Orientation
Universal	Team members contribute both as specialists and as generalists; they do not hesitate to offer opinions on areas outside their own specialties; the most valuable team participants can analyze issues from a broad strategic perspective	Team members each represent highly specialized functions; they solicit opinions and defer to each other's expertise on technical matters; the strong professionalism of team participants makes the whole team strong	**Situational**

Recommendations for Building Global Teamwork

Several topics deserve focused attention on the part of multicultural teams and team leaders to optimize team performance. These include the initial stage of team formation, team meeting practices, communication across technology for dispersed teams, and team systems such as decision making or problem solving.

Team formation.

The startup phase is particularly important for multicultural teams. When team members come from very different backgrounds, it is all too easy to create misunderstandings that can have a long-term negative impact on performance. Creating positive team chemistry can be a challenging and complex task. For such teams to be effective, it is imperative to invest the effort to create a shared context and to build relationships of trust and rapport among team members. Specific suggestions are listed in table 9.

Team members from more egalitarian business environments often underestimate the critical role of the team leader. With diverse teams it is ideal to have a leader who is both well positioned within the organization and highly respected by each member of the team. (For better or worse, seniority and a touch of gray hair may be helpful for leaders on certain

Table 9. **Building a Multicultural Team**

- Explain how the team and its objectives are positioned within the global organization and underline the importance of the team's efforts
- Select and support a leader that team members of all nationalities will respect
- Have the team leader meet with team members individually to build rapport and trust
- Disseminate biographical information on team members before they meet
- Create opportunities to meet in comfortable social settings
- Offer the team written background information and a structured orientation to the project
- Take time to clarify the team's collective mission and to clearly delineate the roles and responsibilities of each team member
- Enable team members to build "face" with the others by giving them opportunities to utilize their experience or expertise

teams where competing national interests and personal titles are at stake.) If this team leader then takes the time to build his or her own strong relationship with each member of the team, the chances that these team participants will respect each other are much greater. The team leader can communicate with them one-on-one to plan what will be done in meetings, and later orchestrate group interactions so that each member is able to make a visible contribution toward achieving team objectives.

There is a certain conditioning process that goes on in multicultural teams. This takes planning, discipline, and patience—similar to the preparations for a demanding athletic event.[1] Many people question whether the time and effort involved are worth it, or claim that they do not have the luxury, for instance, to hold pre-meetings. But on a multicultural team, working under the pressure of ambitious goals and tight deadlines, the different assumptions held by team members can easily become accentuated and pull the team apart. Building a supportive organizational context for the team's activities, while starting out with an emphasis on the creation of solid, trusting relationships between team members, gives the team room to establish its own collective definitions and operating style. When these initial steps are taken in a careful, comprehensive fashion, the different perspectives of team members can be focused on common goals with a shared commitment to achieving them. The diversity of a multicultural group is thus transformed from a hindrance into a strategic advantage.

Team meetings.

Multicultural team meetings often suffer from uneven contributions made by team members. As one interviewee commented, "To me, the biggest challenge of a cross-cultural team is that in that process of teaming we leave room for others to truly give their input. Otherwise, why do we need to have a cross-cultural team?"[2] The readiness of team members to speak up and contribute opinions, to tackle controversial or delicate subjects in a public forum, or to offer constructive feedback to one another is strongly influenced by their cultural background. It is critical for team members to have the shared commitment and the skills to engage in a productive exchange of views, bringing out the maximum possible contribution from each meeting participant.

Meeting facilitation techniques become particularly significant when working with diverse groups. The facilitator should of course try to establish a clear meeting agenda and shared ground rules. He or she is also responsible for regulating the flow of the meeting dialogue and balancing the speaking time of different members. This may mean holding back those who are speaking too much or encouraging others to provide more input. Recommended facilitation techniques include those listed in table 10.

The facilitator, however, is not the only person with the responsibility for creating a balanced team meeting format. All team members share the responsibility for helping the group to work effectively together. (See table B-1 in appendix B for some techniques that participants can use to enhance the value of their own contribution as well as that of others.)

Table 10. **Multicultural Meetings: Techniques for Facilitators**

- **Changing speakers.** When one or two people begin to dominate the team discussion, the facilitator should invite others to express their views.

- **Drawing out team members.** Team members who are non-native-language speakers, or members of cultures in which reserve is considered a virtue, may avoid making a contribution until they are asked. It is also often necessary to give such persons more time in which to answer the question or to come forward with their ideas or opinions. Asking a person to provide advice to the team can be a nice way to invite them into the conversation: "You have lots of experience in this area—what has worked for you in the past? How do you see this situation? What improvements could we make?"[3]

- **Initiating turn taking.** Give each person at the table, one by one, the chance to express his or her views before beginning a discussion. This provides those who are less comfortable speaking up with a chance to prepare, a predictable entry point into the conversation, and an audience that is primed to listen.

- **Using small groups.** Some participants are likely to feel more comfortable expressing their thoughts to a smaller group of colleagues and reporting the views of their subgroup rather than their own personal opinion. Small group discussions are a good way to help surface views that the whole team needs to hear.

- **Requesting written input.** This can help to initiate a discussion because it allows people to contribute who are not fluent in the primary language being used or who do not tend to speak up. People who are inclined to say little in a meeting will commonly have plenty to write if a well-structured opportunity is provided to them.

- **Balancing tasks and relationships.** On the task side, the facilitator must keep the group on track, but it is also imperative that he or she cultivates a positive group atmosphere that encourages everyone to contribute.

The most vital skill for any participant in a multicultural meeting is to recognize that there is a wide variety of effective meeting styles. Flexibility and mutual adaptation are essential. Successful teams ultimately create their own "third culture" that blends the contributions and styles of all team members.

Communicating across technology.

The challenges for cross-cultural productivity are perhaps most acute for the geographically dispersed project team whose members can only meet in person occasionally. Many companies are now relying increasingly on virtual teamwork to accomplish critical business objectives.

Establishing an overall communications strategy helps to ensure that virtual communications technologies are used most effectively. When creating such a strategy, it is worth considering the amount of "context" available through different types of interactions, as illustrated in table 11. A person-to-person meeting, for example, affords a large number of contextual cues through a range of possible interactions: informal contacts (e.g., in the hallway outside of the meeting), direct physical exchanges (e.g., handshakes or bows), environmental setting (e.g., table seating order), nonverbal messages (e.g., facial expressions, hand gestures), immediate feedback, voice tone, control over the format of a given message, and words themselves. Each step on the way from personal meetings to e-mail involves a significant loss of context.

The point here is not that the forms of communication that offer more context are always better, but that it is essential to select the communication style most appropriate for the people and the purpose involved. In general, more important messages are best communicated through higher-context means. Universally, most people would prefer to make vital decisions or receive really good or bad news in a face-to-face setting. But this preference does vary relative to culture. In the U.S., for instance, it is perfectly acceptable to introduce oneself, to approach customers, and even to transact large business deals over the telephone—a custom perhaps influenced by the sheer breadth of the country—whereas this may be unacceptable elsewhere. E-mail, too, is increasingly used for crucial business dealings, in spite of its low ranking on the context scale.

What frequently works best in a multicultural setting is to build context by arranging for a personal, face-to-face meeting early in the relationship. Through this meeting a regular, mutually acceptable pattern of communications involving different media—videoconference, telephone, e-mail—can be discussed and established. If frequent personal meetings are not possible due to the time, distance, and expense involved in international travel, multiple media can be used to increase the context available: an intranet site containing background information helps an

Table 11. **Communication Technologies and Context**

Comm. Technology	Context							
	Words	Control over Format	Voice Tone	Immediate Feedback	Nonverbal Cues	Environmental Cues	Direct Physical Exchange	Informal Contacts
Person to Person	■	■	■	■	■	■	■	■
Video-conferencing	■	■	■	■	■	■		
Web/Phone Meeting	■	■	■	■				
Telephone	■	■	■					
Voicemail	■	■						
Fax & Groupware	■							
E-mail	■							

Source: Based on suggestions from George Renwick.

overseas counterpart to prepare for a phone call, which may be followed up by an e-mail message to confirm any agreements made.

Context is also created through the use of facilitation techniques commonly applied to face-to-face meetings. Prior to a videoconference, for instance, it helps to circulate written background material, an agenda and seating chart, and biographical information about participants who are new to each other. During the videoconference a facilitator can make introductions, act as a gatekeeper to bring everyone into the conversation, and define unfamiliar terminology or concepts. Similar techniques are applicable to conference calls held over the telephone. (See table B-2 in appendix B for conference call guidelines.)

It is essential that context be a joint creation and not something that is imposed. Some team members simply assume that English is the language of global business and shower their colleagues abroad with rapid-fire speech or a deluge of complex documents. Even when English is spoken by other team members, modifying speech and being more selective in the circulation of materials will help to create a greater sense of consideration and mutuality. Another aspect of shared context is the time at which a communication takes place. Does it always end up being midnight for someone else, or are the burdens of the time difference borne together?

At minimum, no matter how superb our technologies, it is always worth asking the various parties involved for their preferred method of contact. The ultimate purpose of such communication is to enhance human relationships, not to replace them. While technology is changing the way we relate with one another on a global basis, it must also fit with existing human preferences and work habits across cultures to be readily effective. By committing to the form in which a conversation will occur, participants from different parts of the world become more willing to make an active contribution to its substance. The ten strategic considerations listed in table 12 can help multicultural teams to determine the appropriate mix of communication technologies while promoting their optimum use.

Team systems.

Different viewpoints and assumptions held by multicultural team members can lead to hours of unproductive discussion and wrangling. Personal feelings get hurt, and decisions seem to take forever. It is essential to develop mutually agreed-upon team systems, including methods for organizing common tasks as well as shared values that encourage team members to work together effectively. Among the key team systems are procedures for the following:

Creating a common team vision. First of all, team members need a collective vision of what they are trying to achieve that enables them to rise above their individual or national concerns. This is more than an objective or numerical target. Diverse participants will only begin to mesh as a team when they have committed themselves to a vision that transcends the national or local interests that will inevitably emerge at some point in the team's work together.

Table 12. **Virtual Communication: Building a Global Team Strategy**

Availability	To what extent are the various technology options readily available to everyone involved in a geographically dispersed team? What are the technologies that can be used on a regular basis without putting anyone at a disadvantage?
User skills	Is everyone adequately skilled at, and comfortable with, all the different technology options, including voicemail, videoconference, or intranet systems?
Cultural variables	Do team members represent cultures that favor low- or high-context communication? Are there other cultural requirements or preferences?
Level of rapport	How well do the people who are communicating know one another? Does rapport, or the lack of it, affect the level of context necessary?
Importance of the message	Is this a message with sufficient priority to dictate a more high-context medium, or will a lower-context form of communication suffice?
Methods for building context	Are there means that can be employed to build greater context to enhance team member participation, such as personal meetings, multiple media, or facilitation techniques?
Regular pattern	Is there a communications rhythm that allows each participant to know when to expect messages and in what form?
Language modification	Where a single language is used, are native speakers considerate in their speech and in the transmission of written materials to non-native speakers?
Time windows	What are the most convenient times for all co-workers to send and receive messages across time zones? Are there ways to share private contact numbers that will improve communication while respecting home life?
User choice	Have the participants in a given transaction been asked how they would prefer to communicate?

Information sharing. Any team needs to establish a regular rhythm or pulse of communications that gives people the information they need to do their jobs. Ideally, this rhythm combines face-to-face meetings with other forms of contact and allows each participant to know when to expect messages and in what form. Mary O'Hara-Devereaux, from the Institute for the Future, notes that

> *Good leaders and good managers use technology to support drumbeat communications—something people can count on, whether it's an e-mail that gives the highlights of progress every week or every two weeks, the audioconference for a project team every week, Thursdays at 10:00... It doesn't matter so much what the medium is or what the frequency is. What matters is that the medium and the frequency have a drumbeat that people can count on. And that becomes part of the structure that keeps the communication strategy in place.*[4]

A combination of communication practices that establish a dependable pattern for information exchange might include

- Mutually agreed-upon response times
- Regular (weekly, semiweekly, or monthly) virtual meetings
- Regularly rotating meeting roles
- Routine meeting flows, with some variation but set up to help remote team members anticipate the process
- Occasional celebrations of success

Decision making. There is no one correct decision-making process for a global team. In parts of Asia or Latin America, employees may count on their leaders to set clear goals and provide instructions on how they should achieve them. In other locations such as North America or Scandinavia, where independence and egalitarian values are deeply ingrained, employees expect to discuss with leaders the goals they would like to attain and then exercise their own independent initiative in achieving them. Leaders of global teams need to be aware of the differing expec-

Table 13. **Decision-Making Processes: Examples**

- **Situation 1:** The majority of team members come from hierarchical cultures and have limited business experience.

  Possible response: A team leader accustomed to an egalitarian decision-making style takes on a more directive role, providing instruction and detailed consultation for each person.

- **Situation 2:** Most team members are accustomed to an egalitarian decision-making environment and have a strong track record of past performance.

  Possible response: A team leader accustomed to an authoritarian decision-making style resists the urge to provide precise and detailed instructions and takes a more egalitarian approach, asking team members what approach they would take.

- **Situation 3:** Team members represent a variety of different cultural backgrounds and levels of experience, while the company's business approach aims to flatten the organization and to push responsibility and authority down into the organization.

  Possible response: A seasoned team leader with experience in several global business environments introduces a decision-making style that requires significant input from each team member. The leader works deliberately to draw out the views of those who are unaccustomed to this process, enlisting the help of other team members to encourage participation.

tations that team members may have of them and what level of responsibility each person is willing to accept.

To create an effective decision-making style, the leader of the team and its members need to consider a complex array of factors: national culture, corporate culture, individual personalities, functional differences (e.g., between Sales and Engineering), and the experience levels and capabilities of team members. Another important factor is the team leader's own preferred style and degree of flexibility. In order for decisions to be sound and supported by the team through the implementation phase, however, the preferences and input of team members must in some way be taken into account. Mutual adjustment is frequently required. Table 13 includes some typical examples.

Often the single biggest obstacle to good decision making is team members' lack of a common vocabulary about different methods for making decisions. (See table B-3 in appendix B for a description of five common decision-making strategies.) It is essential to explain clearly the decision-making process to team members, address questions that come up, and coach those who may be unfamiliar with this form of working together.

Some team members may be satisfied with having their opportunity for input into decisions consist simply of being able to speak up in team meetings. Others will appreciate being consulted in a one-on-one meeting. Still others are unlikely to offer frank input unless they meet with the team leader in a relaxed, informal setting where they can air a variety of concerns without risking confrontation or loss of face. It is up to the leadership of the team to identify and utilize all the necessary input channels; at the same time, team members should try to offer their views in ways that go beyond their normal comfort zone.

Problem solving.

Multicultural teams need to be particularly aware of the different approaches—for example direct or indirect, verbal or nonverbal—that members may apply to problem solving. Taking a vote to decide on one style or another is not advisable. If there is an imbalance in preferred styles among team members, it may be necessary for the minority members to do more accommodating. However, the team should consider what is going to work best in the long run and find a creative way to develop a problem-solving style that combines elements of different approaches.

Clarifying roles and responsibilities will help team members to know whether they can take the initiative to solve problems or if the team has established a different process for dealing with them. The team leader must also express his or her own expectations about how problems should be solved. In many cases the fact that these expectations are assumed rather than explained leads to further misunderstandings and problems among team members.

Some of the common points of confusion that multicultural teams need to address include the following: When should individuals try to solve problems on their own, and when should they bring them to the team leader or to others on the team? What is the proper procedure for escalating a problem inside or outside the team if a team member cannot find a solution? How should potential conflicts between team members be addressed?

Regardless of the particular approach that team members choose to take, there are several general problem-solving principles that are effective for multicultural groups:

- Refrain from leaping to quick negative judgments about other team members
- Describe as objectively as possible the specific behaviors that contribute to the problem
- Seek various interpretations of those behaviors, including interpretations from people who are familiar with the cultural background of the people involved. Assume good intentions to start with and try to understand the motivations of team members on their own terms. The key to problem solving is deep listening. (See table B-4 in appendix B for a mutual listening exercise).
- Reevaluate the problem and the people involved based on the new information and knowledge gleaned from seeing the situation from various perspectives and hearing the viewpoints expressed
- Find a way to refocus everyone on common goals and shared interests

Teams that have a well-established procedure for solving problems report that their members do not blame one another but rather seek solutions together. As a sales manager in Singapore said,

> *We are so close, as a team, that when there is an issue we try to work together to find out how we can help from the region or the U.S. or the factory. There's no finger pointing. It's very much like, "If we survive together, we survive. If we fail, the whole team fails." So there's this very strong emphasis on team effort.*[5]

Rewarding team members.

Global teams often experience conflicts between team priorities and reward systems that reinforce conflicting goals of country or business units. Team members will be torn in different directions if the reward system does not support behaviors that benefit the team. A critical long-term factor in the successful implementation of any global team reward system is the creation of a matrix mind-set among key managers that makes them willing to balance conflicting priorities for the good of the company as a whole. This attitude can be reinforced by executive profit sharing and stock grant programs based on general business results for the firm.

Another way to reinforce the importance of team participation is to measure contributions to the team and its business results instead of just individual performance. Teamwork is taken more seriously by employees who may only rarely meet face-to-face when it is measured in performance evaluations and feedback systems and when it becomes an explicit criterion in determining performance ratings, compensation levels, and employee rewards. Without this, teamwork principles are empty, and everyone will ultimately go in their own direction. When members realize that they will receive a positive evaluation only when the whole team succeeds, there will be increased motivation to collaborate and work together.

Taking part in the work of a high-performance global team offers many psychological rewards—for some team members it can be the highlight of a career. A distinctive team identity might be cultivated in several ways; for example, let team members choose their own name and create a logo, encourage competition among teams rather than between individual team members, or provide a modest budget for team gatherings and social events. Some organizations with dispersed team members have even begun to report success with "virtual celebrations" held when important milestones are reached. Such methods can be particularly effective in group-oriented cultures and are a good means of creating a bridge between individualistic team members and those with a collectivist orientation.

Making collective improvements.

The best teams have a joint process for critical reflection and improvement that helps them to build a common learning base. What did we do well? What did we not do so well? What could we do better next time?

My Mistake: A Multicultural Team

A multicultural team I was helping to lead conducted an assessment of its work together. We identified some significant team strengths, but one of the items that the team scored as a "weakness" was its reward system. I felt a sudden flash of anger when I heard this and pointed out that we had been meticulously fair in determining compensation and that even the team leaders were not earning a whole lot more than many team participants.

However, as we began to dig into this issue and look for ways to deal with it, I found that my initial assumptions were largely incorrect. Team members weren't necessarily saying that they wanted more money, although this was true for a few. In fact, they offered a variety of different and even conflicting perspectives. With some participants there was the sense that there should actually be larger discrepancies in rewards between people based on contribution level. Others simply did not understand the reward system that we had in place or had confused it with elements of a prior system and concluded mistakenly that they were being shortchanged. Still others felt that we needed to restructure rewards to promote greater cooperation between team members with different tasks and objectives. Finally, some interpreted *rewards* as meaning opportunities for professional growth or for more of a sense of friendship and community. There were significant differences in viewpoints on rewards according to both national origin and the role that each person had on the team.

My initial angry reaction to the low score on the subject of rewards was based on a narrow and overly simplistic interpretation. I belatedly discovered that as a team leader I needed to learn a lot more about what motivated each person in this very diverse group and to link that to the reward system for the team as a whole in order to get everyone aligned in the same direction.

How can we learn together in a way that the experience we are accumulating can help take us to the next step? This is an area where the diverse perspectives of multicultural team members can provide keen insights and a powerful boost toward higher team performance.

Try to seek out fresh benchmarking data or outside perspectives as a source of new ideas and an objective view on current team performance. Be sure to include viewpoints that reflect or even go beyond the diverse composition of the team itself.

Informal team systems.

Team systems have both formal and more informal aspects. While the more formal, explicit systems such as the team's vision or reward system are important, equally critical is the set of core intercultural values that the team members can come to share and that ultimately becomes the glue that binds the team together. Chapter 2 described the values of trust, respect, listening, observation, empathy, flexibility, informed judgment, and persistence. These can become an informal team discipline or skill set, with team members challenging themselves, Can we as a team incorporate these values? Can we find a common definition for them, and can we enact them in our work together on a day-to-day basis?

Another value worth mentioning here is humor. Some experts suggest that humor should be avoided in intercultural situations. This advice is worth considering in initial encounters with people from unfamiliar cultures, especially when those who are meeting together do not share the same language. Inappropriate humor can be offensive, reflecting badly on the person who uses it and offending, angering, or confusing the others who are on the receiving end. Even well-intentioned teasing may cause a perceived loss of face to other team members and become an unspoken source of resentment. Time and place are critical—one culture's sense of the best occasion to laugh seldom fits exactly with another's.

However, humor is also a key ingredient in building good intercultural teamwork. Teams that find truly shared ways to laugh together are better able to build the trust and rapport they will need to accomplish joint tasks. One of the safer forms of humor in an intercultural context is directed toward one's own shortcomings. Self-deprecating humor can be a good way to break the ice and enable others to feel freer about admitting weaknesses of their own. It also avoids the damage done by teasing that backfires and becomes a source of private dismay or anger from the person being teased. Shared humor—when all team members have a good time together around a particular experience or theme they all understand—is part of what makes being a member of an intercultural team a rewarding experience.

The members of an intercultural team begin further apart from each other and are more difficult to bring together into a cohesive whole. But when formal team systems are infused with these core intercultural values and the team is focused on real customer needs, there is no greater asset for a global company. This kind of teamwork also brings significant personal and professional rewards for team members.

Issues and Action Steps

The recommendations outlined in table 14 revisit the case of the global purchasing team outlined at the beginning of this chapter. A carefully integrated combination of measures drawn from best practices in team formation, team meetings, virtual communication, and team systems is more apt to produce positive results for this global team than any single panacea.

Table 14. **Global Team Issues and Possible Action Steps for Team Leaders**

Level	Issues	Possible Action Steps for Team Leaders
Individual personalities	Friction between Gerhardt, Mirjam, and Teresa, and between Adam and Sombat	• Talk or meet one-on-one with team members to hear their views and look for ways to help them establish stronger relationships with others
Mutual trust	Gerhardt and Adam doubt the competence of key counterparts on the team; Sombat feels that Adam is creating problems without realizing it	• Hold a face-to-face meeting that permits team members to get to know one another better and engage in a deeper discussion of major issues; include social venues where team members can relax together • Seek out opportunities to position people who have different viewpoints and communication styles with each other in a positive way
Communication styles	Direct vs. indirect and verbal vs. nonverbal styles create an imbalance in the contributions of team members	• Facilitate meetings to draw out views of less-vocal participants (e.g., Sombat); solicit written input in advance or change speakers if necessary • Use higher-context communication methods (e.g., videoconference or a combination of other methods) to encourage more balanced participation
Team systems	The team has a clear cost-cutting objective but lacks a broader vision; team members do not have a shared definition of how they should make decisions and solve problems; the company reward system does not reinforce cooperation	• Establish a common vision for the whole team that can serve as a touchstone for better decision making • Meet with individual team members who are at extremes of the problem-solving spectrum (e.g., Gerhardt, Adam, Sombat) to gain their understanding and cooperation • Hold a role clarification discussion with the team to sort out the question of country vs. global priorities • Revise the reward system for team members to reinforce contributions made to the team and to achieving global business goals

Table 14. **Global Team Issues and Possible Action Steps for Team Leaders (continued)**

Level	Issues	Possible Action Steps for Team Leaders
National interests	Members of the team tend to defend the interests of their particular geographical location	• Remind the team of its shared vision • Work through top management to gain greater buy-in from local managers for global supply chain initiatives
Global business challenges	The team faces business challenges that are common to any purchasing operation: achieving greater cost efficiency from global suppliers and finding new low-cost local sources of supply near manufacturing sites	• Examine global benchmarks as a team and use them to stimulate discussion of new ideas and practices • Anticipate generic issues and depersonalize them through ongoing discussion and mutual learning

Working on a Global Team

SUMMARY AND REVIEW QUESTIONS

1. Have you experienced any of the common multicultural team issues listed below? Which have been the most difficult to resolve? How were these types of problems linked with one another?

- Personality conflicts between individuals
- Lack of mutual trust
- Different communication styles
- Inadequate team systems (e.g., for decision making, problem solving, rewards)
- Competing national interests
- Global business dilemmas (e.g., cost reduction vs. local customer service)

2. What approach would you take to form a multicultural team? What role would you expect the team leader to play in this process? How would you go about the following tasks?

- Defining member roles and responsibilities
- Setting meeting practices
- Motivating team members to perform
- Establishing common commitments and accountability

3. During team meetings, what strategies do you use for drawing out contributions from less-vocal team members? How would you go about asking an overly talkative meeting member to cooperate in asking for the views of others?

4. Does your team make optimum use of communication technologies? Are these technologies used in the proper balance with strong personal relationships? In your experience, what kinds of issues can be addressed through a "low-context" medium, and which are best dealt with through "higher-context" means? Is the choice of technologies open for discussion, or imposed by some team members on others?

5. How have you gone about creating a team vision that fosters a sense of shared direction? Is information shared among team members according to a steady "drumbeat"? Do team participants support the team's decision-making and reward systems?

6. What advice, if any, would you give to a new multicultural team leader regarding the use of humor?

CHAPTER SIX

Training and Development

The world of training and developing personnel has experienced a relentless stream of changes in recent decades. Companies want their employees to learn more, better, faster, and for less money. E-learning has come into vogue for some forms of instruction, along with "blended" models that combine in-person and Web-based training. Yet even with all these changes, training remains a primary vehicle for enabling employees to meet corporate objectives, and training programs are increasingly designed and delivered on a global scale.

Global People Skill #6: Training and Development

What happens when training programs are taken across borders? Training and development objectives are relatively universal: organizations want to disseminate selected knowledge, attitudes, and skills that will make their employees more effective in their jobs. But learning styles and instructional methods are both deeply influenced by culture. When and how should training and development practices be modified to accommodate cultural differences?

A Training Program in Nairobi

Looking back on the ten-day management training program she had just conducted at the facilities of a major telecommunications firm in Nairobi, Sondra Jackson was both exhausted and grateful to have made it through to the end of the program. A vivid collage of events passed through her mind as she tried to sort through her experiences and the adjustments she had made along the way.

The initial atmosphere was one of suspicion and mutual distrust among the Kenyans and the multinational hodgepodge of expatriates who made up the audience. There were too many inappropriate side remarks and put-downs, sighs and rolled eyeballs. The non-Africans in the group had received previous management training of sorts at their past companies and in schools—they clearly had an advantage and were dominating the discussions while being subtly condescending toward, and ridiculing, the Africans. This did little for the willingness of participants to work and learn together.

Everyone seemed to be distracted with the business of establishing a pecking order within their own subgroup. During the breaks they would form separate clusters divided by nationality and rank. As time passed, Sondra realized that there was an odd dynamic among the Kenyans themselves—several appeared to be a bit aloof from the others, who in turn deferred very cautiously to them. She discovered on the second day of the program that the three individuals who stood apart were members of elite and powerful family groups. The others not only treated them with respect, but appeared to be intimidated by them and went out of their way to avoid disagreement.

One of the most effective changes that Sondra had made along the way was to open up time during each day for one-on-one meetings—two hours at lunch and another two hours after an early close to the group training at

4:00. These meetings created the opportunity for more individualized coaching and discussions on how to apply the skills in the program to the daily work of trainees. The trainer herself also learned many things during these private sessions that never appeared in the needs assessment comments. For example, one of the trainees, the same person who told her about the elite program participants, confided, "Colonialism never went away. Now it's just economic instead of political. The privileged people with the right connections go to the best schools, and then foreign companies like this one hire them for management positions. We're just seeing the same faces in new buildings. I am not going to get on the wrong side of anybody." Another person gave her the blunt feedback that the management training materials she had brought from headquarters contained too much unhelpful jargon: "This is the company's clever way of manipulating us. They try to tell us that this is a common global language, but it's one that only they can speak. They're not fooling anybody."

A breakthrough had come on the second day when Sondra threw away her initial program design and increased the amount of small-group work, which everyone seemed to take to immediately. Participants could ask questions more openly and explain or provide examples to each other without running the risk of public embarrassment by having to ask the trainer in front of everyone else. These small group sessions became very lively and dynamic, with conversations spilling over into breaks.

The small group sessions helped to open up discussions in the whole group as well. At one point a senior participant responded to Sondra's presentation on consultative decision-making strategies by launching into a story. She considered interrupting him as he headed off into what appeared to be unrelated subject matter, but then noticed that the rest of the audience was riveted by the vibrancy, the rhythm, and the colorful punctuation of his tale. The man recalled the tough times the subsidiary had faced during an economic downturn several years back—how their company had almost pulled out of the country due to political interference and the lack of profits. After several more long minutes during which the trainer wondered where this lesson in local corporate history was going, the storyteller returned to the way that the foreign subsidiary president at the time had consulted with others, testing several alternatives before deciding on the proper course of action. The story culminated with a perfect illustration of the trainer's point as the listeners nodded and murmured their assent. Sondra herself was so impressed by the richness of his story that she not only thanked him warmly but also felt embarrassed to go back to the now sterile-looking bulleted items in her slides.

In subsequent days, as Sondra learned how to trust the story-telling capabilities of participants, the group talked in an increasingly open way about a variety of topics that were both directly and indirectly related to the program curriculum. Participants spoke of their faith in God, longing for heaven, AIDS, and family problems during the training, making little distinction between work and the rest of their lives. One entry in Sondra's notes read, "I can't believe how far we have come. It's been a very intense program, and the content has been covered—but certainly not in any kind of linear manner! There hasn't been anything linear that's happened over these past few weeks of training. Yes, they do like to talk and dramatize and tell stories and talk some more—but it works for them, even though it might look chaotic and loud. They have an amazing spirit!"

Perhaps the most difficult parts of the program for Sondra had been the times when she felt the widest gulf between herself and the audience. She had launched into a new segment on strategic planning, for instance, only to have a participant quip to her during a break, "I'm just happy to be alive today. If you're a privileged person, you can think about planning. If you're not, you must deal with whatever God gives you." She also found it difficult to link management techniques with the constructive application of power—what one nationality saw as positive and constructive, another had experienced as repressive, oppressive, condescending, or in some other way resulting in negative consequences. A common line of skeptical questioning was directed at her depiction of management's role in delegating tasks and "empowering" employees to carry them out. Delegation was fine in the participants' view, but they would ask, "Who is really going to give away power? If you trust such people, they may pretend to represent you and support you, but then they will misuse the information you provide them or turn against you to serve their own agenda. When you make a fine show of empowering others, then it is easier to blame them when things go wrong!"

Sondra was proudest of the success she had with participants in leveraging their own concepts to take a different approach to the profession of management. Trainees often spoke of insiders versus outsiders in a way that related to other common themes such as trust and power. One's "inside" circle, as they defined it, was of course treated in a very different way from how those on the "outside" were treated. She urged them to reframe the way they saw themselves within the company, their divisions, and management teams by adding new and expanded groups of insiders. This was a challenge that they took quite seriously and which had a visible impact on the way that group members related to one another.

Sondra also made discoveries about the learning styles of participants that she was able to use for the benefit of the group. As members of the audience became less skeptical and more receptive to the contents of the program, they asked her to "drill" them and "mark" them to make sure they would "pass." During the final couple of days they mobilized each other into an arrangement that was comfortable for them: seats in straight rows. Then they stood up and responded to questions as Sondra and fellow participants quizzed them and had them engage in tough skill exercises. In the final program hour, as she handed out certificates of completion to each member of the group, she had to admit to herself that the awards were well deserved and that these participants had probably made greater strides by dint of their enthusiasm, questioning, and intensive practice during the program than any other group she had ever worked with in the company.

Cultural Comparisons

Many of the assumptions, experiences, and perceptions of the Kenyan participants were difficult for the trainer to understand or accept. These included

- The prominence of nationality and race in shaping interactions among trainees and their perceptions of the opportunities open to them
- Their lack of positive experiences with the exercise of power by professional managers, coupled with deep suspicion of those currently occupying positions of power

- A preoccupation with the present or the past, coupled with the difficulty some had in regarding future planning as a realistic or helpful exercise
- The value of story telling, drills, and testing as learning techniques in a management development curriculum

Table 15 outlines a set of contrasting expectations regarding the form that a training program ought to take based on the perspectives of both the trainer from U.S. headquarters and the African members of her audience.

Recommendations for Training

Taking a training program successfully across borders is a complex and demanding job. What follows is a wider set of thoughts and recommendations based not only on the Kenyan example provided above, but also on the experiences of foreign trainers in Asia, Latin America, and Europe.

Targeting training contents.

When trainers work in a familiar business environment, a proper needs assessment will usually provide sufficient information to gear training program contents to a suitable level. However, even experienced trainers who take their programs abroad often make the mistake of presenting their materials at a level that is either too advanced or too simple for their foreign audience. Another type of issue is program contents that do not fit well with local circumstances. The gap in assumptions between the trainer's prior experiences and those of program participants in each of these cases can be so large that the trainer simply does not grasp how great an adjustment is necessary.

Too complex. One of the first adjustments that the trainer in Africa made was to hone down the contents of her program, prioritizing the materials from "must know" to "nice to know." Given language issues, the need for time to discuss or review unfamiliar concepts, and communication style differences, trainers are commonly able to cover only a fraction of the content abroad that they would in their own country.

Table 15. **Training: Comparative Styles**

Cultural Orientation	← Expectations and Behaviors for Training →		Cultural Orientation
Individual	Trainees are individuals and should be dealt with as such; a major challenge for the trainer is to create a common agenda that will accommodate different individual skill levels and interests	Trainees belong to different subgroups; the group that each person belongs to shapes his or her identity and role in the program; a major challenge for the trainer is to integrate the various subgroups	**Group**
Task	The program provides an objective presentation of knowledge and skills that participants can immediately put to use in the workplace; practical questions about implementation can and should be asked at any time	A strong relationship with the instructor helps participants to understand the real meaning and purpose of the program and ensures that knowledge is internalized; questions regarding implementation are sometimes easier to pose in private or in a smaller group of peers	**Relationship**
Direct	Direct dialogue and discussion are expected; it is the trainer's job to create an atmosphere where it is possible for participants to ask questions and express opinions; doubts or concerns about the program can be raised directly with the trainer	Direct dialogue and discussion may be inhibited by hierarchical relations among participants; personal opinions are often expressed in private; stories and other nonlinear devices may be the best way to convey key learnings	**Indirect**
Equality	The trainer is a well-intentioned peer and partner; trainees can request that materials be modified to better meet their needs; trainees participate in the program as relative equals	The trainer is a representative of the corporate power structure and serves an agenda determined by that structure; program participants remain very conscious of status differences among themselves	**Hierarchy**

Table 15. **Training: Comparative Styles (continued)**

Cultural Orientation	Expectations and ← Behaviors for Training →		Cultural Orientation
Future	The focus of training is on developing skills that will enable participants to contribute to the future development of the organization—and to build more productive professional careers	The training program needs to take into account the past history of the subsidiary and its role within the larger power structure of the corporation to have any meaningful impact; trainees from less privileged backgrounds might feel it is unrealistic to think too far ahead	**Past**
Informal	Skilled trainers use humor and a relaxed but focused communication style to create a positive learning environment	Skilled trainers begin with a formal tone, a carefully structured agenda, and polished materials to create a professional atmosphere, gradually loosening up and becoming more spontaneous as relationships are established	**Formal**

Many of the Western business concepts that have been taken into former communist countries assume a certain foundation of shared knowledge and experience. Trainers have been stunned by fundamental questions that suggest they are several steps too far down the road already with their program contents. Questions such as, "Why is the customer important?" or, "Why is marketing necessary?" make perfect sense from the standpoint of a person raised in a state-controlled economy where customers were at the end of the food chain and government bureaucrats at the top—customers were willing to take whatever they could get, and marketing was unnecessary because there was no real market. Also, in some cases trainees do not have the educational foundation they need to be able to absorb a highly technical explanation.

Too simple. The training equivalent of carrying coals to Newcastle is another hazard. For instance, a training program on quality control delivered by a pair of U.S. corporate trainers in Japan was a complete disaster. The two trainers worked through an interpreter to deliver the program right out of the parent company's manual while the Japanese sat politely and listened. Questions were minimal throughout the two days of the session, and the U.S. trainers struggled for traction with their audience. Afterward it came out that most of the audience was silently fuming that the real quality issues originated in the company's U.S. factories, doing considerable damage to their relations with Japanese customers. The program participants in Tokyo were already quite familiar with quality control practices—they just wished that the parent company would make better use of them to fix the seventeen major product quality problems that they had already identified and communicated to headquarters!

Lack of content fit. Examples of training contents that do not fit circumstances abroad ironically include U.S.-based diversity programs that have been mandated corporate-wide. General diversity principles such as creating an equal-opportunity workplace and rooting out acts of bias unquestionably have global implications. Yet, overseas employees with limited exposure to U.S.-specific diversity matters pertaining to ethnicity, gender, sexual orientation, and so on are sometimes left scratching their heads over how to apply the program contents. Meanwhile, diversity issues truly relevant in their own environment—for example, Muslims in India, North Africans in France, Burakumin in Japan, or relations between Afrikaners, Xhosa, Zulus, and Indians in South Africa—are neglected by trainers without the background or expertise to handle them.

Trainers who suddenly realize that their program contents are not properly geared to fit their audience face a variety of undesirable choices, most of which fall under the category "Back up and start over again." A preferable course of action is to insist on a needs assessment prior to the program that consciously looks beyond superficial responses. These responses may include reassuring voices from our own home country that say, "Oh, just go and present what you already do here and every-

My Mistake: Training and Development

We were asked to carry out a training program in negotiation skills for a group of Russians. The U.S. client, based on the East Coast, felt that the Russians from their own Moscow branch were using very different negotiation methods than those to which they were accustomed, and they wanted their company to have a shared set of internal practices. In spite of a lack of opportunity for a good needs assessment, the U.S. headquarters personnel insisted that their negotiation training materials based on a "win-win" type of principle would be perfectly adequate for the Russians.

The response of the Russians from the start of the training program, however, was skepticism and amusement. They saw their U.S. colleagues as narrowly technical and unsophisticated. In their view, the "win-win" approach was Pollyannaish (as they pointed out, "In Eastern Europe, there are always losers"). The Americans' approach encouraged a "dialogue about options," but the Russians preferred to provide them with a forced choice between just two alternatives, both of which they had thought out in great detail, understanding all the possible contingencies. The U.S. text promoted open communication and clarity, while the Russians would swamp their opponents with complex language and mathematical equations.

So the real problem was not that the Russians needed to be trained in negotiation—they were already master negotiators. The problem was that they were running circles around the Americans when competing for internal company resources, and the Americans didn't like it because they wound up agreeing to proposals that they hadn't thought through fully. The advice of the Russians was to "Go back to the U.S. and train them to debate with us."

thing will be fine." Another danger is local employees who are anxious to please—not to mention proud of their own capabilities—and offer similarly bland reassurances for different reasons. "Yes, we'd be glad to have the same program that you deliver at headquarters."

Table 16. **Adjusting Instructional Techniques: Examples**

• Credentials	• Small groups
• Level of formality	• Models
• Background or context	• Role-playing and action learning
• Agenda	• Tests
• Questions	• Rewards
• Discussion or debate	• Program evaluation

Instructional techniques and learning styles.

In addition to program contents, another crucial match is between trainer instructional styles and common learning patterns of trainees. Does the trainer understand the preferred learning styles of training participants, what motivates them, and the most conducive types of environments for their acquiring new knowledge and skills? Table 16 lists examples of adjustments that are frequently required in working with trainees from other cultures.

Credentials. Trainees probe the credentials of trainers in various ways. In the U.S. the usual questions are focused on the trainer's direct experience with the topic at hand. In the African example above, a key transition point for the trainer was establishing that she was "humane." Participants seemed to assume that she was a content expert but were interested in her compassion as demonstrated by her flexibility in meeting them one-on-one, dealing with story telling, increasing the number of breaks, and providing opportunities for them to question one another without being humiliated in front of a larger group of peers. Other cultures may rely on more indirect cues such as the trainer's educational qualifications or the strength of his or her introduction.

Level of formality. The host culture represented by trainees might be more or less formal than the one to which the trainer is accustomed. It is hard to gauge the best way to use humor or how to time the move from a formal atmosphere to a more informal one. U.S. trainers working abroad typically try to insert humor and informality before their audience is ready for them, leading to questions about their credibility and seriousness of purpose. In the Kenyan example, the trainer found it best to begin in a very structured, methodical, and directive manner and then be prepared for a whole series of impromptu events. Thus, her program was probably more formal than the U.S. norm at the beginning and less so as it progressed.

Background or context. With trainees who come from high-context environments—for instance, those from Asia or Latin America—it is often a good idea to provide ample information about the purpose of the program, how it was created, who sponsored it, when it was begun, what groups have already been through it, and what is expected of the people who complete it. This kind of information can be furnished in advance or introduced at the beginning of the session to set the audience at ease and allow them to devote themselves to the training curriculum. It is also helpful to have an executive introduce the program and for trainers to demonstrate local management support for the training effort.

Agenda. Expectations about how closely a trainer should follow the agenda also vary by culture. A U.S.-designed program is likely to be relatively linear and time-bound in spite of the atmosphere of informality—this could make it difficult for a trainer to cope with apparent digressions or extended narratives unless their immediate relevance is demonstrated. The program in Kenya diverged substantially from the scheduled agenda as the trainer adjusted to the participants' fondness for storytelling and animated discussion. In Brazil as well, to mention another example, it is best to factor in the general disposition among many training participants toward spontaneous verbal exchanges. Trainees may use circular conversation styles and need longer periods of time to discuss several angles of the subject matter. In this cultural context, the particulars of each case are important, as are the subjective experiences and feelings of the participants. Brazilian trainees will actively seek to share their perspectives and may solicit personal examples from the instructor—all of this could take the group far from the original agenda in a way that trainees find to be perfectly acceptable. More traditional audiences in Asia, on the other hand, will question major departures from the agenda and expect that the points in the written training materials be fully covered according to a preset plan.

Questions. Trainers who are used to getting a lot of questions from their audiences may find that they get a very different reaction when they take their program to other locations. In Nairobi, the questions began with participants first trying to sound out the real purpose and objectives of the training program. The initial atmosphere of mutual suspicion among trainees extended to their attitudes toward the course itself. Such questions, whether raised in public or in private, must be addressed for participants to begin to open up and become engaged.

In locations such as China, Korea, or Japan, where hierarchy and reserve are valued, the problem may be how to elicit any questions at all. The trainer makes a rousing presentation, confidently invites questions, and is met with a stolid silence from the audience. He or she then asks a leading question that usually is quite good for getting a discussion going, receives little or no response, and moves on, presuming that there is a lack of interest or comprehension. The key issue is often pacing. When trainers have a bit more experience, they can almost see the wheels turning as members of the audience ponder their response and then look out of the corner of their eyes for cues as to whether it is okay to speak up. Providing that the topic or question is clear to participants, the trainer can deal with this situation in several ways: (1) speak with the senior member of the audience beforehand and request that this person start off the Q&A session with a question; (2) call on specific individuals who look as if they could have an opinion to offer; or (3) wait them out, letting the silence put pressure on the participants to reply rather than on the instructor.

Discussion or debate. Some audiences will grill a presenter or initiate a debate regarding factual claims. Trainers should be prepared to defend their factual claims with rigorous and logical observations. In France, for instance, the formal secondary and postsecondary educational system is recognized to be among the best in the world. French businesspeople begin work not only with a substantial knowledge base, but also with strong deductive abilities, well-developed argumentation skills, and high expectations for ongoing training. Argumentation is a key aspect of the learning process in this environment; ideas are tested and challenged and discussions may become heated. A good trainer will be able to tolerate open challenges from trainees. Whenever possible, it is also important to allow debates and discussions to take place in French. Learning is enhanced through the articulation and exploration of ideas; without this element, or if this element is restricted to a second language, training will not be as effective.

Small groups. The use of small groups provided a key breakthrough for Sondra Jackson in Kenya. Participants who are reluctant to speak up or ask questions in front of a large audience are often quite willing to engage in discussions in groups of four to six people. This allows them the security of speaking with a more limited set of colleagues, makes it easier to consult back and forth with other second-language speakers, and helps them to digest the knowledge that has been presented to them—they are able to ask questions, hear things explained again by their peers, and clarify points of misunderstanding. It also permits the group to plan a response together rather than offering one up spontaneously; the person who speaks up on behalf of the group is expressing a collective opinion rather than taking the risk of voicing a personal opinion that others might deride or disagree with. One way to begin to integrate subgroups in the training room is to gradually alter the mix of people in the small groups, beginning with the preexisting divisions and then shifting them to make each group more inclusive.

Models. Offering examples of excellent performance helps in several ways. First, in an environment where people may simply not have prior exposure to the training concepts, such examples lend a greater sense of reality to the presentation. In addition, trainees who are conscious of maintaining face in front of other participants, as was the case with the Kenyan audience, may be a lot more comfortable trying out a new skill if they have already seen a graphic illustration of the ideal behavior. Learning through models is a classic form of education in many parts of the world. China, for instance, has designated model factory workers, model farmers, and even an unofficial model plumber. So, letting an audience see a model or preferably even a "master" in action can be an extremely effective training device.[1] Models serve to demonstrate not only technical skills or management competencies, but also more complex examples of service environments or quality systems. Exposure tours where trainees visit other locations to benchmark outstanding examples are useful in lending credibility and substance to the topic at hand while challenging participants to meet or surpass the levels of performance already set by others.

Role-playing and action learning. The use of experiential learning formats is sometimes awkward with audiences who are accustomed to learning through more passive, lecture-style instruction. What appears to be most critical, however, is the way the exercises are presented. Participants who will not eagerly volunteer to jump into role-playing at first nonetheless tend to join in quite happily if there is sufficient preparation. This could mean providing a careful explanation, a model demonstration of a specific skill (including both how to do it and how not to do it), and the chance to plan what to do in small groups. An important difference with the group in Kenya turned out to be the need for explicit instructions about what was expected in terms of both process and outcomes. The trainer in Kenya found that, in contrast to many U.S. trainees—who would be willing to throw themselves into a role and improvise based on minimal instructions—participants in Kenya were extremely self-conscious about making mistakes in front of others, so she had to do much more than usual to set up each exercise and make them feel comfortable.

Project work is also an effective learning strategy in most places. There is one caveat: participants should not feel that the project contents involve such a big stretch beyond their normal work that they are unable to contribute in a professional way. Other forms of action learning can be quite effective as well. A veteran trainer who was trying to help his audience learn about electrical circuitry cleared the training room early in the morning and drew out the design of the circuit many times enlarged on the floor of the training room. He then had each participant walk through the circuit just as the electricity would follow through it. At every step there was a description and discussion among trainees of how the circuit worked to channel the flow of the current. After this exercise, the participants understood much better the function of the circuit because they themselves had simulated it, and this knowledge stayed with them well after the program.[2]

Tests. While many corporate audiences in the West are allergic to tests except with very technically oriented training, there are other locations around the world where tests are not only accepted but expected. This proved to be true in Kenya, where the participants actually asked the trainer to be tested and caused her to alter the agenda to make it possible. In China, too, testing is common—the educational system uses testing heavily throughout the curriculum. A training program without a test might be regarded as lightweight or incomplete in this kind of setting, and testing can be used in a positive way to motivate trainees or to encourage a comprehensive review of points covered. A contradictory twist, however, is that younger, urban audiences may associate testing with the part of their education that they did not like, and a program that is deliberately positioned as different from the norm could be regarded more favorably. In either case, the trainer needs to take into account the prevalence of testing in both education and industry and design the program with this in mind.

Rewards. When training is not taken for granted but regarded as a special opportunity, trainees will look for extras that help them to make the most of the experience and share the news of their participation with others. This can be accomplished in part with special one-on-one "office time" meetings as in the Kenyan example. Other possible rewards could include books, copies of articles, photos taken together—there are many ways of demonstrating trainer attention and interest.[3] Certifications of course completion that might be spurned by more jaded U.S. trainees are received in some locations with pride and later displayed on office walls. Public recognition in the form of pictures and feature articles in newsletters, dinners, formal ceremonies, framed group photos, and introductions to senior people are often remembered and even treasured.

Program evaluation. Training participants with relatively indirect communication styles will not necessarily express any dissatisfaction directly to the trainer or on a training evaluation form. They may, however, vent their frustration to other trainees or to colleagues who are not directly involved in the program. Training evaluation processes should seek out feedback on a pro-

Table 17. **Ideal Trainer Profile**

• Rich practical experience • Hands-on work style • Seniority • Ability to explain complex issues simply • Flexibility • Patience	• Humility • Willingness to learn from training participants • Ability to teach others how to teach • Ability to link training to the wider organizational context

gram from multiple sources, including informal contacts with trusted third parties who can listen carefully to what trainees really think.

Trainer availability and profile.

The more challenging the learning curve for participants, the more important it is that instructors be available on site for an extended period. An ideal program design calls for the trainers to arrive at least a few days before their session begins, enabling them to better understand the work environment and to meet and become acquainted with participants. After the program is over, it is also a good idea to have trainers remain for several days or even weeks so that participants can ask follow-up questions and learn how to apply new knowledge to their work. Having trainers parachute in for a few days and then depart as soon as the program finishes is less likely to achieve satisfactory results. Obviously, the appropriate time period depends on the program contents. Corporate training and development managers in China, for example, recommend that visits be for a minimum of four to six weeks.

As shown in the ideal trainer profile outlined in table 17, in many places key to success is having rich practical experience and a hands-on work style. Although not essential, seniority can be helpful. There is often a cultural preference for learning from someone who is perceived to be a "master" of a particular craft. Gender also makes a difference in some locations; female trainers frequently have to work harder at first to establish their credibility, and there are a few places—for example, in some Islamic countries—where they would not be welcome.

Trainers in a foreign environment must be able to explain and communicate complex issues simply. Flexibility, patience, and an inner sense of humility are other useful character traits, as is a willingness to learn from new environments and from training participants. Given the wide range of possible settings, trainers should be able to constantly monitor and adjust to what is happening, asking themselves questions such as, "Am I talking at the right pace? Is this example the right one for the audience? What did that question really mean? Are the participants comfortable with the exercise they are doing? Are key concepts being applied? What is the social structure of this group? How can I position the participants to help each other learn?"

The best trainers teach others how to teach and they tie training contents to the broader organizational context. It is seldom possible to have every employee take part in training; meanwhile organizational change does not occur overnight. This makes it essential to build a critical mass of people with fresh knowledge and skills who are able to spread what they have learned to co-workers or suppliers. The trainers who have the most profound long-term impact are those who deliberately seek to build this critical mass by transmitting not only the training package but also the enthusiasm and the capabilities needed to convey it to others.

Employee Development

Building connections between training program contents and other organizational systems to support and extend their application is essential. These systems include the informal employee development that takes place between managers and subordinates on a one-on-one basis as well as more formal practices such as performance management (see figure 11). The "before" and "after" of any training program continue to be as important, if not more so, than the program contents. When training is linked with such systems, it can plant seeds that will be nourished throughout the year. Expatriates or managers of employees visiting headquarters on training and development assignments play key developmental roles that can vastly expand the impact of both training and development.

Figure 11. **Training and Employee Development**

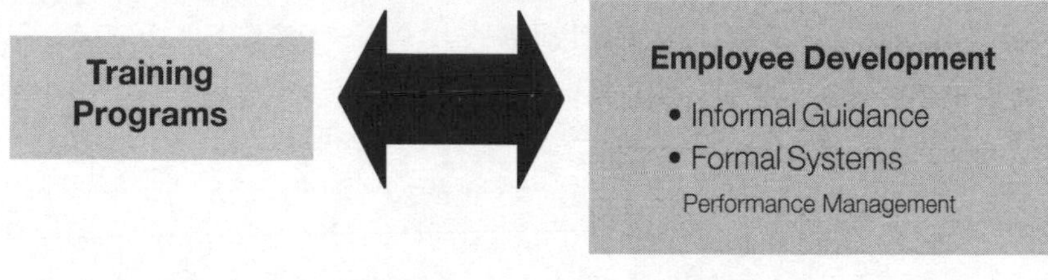

Supervising a Filipino Employee on Assignment

You have been assigned to supervise a Filipino subordinate, Antonio Delgado, who is in your country on a six-month learning assignment. He is a bright young man in his early thirties with a business degree, and he seems eager to learn. Your job is to help him learn how to use customer contact software and explain the techniques used in your customer service department.

After giving Antonio an initial overview of the software and the service department, you've pretty much left him on his own to go through the tutorials, encouraging him to come to your office if he has any questions. Although your relations have always been cordial, over the last few weeks Antonio has become more withdrawn and seems to be working very long hours. You have asked him a couple of times whether he understands the work, as he is now beginning to get into much more advanced features of the software. He has always smiled and nodded without asking questions. Then just today you heard from a Filipino colleague living here that Antonio is confused, unhappy, and worried that he is not going to learn everything in time to serve as a qualified instructor back in the Philippines.

As you think about Antonio's situation, a number of questions come to mind: "Is the problem something I am doing, or something he is doing? Does he really have the skills to do the job? Was he the right choice for the assignment? Is this his way of telling me he is unhappy—by asking someone else to talk with me?"

Recommendations for Informal Guidance

Western managers often take an approach to employee development that could be defined positively as setting out the parameters of a task and then giving an individual room to complete it. Those who demonstrate the individual initiative to accomplish their tasks at one level are then given more difficult and demanding projects. The assumption is that employees will consult with the manager if necessary but only after they try to solve problems independently first. Managers also expect that subordinates who attend training programs will take responsibility for applying key learnings to their own work.

This approach to personnel development, which works well with aggressive subordinates who are used to taking initiative on their own, is seen rather differently in other countries such as the Philippines, where group activities are the norm. The hands-off style of Western managers is described from a critical perspective as "delegate and disappear."

In Antonio's case, he was indeed trying to communicate his distress to the manager through a third party. His expectation was that the host manager would roll up his sleeves and work more closely together with him, asking him regularly what he does or does not understand. This would have made it far easier for him to ask questions of his own from the start. Antonio, who is making his first trip abroad, does not feel comfortable approaching a more senior person in his office to ask questions about the software program. Yet, he is finding it difficult to move beyond the basic tutorials into more advanced applications without assistance. As he works on his own late into the evening, Antonio is probably wondering why he was ever assigned to learn from a manager who is too busy to work with him.

Beyond the rolled-up-sleeves style of employee development recommended in Antonio's case, there are several other practices that appear to travel well across borders. Here are just a few.

Anticipate developmental needs.

Valuable subordinates unaccustomed to learning environments where individual initiative is emphasized will hesitate to step forward and tell a foreign manager what they want. Indeed, their expectation may be that the manager naturally knows more than subordinates about next career steps and should take the initiative in helping them to progress. In order to bridge possible expectation gaps, managers working abroad are well advised to consider and address the developmental needs of employees more proactively than they might at home. Making commitments to develop employees is a good way to build their commitment to the firm.

Establish standards through personal example.

An expression voiced in many factory environments around the world is that you end up with the standard you are willing to walk past. As one foreign factory manager said,

> *When I walk around the factory and something isn't right, that will be the standard we get if I don't make it clear what's required. I go to the packing machine, pick up a package, and put it on the scale. Twenty grams too much weight. I take some out. When I've done that the third time, then each time when I'm in that part of the plant, fifteen people at the fifteen packing machines are finally putting their bags on the weigh scale. And now it is not only me, it is also Mr. Yang, and it's Mr. Zhao, and even the local plant directors have learned this now.*[4]

Expect employees to bring you problems.

Workers in group-oriented cultures commonly assume that the best way to learn is to solve issues together with one's boss. The mark of a good employee might be taking unsolved problems immediately to the manager for joint consultation. If the manager, on the other hand, expects employees to try to solve problems themselves first and to bring solutions rather than problems, there is ample room for misunderstanding. When employees from a different cultural background approach a foreign manager with problems, it is wise for the manager first to try to understand their motivation. Are they shirking responsibility and incapable of thinking for themselves or simply accustomed to solving problems together?

Through intensive coaching over time, managers can instill greater employee initiative by first solving problems together and then gradually encouraging employees to take on more responsibility. Those who turn away the first approaches from employees, however, will never develop the close relationships with them that make the transfer of responsibility possible. Instead, problems will fester in silence as employees feel that they cannot approach their manager but also are unequipped to find a solution on their own.

Expect to be approached on personal as well as business matters.

Many cultures do not make a strict distinction between work and private matters. In places where family enterprises dominate, co-workers are literally "family." Providing assistance or advice on spousal relations, family finances, health conditions, and so on is thus assumed to be part of a manager's job and also part of employee development in the broad sense of the term. The foreign manager may not be suited to take on some of these duties, including sensitive tasks such as finding marriage partners for subordinates or serving as mediator in marital disputes. But handling personal requests respectfully and not dismissing them out of hand could help to shape a positive employee development context.

Recommendations for Managing Performance

Performance management is commonly seen as a prime vehicle for ensuring systematic progress toward achieving business and professional development objectives. Yet, much can go wrong when Western-style performance management systems are introduced into work settings in other countries. These systems embody a number of culturally based assumptions. For instance, managers have to make judgments that are based objectively on performance results rather than on relationships, and they must provide praise and criticism openly and directly. Employees should also be able to distinguish comments about their performance from comments about personal character and accept that certain individuals will receive both higher evaluations and greater rewards, even when they are supported by the efforts of other team members. When a new performance management system is brought in without adequate thought or preparation, the consequences can include those listed in table 18.

One alternative that some experts recommend is to simply leave the Western-style performance appraisal process at home and use other means to assess or improve performance.[5] For companies that choose to press forward with the rollout of this kind of system, here are some suggestions.

Comprehensive training for managers and employees.

Training for managers who have little or no experience with formal performance management systems should include instruction in objective setting, preparation for an appraisal session, and constructive feedback. Managers need to be able to notice and gather concrete examples, positive or otherwise, that will support their statements about an employee's performance. General comments such as "poor relationships with coworkers" or "not sufficiently strategic" will likely become sources of conflict. Managers can learn to present the performance management process as an indication that they care about the professional growth of their employees. It's an opportunity to say, "Listen, let's talk seriously. There are things you've done really well. I want you to know I appreciate it, but there are areas I want you to change, to grow, because it's good for you. And if it's good for you, it has to be good for the company."[6]

Employees, too, should understand the new procedures their managers are trying to use as well as the opportunities they have to contribute their own perspective. This helps to depersonalize appraisal meetings and to reassure those being evaluated that their own input is part of the process. Training can also help them recognize that points for improvement should be interpreted within the context of the other feedback that is provided and that substantive improvements will mean self-development, future promotion, and other rewards over time.

Recognition for contributions to a team.

When team contributions are acknowledged along with individual performance, employees are encouraged to continue their contributions to

Table 18. **Cross-Border Performance Management: Pitfalls**

- **Going through the motions.** Managers fill out the forms and hold meetings, but everyone turns out to be rated as a good-to-excellent employee, without the identification of specific areas for improvement. The new system becomes a cover for the continuation of the old system, which may have rewarded tenure rather than performance while granting semiautomatic raises.

- **Confrontation.** Managers and subordinates who have been conditioned their entire lives to communicate indirectly find it difficult to achieve the right balance when describing problems or areas for improvement more directly. Rather than one person sending out subtle signals that the other reads carefully for their hidden meaning, the message is suddenly too blunt and/or overinterpreted. Supposedly objective discussions produce tension-filled relationships where subordinates feel unfairly accused or are offended by perceived attacks on their character.[7]

- **Ostracism.** Individuals who are scored and compensated at higher levels become the subject of resentment by other employees, who soon become less inclined to offer cooperation and support. This trend can be accelerated when Western-based criteria such as "assertiveness" or "bias for action" produce a positive evaluation of people already held in low regard by local employees for being overly aggressive or poor team players.

- **Demotivation.** In cultures where the sense of fairness is closely tied to equality of rewards—the most extreme version of this having been the communist "iron rice bowl"—visible distinctions in evaluations and rewards might be attributed to favoritism. A related consequence of such distinctions can be poor morale among the bulk of the employee population not rated in the high-performing category or designated for special remuneration or benefits. Rather than seeing performance management as a system that offers real rewards for anyone who tries hard enough, they may come to see it as a new kind of class system that separates them from the most desirable opportunities.

team efforts. At the same time, they will probably be less inclined to regard top performers as selfish individuals who have been unjustly singled out for praise. As everyone becomes accustomed to the new system, standards for individual performance can be gradually raised.

Clear quantitative measurements.

A useful method for making performance criteria acceptable to everyone is to tie them directly to the operation's business goals. Company goals are translated into specific targets for divisions and for teams. Each individual has a job description and goals that are set as part of the general planning process at the beginning of the year. When performance on these measures is tracked throughout the year and becomes the basis for year-end evaluations, then even skeptical newcomers to the process will perceive it as more rational and objective. Bonuses and salary increases can also be very clearly linked with performance results.

Several companies have experienced success with the public display of numerical performance results. In cultures such as those of Japan or China, where these practices have deep roots, open posting of quantitative results relative to targets can be used to shift the focus from one-on-one relationships between managers and subordinates to collective performance—and to convert the issue of individual loss of face into socially driven peer pressure to improve.

Frequent informal feedback.

Formal annual or biannual performance appraisal meetings are normally required to discuss overall results and to create a record that can be tied to compensation adjustments. But, these meetings are seldom a satisfactory solution by themselves. More casual feedback given on a regular basis will have the greatest positive effect on performance, especially among workers used to a hands-on management style. Try pointing out something specific that a person is doing well while providing on-the-spot suggestions or demonstrations of how a task could be done differently. Ask questions such as, "How are you doing? What's working for you and what isn't? What can I do to help?" Such everyday feedback and assistance prepare individuals new to performance management for formal meetings. This way there are no big surprises, and the transition to evaluation based on performance-based criteria becomes easier to accept.

Creating a culture of openness.

Employees who have experienced an organizational climate where performance information is not typically shared may welcome greater openness. Company-wide improvement practices that allow employees to discuss business results along with how each person can improve help to create a shared stake in better performance. It is possible to cultivate such a constructive, objective atmosphere even in cultures that have traditionally been relatively hierarchical and indirect. This may actually be preferable for young people who want to move beyond traditional ways of doing things. Yi Qing, a young Chinese employee of a European firm, describes her work environment with enthusiasm:

> *It's very open. People can really discuss and agree on what you did well, and what you didn't, and what you should improve in the future. And for my staff, I think it's also very clear. It's not like Old China, where if my staff member has a really good relationship with me, she can get a better score. And if she doesn't have a good relationship with me, she won't get a good score. It's not like that. It's very…you can say objective…*
>
> *When you review your past, you know what is right and what is wrong and what you can improve in the future. And, I feel that young people want to improve themselves. They don't want to stay the same.*[8]

There is of course no single formula for companies seeking to establish an optimum global performance management system. It may be that some are actually better off not forcing foreign practices onto an older, more traditional work force or a reluctant joint venture partnership. On the other hand, some employees in those same countries may welcome opportunities to improve their professional skills that are combined with rewards determined on the basis of their achievements. Each organization must strike a balance between adjusting to local circumstances and trying to create a new kind of culture—at least within its own buildings.

Training and Development

SUMMARY AND REVIEW QUESTIONS

1. In what ways, if any, would you modify your standard needs assessment methods to collect information that reflects local conditions in another country?

2. How do you change your approach when the training group you are working with speaks English as its second language? What kinds of changes would you make if the trainees spoke several different first languages?

3. Can you identify a situation in your past experience where local cultural or social factors strongly affected the outcome of a training program? What adjustments did you make at the time? How would you adapt your approach in areas such as those listed below to deliver training in an unfamiliar setting?

   - Establishing credentials
   - Using small groups
   - Setting the training agenda
   - Introducing models
   - Handling questions
   - Testing and rewarding
   - Handling discussion or debate
   - Evaluating the program

4. In your preferred approach to training, what role do testing and action learning play? Under what conditions might you emphasize each of these techniques?

5. Do you prefer a more formal or more informal style of training? When has your preferred approach worked well? When might it require modification?

6. What is your approach to employee development? Is it possible that you might be seen by your counterparts from other countries as someone who "delegates and disappears"? How would you respond to an employee who brings problems to you and expects to solve them together?

7. In many cultural settings, managers are expected to respond both to employees' work-related and personal needs. How would you handle this kind of dual role?

8. Is your company's performance management system the same around the world, or is it applied differently depending on the country? How could it be modified to make it more effective both globally and locally?

CHAPTER SEVEN

Selling

Among all the different occupations, sales is probably the most resistant to globalization. Unlike the employees of a multinational firm, who must adapt to some degree to their employer's way of doing business, customers ultimately retain the power to spend their own money. Buyers can exercise varying degrees of leverage to induce the seller to meet their own terms. There is no other discipline where personal relationships matter more—buyers everywhere are most comfortable with a salesperson who literally and figuratively speaks their own language. Most countries even have cultures within cultures that require a special approach: distinct regions, ethnic groups, or particular segments of the economy.

Global People Skill #7: Selling

The skill of selling across borders must successfully address the ambivalent state of mind of customers who are considering the purchase of foreign products. These customers are simultaneously attracted and repelled. They want the latest technology and prestigious foreign brands. They are generally well aware of both the strengths and the weaknesses of domestic sources of supply, which may include significant flaws such as limited features, shoddy quality, or poor service—drawbacks that could make foreign suppliers look very attractive. Yet, the same customers do not want to work with a large foreign enterprise that is perceived as trying to control them or tell them what to do. Nobody wants to be colonized, particularly people from countries that are actually former colonies!

Indeed, potential customers harbor a broad range of concerns about dealing with a foreign vendor that must be addressed before any purchase will be made:

- "How much more will it cost me to deal with a foreign supplier?"
- "Do we really matter to them, or are we just another sale? How much of a priority for them will our company be if they have customers all over the world?"
- "Will they be available to help if we have trouble after the sale?"
- "Are their local representatives competent and trustworthy?"
- "Are they going to be a long-term player in this market?"
- "Can I trust them, or are they going to try to exploit my company, my country, or me?"
- "How will I convince others in my firm that this supplier is a good choice?"
- "What are the possible risks and rewards for me within my own organization if I advocate a purchase from a foreign vendor?"
- "Is the value of the products or services they offer worth the trouble and risk of dealing with somebody 'different'?"

The process of addressing these concerns and making a sale is a multistage effort. Although it is possible that one could encounter a buyer (particularly one who has been studying English or watching too many movies) who will say, “Okay, let’s cut to the chase,” chances are that the sales cycle will be more protracted and demanding. This chapter illustrates common problem areas along the way to a sale, including

- Initial contacts
- Discovery
- Relationship selling
- Handling of customer concerns
- Persuasion
- Closing the sale

Initial Contacts

Many of the forms of initiating contacts that work in a task-focused environment—cold calling, e-mail messages, advertisements in trade magazines, and so on—are less effective in foreign contexts. The preferred way to strike up a new business relationship is still frequently via the introduction of a mutually respected third party. Once this introduction is made, the salesperson must leap a number of additional hurdles to have any chance of getting further.

Meeting a Potential Customer in France

Gwen Davis, a salesperson for an electronics company, has just been introduced to a potential new customer in France by a mutual acquaintance, a banker. The banker suggested that she contact Christian La Fontaine, a purchasing manager at a large French conglomerate, as soon as possible. She calls his office to schedule a phone appointment, hoping to get acquainted and to explore the possibilities for a visit to France, during which she would present her firm’s product offerings. M. La Fontaine, however, seems rather terse during the phone conversation and stays on the call only long enough to arrange dates for her trip to his office in Paris.

Upon her arrival at the Paris hotel that had been recommended to her, Gwen is surprised to find a message from M. La Fontaine asking to change the meeting to the day after she had expected. Once she finally arrives at the customer site, she is ushered into a room with several people present. M. La Fontaine introduces her to two of his colleagues whom Gwen understands to be engineers with technical background in her product area. Another person is present who serves as the interpreter, even though Gwen's colleagues seem to speak quite a bit of English. She struggles to learn their names but has trouble with the pronunciation. There is a brief discussion of Paris, and her new acquaintances seem keen to know about her familiarity with its history and famous sites. Gwen responds briefly but soon finds herself at the limits of her knowledge. Early on in the conversation she attempts to learn more about their company and their needs, but they steer the discussion to other subjects such as her own background. They even seem interested in topics such as what graduate school she attended.

M. La Fontaine encourages Gwen to begin her presentation, and she starts with the usual focus on customer benefits that accrue from the technical advances that her company has made. Her idea had been to offer them a product overview and then get into a more specific discussion of their business direction and needs. Instead, they begin grilling her on general market trends as well as technical aspects of the products. Gwen finds herself wishing she had brought along her own engineering team and a lot more technical data. As the discussion goes on, she begins to get a headache that is not relieved by the wine at dinner.

Getting Started on the Right Foot

The first test that any salesperson faces in an unfamiliar environment is learning how to move forward according to a sequence of mutual exchanges that the customer regards as natural—like learning a set of dance steps with a new partner. In the short case above, the foreign salesperson expected a more expansive phone conversation at first, but the customer was not comfortable having a long discussion at that stage. After stumbling over names, the salesperson faced a quiz about Paris and its environs that caused her to struggle. And, even though she tried her best to ask the right questions about the customer's organization and its needs, the conversation veered again toward her own background.

What could Gwen have done differently? Learning a few do's and don'ts—while also assuming we will need to learn a lot more—sends the symbolic message that we have made a step in the customer's direction. From the French perspective, the discussion of Paris is a meaningful first probe because it is an obvious symbol for things that are vital to them. If we have followed a major "do" and made the effort to learn about their capital city, that will be apparent from our first words—not that we need to paint ourselves as experts on Paris. At this point in the relationship it is more critical to indirectly reassure our French counterparts regarding our overall intentions than it is to begin asking about their needs. If we don't pass this simple test, why should they bother to provide us with more information? In local terms, our response even to this simple query is a preliminary answer to their deeper questions about whether we are going to treat them as a priority and become a long-term player in their market. The salesperson in this case has already dug herself a hole through the double faux pas (French for a "don't") of assuming that someone will speak English and depending on the customer to furnish an interpreter. The message she unwittingly conveys is: "If there is a difference between the way you do things and the way my company does things, it will be up to you to fill in the gap."

A series of gaffes made during these initial symbolic exchanges will generate obstacles to proceeding further and possibly even lead the host organization to usher the salesperson out the door of the relationship. Smooth participation in the small-talk phase, on the other hand, shapes a positive perception on the part of the customer—progress in the sales cycle is most likely when we can enter the cultural world of the buyer and create an immediate sense of comfort. For example, the questions about educational background in the scenario above stem from the considerable value placed on higher education in France, an "ascriptive" orientation that makes advanced degrees from a prestigious institution as important as one's recent achievements might be elsewhere. Detailed questions and challenges about market trends and product specifications from French counterparts are another way to test the waters of a potential relationship—their common passion for discussion and debate is put to use here to test the seller's professional qualifications. Unfortunately, the salesperson in this case was taken by surprise. A more positive result to such a grilling could have been respect on an intellectual level from the French side that translates into a greater willingness to depend on Gwen and her company.

Discovery

Every good salesperson will want to move on to learn about the customer organization and its needs as a prelude to the transaction. By keeping in mind the national background of the customer, we can anticipate behavior that might otherwise seem incomprehensible and formulate an effective response. Consider the following discussion that occurs partway through a meeting between Mark Thomas, a new regional marketing manager, and two members of a Korean company that is an important customer. Mark has been called in to replace the previous marketing manager, who left the company to take advantage of another job opportunity. Mark regrettably had little time to spend with the former manager.

Mark: *What do your production plans look like for next year?*

Mr. Lim (purchasing manager): *We expect to produce the same volume of product or perhaps slightly higher.*

Mark: *Will there be any significant changes in product types?*

Mr. Lim: *No changes except for the new R-5 line of products that we talked about before.*

Mark: *Can you tell me something about the features of the R-5?*

Mr. Lim: [Provides short explanation.]

Mark: *It sounds like the technical requirements are similar to those for the R-4. What can we do to serve your requirements on the R-5? Do you expect to be using the new chip set from us?*

Mr. Lim: *What quantities will you be able to deliver, and what will be the time frame for delivery?*

Mark: *I estimate that by March of next year we could deliver ten thousand sets per month within five weeks of the time you place an order.*

Mr. Lim: *Last year we were promised eight thousand units a month of your current chip set for the R-4, but only six thousand were available. And delivery took seven weeks, not five.*

Mark: *Yes, but that was before I came to this job. And I thought that the delivery issue had been resolved. If I can assure you a steady supply and five weeks for delivery, what quantities would you want to have on a monthly basis?*

Mr. Ahn (purchasing director and Mr. Lim's boss): [Briefly confirms delivery time frame estimate with Mr. Lim in Korean and then slams his hand on the table.] *You have never delivered so much new product on time. Don't you know your own company?*

Mark: [Stunned silence.]

Mark is blindsided here by the Korean customer's reaction. From his standpoint, he is trying to ask good questions about the customer's needs that will lead toward a sale, has presented valid projections of available unit quantities and delivery time, and is willing to take personal responsibility for moving things forward. Instead, he has been hit with a complaint about an issue from the previous year that he thought had been resolved. The projections he is offering are based on his own best-faith estimates of what his company will be able to provide, but the customer representatives are questioning his credibility based on their prior experience.

It is useful to examine the Koreans' point of view as well. For them, Mark is the third in a chain of marketing managers. This turnover leads them to question the loyalty of the managers to their own company, let alone to a customer in Korea. In addition, the previous marketing manager made commitments (although he may have thought they were estimates) that were not completely fulfilled. Here is a conversation between the senior and junior Korean managers that took place before the meeting with Mark.

Mr. Ahn (purchasing director): *How could you waste my time with a vendor like this? You did not check them out well enough to begin with! Their personnel are constantly changing, and they have no company loyalty. This is the third marketing manager in three years. They don't seem to take responsibility or apologize for the problems they are causing us. All we get from them are weak excuses and unrealistic commitments that they are always breaking. I hope you have worked out the arrangements carefully this time. There had better not be any more problems…*

Mr. Lim (purchasing manager): [Bows silently.]

In terms of the dimensions of culture that have been discussed previously, Mark is a task-focused individual who has his eyes on future business prospects. His Korean customers are more concerned with a long-term, company-to-company relationship that has been seriously damaged in their eyes by the past performance of this foreign vendor. At this moment, Mark's forward-looking discovery questions and optimistic estimates are pointed in the wrong direction.

If Mark wants to win future business with this customer, he first has to rediscover what happened in the past and then go back and fix it rather than push for a quick close. The sale will be decided based not on what he offers as an individual, but on the customer's perception of his firm's collective performance. Mark could have gotten off to a much better start with the customer if he had done a more thorough investigation into the prior relationship between his company and the Korean firm, ensuring that all past issues had been resolved to their satisfaction. It would also have been helpful to have an in-person introduction by the previous marketing manager or by an executive from his own company who knows the Koreans well. A sincere apology for previous problems and a specific, detailed action plan for addressing any remaining grievances would allow the Koreans to let go of their concerns about the past and begin to think about the future together with him.

There are a number of other cultural dimensions that influence the conduct of potential customers in a cross-border transaction. Table 19 shows key dimensions with the behaviors that might go along with either side of the spectrum.

Keeping in mind such dimensions and the different practical perspectives they bring helps us to listen for the unexpected. To discover real customer needs it is necessary to both ask the right questions and be able to hear and make sense of the response. In a global business setting, so-called common sense can easily be reversed: customers may be focused on the past rather than the future; they may react better to questions aimed at their personal rather than business interests; and, instead of becoming a partner, they may expect to be treated as royalty. An apparently simple question such as, "Who is the decision maker?" can lead to unanticipated results. It might be seen as brazen and overly direct when the salesperson has been assigned without being aware of it to a place in the customer's hierarchy (e.g., the president of a small vendor is unofficially paired with a director-level person in the customer organization). It could also be naïvely simplistic in a culture where multiple interlocking groups of stakeholders must all be satisfied before the transaction can move forward. A better question that accommodates different cultural perspectives is, "Could you please tell me how the decision will be made?"

Relationship Selling

Relationships are not static—they are not "built" to completion so that we can move on to other things. Business relationships in fact continue to grow and develop over time and bring with them a web of ongoing mutual obligations that are a key ingredient to the sales process.

Types of relationships.

The terminology used for customer/supplier relationships in the U.S. tends to obscure the advantages and the costs of relationships in other locations. Terms such as *vendor, preferred vendor, outsourcing solution,* or *strategic partner* suggest increasing levels of association and

Table 19. **Selling: Comparative Styles**

Cultural Orientation	Expectations and Behaviors ← for Selling →		Cultural Orientation
Individual	Find a qualified decision maker; sell to the individual personality and preferences of the buyer who has the power to make a decision	The individual customer is a representative for a larger group—help your contact sell to that group; other groups may be involved beyond the immediate purchasers	**Group**
Task	Focus on product features, quality, delivery, price; build trust through delivering on commitments; fulfill the letter and the spirit of the contract	Find common ground and build trust through deep friendship and shared experiences; your word is your bond—breaking your word damages the relationship	**Relationship**
Direct	Sell based on a match between customer needs and the benefits of a product or service; expect vigorous debate and discussion on the merits of the offering; talk about money frankly and specifically	Sell based on a spiral approach to the buying decision; customer questions may come later or in the form of written requests for information; money is treated as a secondary topic or may be handled in a separate discussion	**Indirect**
Equality	Build a constructive partnership with the customer that provides mutual benefits	Provide the customer with loyal, faithful service; respond rapidly and efficiently to customer requests (even sometimes unreasonable ones)	**Hierarchy**

cooperation between the buyer and the seller. But, each type of transaction continues to retain a sense of distance even in the closest commercial relations.

Table 19. **Selling: Comparative Styles (continued)**

Cultural Orientation	← Expectations and Behaviors for Selling	→	Cultural Orientation
Future	Present forecasts and projections; outline prospective benefits and advantages; build a scenario with the customer that promises shared benenfits	Build continuity with past history—make decisions about the future based on past performance; apologize for previous problems; identify root causes and solutions before moving forward	**Past**
Universal	Maintain standards that are fair across the board; make adjustments according to objective factors such as purchase volume	Special circumstances naturally influence the terms of a sale—prices differ for insiders and outsiders	**Situational**
Neutral*	Provide facts and strong supporting detail; avoid flashy tricks or glitzy advertising	Project a lively and entertaining presence—show your passion for what you are selling; present yourself and your company stylishly, with an eye for aesthetics	**Emotional**

*The neutral/emotional, or affective, dimension is another commonly used cultural comparison that is part of the model presented by Fons Trompenaars and Charles Hampden-Turner. It contrasts the extent to which displays of emotion are viewed as appropriate in different cultural settings. See *Riding the Waves of Culture: Understanding Diversity in Global Business*, 2d ed. (New York: McGraw-Hill, 1998), chap. 6.

In other business contexts around the world it is more accurate and revealing to think in terms normally reserved for friends and family—indeed, business and family relationships may overlap. The progression of our relationship status from acquaintance to friend to relative to family member entails a distinctly different set of business consequences. Being an outsourcing solution or a strategic partner is not the same as being a relative or family member.

Customers may offer a foreign vendor incremental opportunities to prove itself, initially as an acquaintance or friend. Because these opportu-

Table 20. **Relationship Selling: Types of Relationships**

Vendor	Preferred Vendor	Outsourcing Solution	Strategic Partner
Benefit: Considered equally among other potential candidates	**Benefit:** Company employees are encouraged to use it	**Benefit:** Considered the primary source for a particular product or service	**Benefit:** Regarded as a business ally; can leverage "lead user" arrangements with customers to pilot new products or services
Obligation: Provides good value in exchange for fair payment	**Obligation:** Provides good value in exchange for package payment	**Obligation:** Provides good value in exchange for a cost lower than the customer could achieve on its own	**Obligation:** Makes new technology available; provides strategic value to customer at a fair price
Drawback: Receives no security and no guarantees; relationship could end tomorrow	**Drawback:** Several preferred vendors may exist; has security only for the duration of the agreement	**Drawback:** Has security only for the duration of the contract	**Drawback:** Partnership duration depends on continuous mutual advantages; there is less freedom to work with competitors

nities appear to be relatively minor at the outset, if they are evaluated from an economic standpoint without the implications of closer family status in mind, their significance could be misjudged. Table 20 compares the benefits, obligations, and drawbacks of the different paths that lead to strategic partner or family status.

Salespeople who work across borders should become very familiar with the potential advantages and disadvantages of family or quasi-family relationships. Global sales strategies must take into account the types of relationships common to many locations and consider ways to win potential benefits, fulfill obligations efficiently and legally, and avoid the most serious drawbacks. Following is a positive example of the benefits that are available through family-style ties.

Table 20. **Relationship Selling: Types of Relationships (continued)**

Acquaintance	Friend	Relative	Family
Benefit: Has the opportunity to progress to status of friend or relative	**Benefit:** Is favored over others when most factors are equal	**Benefit:** Is favored for new contracts; receives ready introductions to other customers	**Benefit:** Has free access to inside information and contacts; customer uses even when other vendors are superior; can ask customer for help
Obligation: Competes with others; must be willing to go the extra mile to advance status; provides excellent value at reduced prices	**Obligation:** Provides good value in exchange for fair payment; needs to maintain relationship on social as well as business level	**Obligation:** Provides acceptable value in exchange for fair payment; uses products and services of other "relatives"	**Obligation:** Must comply even with unreasonable requests; "what's mine is yours" principle works both ways
Drawback: Receives no security and no guarantees; provisional status depends on strength of introduction	**Drawback:** Security is contingent on continued solid performance; other "friends" may request special treatment; social activities involve substantial investments of time and money	**Drawback:** Has limited freedom to develop alliances outside the network; lacks efficiency and pricing power	**Drawback:** Security of "family" status could mean lack of stimulus to innovate or to grow the business in new directions; pricing power varies depending on family relations

Establishing an Insider Position

Dave Wong has spent the past few weeks in meetings with a potential new customer, an Italian business that would be key to his company's expansion in southern Europe. Dave and his contact person from the Italian company,

Mr. Adamo, have been meeting frequently and have a friendly and open working relationship. Although the meetings often run long, the overall tone has been very positive. Mr. Adamo asks him many questions about the leadership and overall reputation of Dave's company as well as its experience working with other Italian customers.

Dave thinks he is very close to gaining an important new customer, and he asks an Italian manager in his company what would be the best way to cement Mr. Adamo's interest. The manager advises that the most positive thing he can do now to improve the relationship is to set up face-to-face meetings between Mr. Adamo, himself, and selected contact people from his company's other Italian customers. The feedback and endorsement from his other Italian customers will demonstrate to Mr. Adamo that the company is both well respected and well connected in Italy. This will go a long way toward creating confidence and positioning the company as an "insider" that understands the needs of an Italian company. Dave wonders whether such a request will be an imposition on his customers but goes ahead and follows the manager's advice. To his surprise and pleasure, the customers he contacts say they would be happy to meet Mr. Adamo together with him.

Comments

The sales approach described in this case is often a good one in an Italian business environment because transactions are very relationship oriented and Italian businesspeople in general feel more comfortable dealing with people they know well. A reciprocal obligation comes along with the privilege of making this kind of arrangement, however. The customers who have so cheerfully agreed to cooperate in this instance may soon ask the salesperson to return the favor in some fashion.

Levels of relationships.

Besides evolving through progressive stages, relationships also commonly have a hierarchical aspect. A business relationship between two companies in a hierarchically oriented society could easily involve three or more levels of contacts: executives, managers, and workers/engineers. Making a sale in this kind of setting requires strong links with the customer organization at every level. When such links are not present, trouble can result, as shown in the following example.

Taking a One-Dimensional Approach

A Western hi-tech firm was struggling to obtain a design win from a large Asian customer. The Western company was confident in its ability to win this particular contract because it had not only a product portfolio with compelling features, but also solid executive-level relations. Top executives on the customer side had made reassuring statements about their willingness to do business with the Western supplier. Such a significant design contract would ensure a constant flow of business over the next several years and figured prominently in the local subsidiary's revenue projections.

What was not visible on the executive level, however, was a list of complaints voiced by the purchasing manager and the customer's design engineers about delivery and quality issues with the Western supplier's previous product model. The Asian executives were reluctant to broach these nitty-gritty problems too directly—their view was that the executive relationship should be reserved for high-level conversations about strategic direction and the resolution of major issues.

Meanwhile, on the design engineering level, the customer's key engineers were having detailed discussions with a locally headquartered supplier who offered superior delivery terms, had a strong reputation for quality, and also promised to have dedicated local resources in place to quickly tackle any product-related issues that emerged. The Western company's in-country marketing and engineering resources were inadequate to support such regular customer contact on detailed engineering matters, and engineers visiting from headquarters overseas sometimes surprised their counterparts in the customer organization by "revising" statements made by local employees from their own company.

In the final analysis, it was not the executive-level contact but rather the engineering-level opinion that prevailed, and the local supplier got the contract. The Western firm had to revise its sales projections sharply downward, and tension increased between local employees, who felt that they had been undermined, and headquarters engineers, who felt that their local counterparts lacked the expertise to address the customer's needs.

Comments

To ensure a more positive outcome, it is best to employ a carefully orchestrated sales process that leverages the appropriate functions of each relationship level. For this process to work, employees at each level on the vendor side have to share information and work smoothly together with their colleagues at other levels of the company. A common mistake is to depend on a single manager to make a sale when the customer expects to work with a multilevel team. The customer could find this approach to be disorienting and possibly offensive, while the seller misses the benefits that might be gleaned from contacts with customer employees at the levels not represented. Taking a one-dimensional approach to a multidimensional sale can be a major disadvantage when the sales approach of local competitors more closely mirrors the customer's organization. See table 21 for a description of several possible roles in the sales process.

Enabling local employees.

Local staff members, with their firsthand knowledge of local customs and customers, are key allies in making a relationship sale. They can help their company to read the potential of a business contact and sell at multiple levels. Such local talent will be underutilized, however, if it is not developed and positioned properly. "I am just a messenger boy" is the sentiment expressed by sales employees who are not given sufficient leeway to do their job.

Local salespeople have to strike a balance between representing customer needs and the objectives of their employer. This takes a rare combination of skill sets: they must penetrate the customer organization and be treated as a welcome insider and at the same time serve as a bridge and

Table 21. **Hierarchy and Sales Function**

Hierarchical Level	Function in Sales Process
Executive	• Creates entry point for new relationship • Discusses big-picture strategy • Resolves major issues • Provides or requests introductions to other industry contacts
Manager	• Leads sales team for presentation of specific products • Manages ongoing projects • Provides central interface point for customers • Coordinates activities of team members and flow of information between executives and workers/engineers
Professional/ engineer	• Sells product features and specific benefits • Carries out joint design of new products • Implements work plans • Collects inside information through informal contacts

communication link to help colleagues abroad understand and respond to unique customer needs. Immature or inexperienced people may be so strident in representing the customer that home-country colleagues question their loyalty: "Who is he working for, us or the customer?" Or, by crying wolf once too often for help in fixing relatively minor problems, they may also lose the attention of global managers who are trying to allocate scarce resources effectively. At the other extreme are those who are effective at communicating with headquarters but not held in high regard by the customer—they are unlikely to be privy to critical customer information and can produce a variety of false leads.

An obvious step in developing a sales force that can build strong local relationships is to hire people who already have extensive networks or who demonstrate an aptitude for creating them. The employees who are recruited can be ushered through progressive stages of responsibility, depending on their capabilities and the nature of their company's operations. Visitors from other countries should plan joint customer calls carefully so that they learn what information local salespeople possess and help to position these colleagues in a positive way with the customer. As the experience of local salespeople grows, they will typically want and deserve greater pricing flexibility so that they have latitude of their own to manage the customer relationship; such flexibility also decreases the need for time-consuming back-and-forth communication with headquarters. Ultimately, pricing flexibility within general corporate guidelines can also be turned into local profit-and-loss responsibility. The ideal career path for top salespeople is one that progresses from local relationship manager to the head of a global account headquartered in their country. In this way their customer ties and relationship-selling skills can become an asset for the company as a whole.

Handling Customer Concerns

The deepest objections held by customers may not be expressed directly. In many countries there is a hesitancy to broach awkward subjects with foreign "guests." Local employees often report their disappointment that the foreign executive has come away from a customer meeting thinking the relationship is in great shape shortly after the same customer has just raked them over the coals. It is essential to recognize the meaning behind common probes, ask questions that get at underlying issues, and respond in a way that addresses the real concern. For example:

> **Customer:** *How often do you plan to come here?* [Underlying concerns: Do we really matter to them or are we just another sale? How much of a priority for them will our company be if they have customers all over the world?]
>
> **Seller:** *My current plan is to travel here once each quarter. In addition to our quarterly meetings, my colleagues here will contact you on a weekly basis. If you like, we could also set up a regular telephone conference every two weeks or every month that would include all of us. Does this sound okay, or do you feel that more frequent meetings would be useful?*
>
> **Customer:** *How will we handle problems that come up?* [Underlying concerns: Will they be available to help if we have trouble after the sale? Are their local representatives competent and trustworthy?]

Seller: *First, please contact Mr. X, who has local account responsibility. He and I communicate on a daily basis, and I depend on him because he has strong technical skills and knows the people in our main overseas factory quite well. Let me also give you my cell phone number so that you can reach me if there is a serious issue and Mr. X is not available. He or I can contact the right people immediately if there are any problems. Our job is to make you feel as if we were manufacturing product for you right here.*

Customer: *What are your company's plans for investment in this country?* [Underlying concerns: Are they going to be a long-term player in this market? Can I trust them or are they going to try to exploit my company, my country, or me?]

Seller: *As Mr. Y may have mentioned to you when he introduced us, we are planning to build a permanent presence here. We have a small manufacturing operation now that we expect to expand as the demand for our products increases, and we have established a relationship with the university here to contribute equipment and employee instructional time. In exchange, we hope to be able to attract more first-rate employees from the university. What are your own long-term goals? Perhaps there is some way that we can work together to achieve them.*

Customer: *I'd like to receive some more detailed written documentation on the new product features that you're describing. Could you send that to me as soon as possible? And please include a comparison with your local competitors.* [Underlying concerns: How will I convince the others in my firm that this supplier is a good choice? What are the possible risks and rewards for me within my own organization if I advocate a purchase from a foreign vendor?]

Seller: *Certainly. We can have that for you by the end of next week. Is there any other information that you would like us to provide? How many copies would you like? If you want us to arrange a product demonstration for anyone else, we would be happy to do that as well.*

Customer: *If I buy your product, what guarantees can you provide?* [Underlying concern: Is the value of the products or services they offer worth the trouble and risk of dealing with somebody "different"?]

Seller: *The product warranty is for twelve months on any quality-related problems. Our data shows, however, that the frequency of these problems is very low over the recommended five-year usage period, and our repair and maintenance fees are comparable to those of anyone in the industry. Our goal is to earn your business over the long term, so we will do our best to assist you with whatever problems come up. Do you have any specific questions or concerns in this area?*

Persuasion

Nearly every aspect of selling is linked in some way with the art of persuasion. Persuasion involves both a counterpart and a set of methods. With respect to the counterpart, or the buyer one encounters, Western salespeople are trained to sell to an individual customer with a particular personality. One identifies the buyer's type—for instance, "driver," "analytical," "emotive," "amiable"[1]—and then employs the appropriate sales approach.

But what if the buyer is a complex group rather than an individual, and the members of this group engage in dramatically different behaviors depending on the situation? In China, for instance, the stakeholders in a purchasing decision could include one's immediate counterparts in the purchasing department, their managers (who are not involved directly but who must sign off on any agreement), other divisions in the company that will be affected, existing suppliers including close friends or relatives of company members, local government officials who control the infrastructure and enforce regulations, and Communist Party representatives. Moreover, the behaviors of the Chinese managers and employees taking part could be straitlaced and sober in one situation and extraordinarily convivial in another. Figure 12 gives a typology of situations analogous to the personality types mentioned above. It could be equally useful to look for opportunities to persuade based on the type of situation one encounters as well as the individual buyer type.

Figure 12. **Sales: Persuasion and Situation Types**

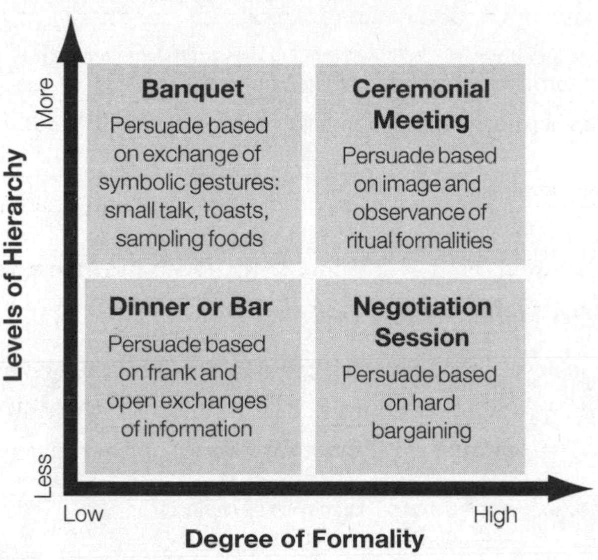

As for methods of persuasion, many people consider them to be a matter of verbal agility. Yet, the powerful forms of logical argument and debate that are so effective in some Western environments may be less useful or even counterproductive elsewhere. Customers from other countries or cultures are likely to place importance on a broad range of verbal, nonverbal, and contextual forms of persuasion.

Approaches to persuasion that may be especially effective in non-Western settings include several steps that have been alluded to elsewhere: introductions or lobbying through respected third parties, associating oneself or one's project with high-status institutions or people, and bringing high-quality written materials, preferably in the local language. The supplier's track record and personal pedigree are obviously important, but they should usually be communicated indirectly. Informal social time allows for the development of friendship and trusting multilevel relationships that enable the other party to say yes more easily. Table 22 lists a variety of worthwhile approaches to cross-border persuasion.

Another, subtler, persuasive method is to allow the customer to control the major transition points in the conversation. Task-focused salespeople often rush the shift from small talk to a discussion of the business. However, a patient approach that lets the customer determine the timing will almost always result in a potential buyer who is more will-

Table 22. **Persuasion Techniques**

- Making introductions or lobbying through respected third parties
- Associating oneself or one's project with high-status institutions or people
- Providing high-quality, localized sales materials
- Communicating track record and personal pedigree indirectly
- Participating in informal social time
- Allowing the customer to control transition points in the conversation
- Citing prestigious local or overseas precedents
- Demonstrating determination and emotional commitment

ing to address concrete issues—the customer has already persuaded himself or herself to move to the next stage of the conversation. The questions that initially come from the buyer, both in the small-talk phase and after the transition to business discussions, also tend to reveal key interests and concerns and are a better place to start than questions brought in by a busybody salesperson.

Citing a prestigious local or foreign precedent for the use of one's product can supplement other forms of persuasion. A gifted salesperson in Korea noted that he sold advanced technology applications to his Korean customers by taking them to Japan and showing them how Japanese firms were using his company's products. His customers, spurred by a mixture of rivalry with Japanese competitors and respect for their technological prowess, would often be persuaded by such a demonstration. George Renwick describes another cross-border example of persuasion in a joint venture context:

> *One large American company was involved in negotiations in China and they wanted to convince the Chinese that certain things should be built into a new facility that the joint venture*

was to construct in China. The Chinese were very reluctant to do this. So, the Americans took fifteen Chinese from Beijing to Mexico, where they all walked through a plant there that had in it exactly the facilities that were being recommended for China. The Chinese got to see it, they got to talk with the Mexican workers and managers about it, and they were able to see the product that was coming from it. Fourteen of the fifteen went back believing that, yes, that was possible, that was appropriate in China.[2]

Buyer decisions are normally based on a largely unarticulated web of factors: the features and price of a product or service, the vendor's reputation, the salesperson's personal background and perceived competence, the strength of personal relationships, precedents that reduce apparent risks, and so on. A further variable that is sensed by the buyer but not discussed is the level of determination or emotional commitment displayed by the salesperson. Demonstration of such commitment is a positive indication of one's seriousness and enthusiasm. This may be particularly important in a situation where the parties involved are not from the same country and have different standards for measuring and evaluating information. The following is an example from inside a company where a junior foreign manager sought to sell senior local colleagues on his idea.

Making an Emotional Appeal

Carlos Herrera, a young American product manager based in Japan, wanted to create a new advertising campaign for his product. He generated a strong base of research data—local consumer data along with comparative data from overseas—and presented it to his Japanese colleagues. But, they were skeptical. It was too risky. It wouldn't work for the local market. Carlos would come back with more data and they would still voice their skepticism. Finally, in sheer frustration and desperation, the product manager broke down and begged the others to go ahead with this advertising campaign as he had conceived it. His counterparts' response was, "Well, if you feel so strongly about this campaign, then maybe we should give it a try."

Comments

What persuaded the decision makers in this case was not all the data that the marketing manager provided, although perhaps that made a contribution. It was the emotional appeal he made—the sheer energy and commitment that he displayed—that helped to convince his counterparts that maybe this young man was someone who could see the project through. They concluded that his passion and dedication to the project could be just as crucial to its success in the long run as the market intelligence that he had assembled. (A point of caution: the degree of open emotional expression considered appropriate varies radically according to the culture and the situation.)

Closing the Sale

Closing techniques are the subject of avid study and training on the part of countless salespeople. It is as if the sale were a big game hunt, with the close being the climax of the hunt—the kill. We have all learned about "power closes" that supposedly work "like a bear trap." Such devices may produce results when selling widgets to domestic clients, but they are not always the best means for selling to customers abroad who are very sensitive about being bulldozed.

Salespeople tend to misread the signals given by foreign buyers because the patterns of communication are so different. They close too soon or too late, are too forceful or not aggressive enough. The classic mistake is to come away from a customer meeting thinking there is agreement when in fact there is none. The mild "yes" from our host can signify nothing more than polite interest. A "yes" accompanied by nonverbal distress can mean, "We don't want to say no to you directly but please understand what we are telling you." Another hazard is the unenforceable contract. Getting the buyer to sign on the dotted line means little in an environment where the legal system favors local firms and contracts are ignored or creatively interpreted.

The close before the close.

The notion of closing the sale is more useful when it is expanded beyond a single climactic event. A better, if more laborious, metaphor than the hunt is the chipping away by a woodcarver or sculptor: the figure being created reveals itself over time. Closing actually begins with hearing out and incorporating the ideas of our counterparts—this shows our willingness to understand rather than dominate or exploit. What foreign colleagues and customers are looking for is often not so much a polished sales pitch as a broader sense of mutual commitment and connectedness. Renwick suggests that one of the best ways to sell a customer or colleague is to examine alternatives together.

> *I find it comfortable for everybody concerned... if instead of trying to persuade them of something directly, we sit with them, look at the situation together, analyze it, and then come up with two, three, four viable alternatives for dealing with it. This gives us an opportunity to contribute our experience, which is often considerable, our insight, and our judgment. We can evaluate pros and cons of each of the options. But we're respecting our counterparts enough to leave it up to them to choose which alternative they are going to pursue.*[3]

Steady follow-up even on minor matters is a sign that we will follow through on major agreements. A small but thoughtful gift—not a bribe or something overly lavish—can be a symbol that we have been listening to what the customer says and are beginning to know him or her as a person. Making ourselves easily available, revising the proposal or providing additional data to help the customer sell it to colleagues, presenting to multiple constituent groups—each of these actions binds us and the customer ever more closely together, wins their commitment to work with us, and begins to cement a working partnership that will continue after the sale.

The circular close.

The style of the close need not be direct or pointed like the teeth of a trap. The value of a more circular approach to a sale is that it offers the seller multiple opportunities to learn more about the customer's circumstances, to gauge interest, and to move toward a sale without forcing a response before the customer is ready. Here is a tactful sales approach that mirrors the indirect style of feedback presented in chapter 3:

Salesperson: *You have a lot of cars in the parking lot.*

Customer: *Yes, it is very full, isn't it? I have a hard time finding a parking place myself.*

Salesperson: *So, business must be going quite well for you...*

Customer: *Yes, thankfully the last couple of quarters have been pretty strong.*

Salesperson: *Does that mean that you will be raising factory production goals in the next quarter?*

Customer: *As a matter of fact, we plan to increase our goals 5 percent beyond the original plan for the year.*

Salesperson: *So, will you be needing more of our components to accommodate the production increase?*

The customer close.

The standard wisdom in most sales training courses is that the buyer needs help to make up his or her mind, and the salesperson must constantly shepherd the buyer toward a purchase decision. However, one of the most effective ways to earn respect and create a sense of mutual comfort is through well-placed moments of silence that let the customer take the initiative. Silence of this kind should not be viewed as a tactic or a kind of contest of wills in which the first person to speak "loses." Rather, it is a way to demonstrate our regard for intelligent buyers and not have them feel rushed or pushed—these latter sentiments are likely to lead to the "yes" that means "no" or "go away quickly."

Once we have replied to customer questions and made a presentation regarding our product or service, reverting to silence gives the people on the customer's team time to think and perhaps consult with each other. This reflects well on our character in a number of countries and can create a felt obligation on the part of the other side to respond. Often at this point the customer will come back with questions that lead toward specific and concrete purchase information: "What quantities can you deliver?" "What is the delivery time?" "When can you schedule this service?" Such questions are very reliable customer-driven closing signals, even from customers who will give us the vague "yes" if we put them on the spot before they are ready.

Careful, complete, and accurate responses to these questions will keep the customer representatives in the driver's seat and give them the information they need, while premature closing gestures will force them into retreat. The final part of this customer-centered close is the simple and friendly act of confirming what each side will do next. This leaves the customer feeling that the choice has been theirs all along and makes likely the chances of an enduring, successful relationship that will bring more sales.

The close after the close.

In societies where contracts are not strictly enforced—which includes much of the world outside the United States and Europe—the "close" doesn't really close anything other than one phase in an ongoing set of interactions. A signed deal must be bolstered by a number of steps in the weeks and months following the agreement to both keep it viable and to win future business. Customer service on an existing contract, for instance, can be a big part of the decision-making process on the next sale as well as ensuring continued payments on the previous one.

A common strategy used by buyers who are distrustful of foreign sources of supply is to offer a relatively small piece of work to the seller and then watch what happens. The vendor must jump through a variety of hoops to make the agreement work. Meanwhile, this vendor also needs to strike a delicate balance between being flexible and being able to set reasonable limits in the face of unreasonable requests. Erring in either direction can be costly. An inflexible seller will find that much larger contracts the customer originally had in mind suddenly vanish like a mirage in the desert. On the other hand, a vendor who agrees to everything will not even want the next contract because a precedent has been set for low prices or extra services that are uncompensated.

Real efforts by the seller to meet reasonable and even somewhat unreasonable demands will normally set the groundwork for the next sale. The salesperson, for example, who takes an overnight train to deliver a part to a customer in time to help meet a deadline has not wasted valuable sales time but rather guaranteed a warm reception in discussing the next piece of work. The more such gestures are made, the more a "family-style" buyer will naturally gravitate toward repeat purchases through a growing sense of obligation. So, a single "close" opens the door to a succession of further closes that both preserve the sale and expand the business relationship.

Selling

SUMMARY AND REVIEW QUESTIONS

1. What unspoken questions do you think potential foreign customers have about you and your company that might make them hesitate to make a purchase?

2. In your experience, what adjustment to selling strategies has your company implemented in response to the business practices of foreign customers?

3. What are some common perceptions regarding customers outside your home country? Does this shared image seem to reflect an awareness of the customers' cultural values?

4. What are your preferred approaches to the initial contact and discovery phases of the selling relationship? How would you adjust your sales methods in a setting where a less direct communication style is strongly preferred? How about where current decisions are strongly based on past experience?

5. In foreign markets you're familiar with, would your approach change if you thought of sales as building family-style relationships? What obligations do you enter into when you sell to "relatives" or to "family" clients?

6. Do you use a sales approach that mirrors the customer's organizational structure and gives you relationships at each level?

7. How would you respond to a foreign customer who asks questions about matters such as how frequently you will visit, your company's plans for local investment, or the guarantees that will come with the purchase of your product? What are the underlying concerns likely to be in a case like this?

8. What are your favorite methods for closing a sale? Are there other techniques that are likely to be more effective in a different cultural setting?

CHAPTER EIGHT

Negotiating

Few activities have as much at stake as negotiations between companies. Significant—and perhaps fateful—commitments of finances and other resources ride on the successful outcome of this back-and-forth process. In a cross-border context, negotiations tend to be intense and demanding not only because of the high stakes, but also because in this type of pressure cooker situation, with so many stakeholders and potentially conflicting interests involved, participants are most likely to have difficulty overcoming cultural and national differences.

Global People Skill #8: Negotiating

Negotiating styles are deeply rooted in cultural behaviors, which differ widely among the world's peoples, regions, and nations. Ample evidence of these differences appears whenever one crosses a national border. For example, a few miles south of San Diego, California, and adjacent to

Tijuana, Mexico, lies the U.S. border city of San Ysidro. There, a tourist can look for a hat at any number of shops or supermarkets and find a variety of sizes, designs, and colors. But in each case, the price will be fixed. Tourists' "negotiation" for purchase of a hat amounts to little more than choosing the store with the design that best matches their needs and paying the sticker price. If they walk ten minutes over the border to Tijuana, however, they enter a different world. There, fixed prices simply don't exist, and they realize quickly—and perhaps painfully—that only a sucker will pay the sticker price. Mexicans expect to bargain so that the purchase price will be significantly lower than the initial price. This expectation is a fundamental part of the Mexican way of doing business.

Because their consumer economies are based on fixed prices, businesspeople from the U.S. and Northern Europe are at a distinct disadvantage when they negotiate in other countries where consumer purchases are negotiated. Their counterparts will have developed keen negotiating skills simply as a result of growing up in their native culture. Instruction in negotiation usually begins when children watch their parents haggle for groceries and other daily necessities. These skills transfer to business negotiations when children become adult professionals, and they confer a huge advantage.

A chapter on negotiation must therefore begin with a stern warning: westerners should beware of overconfidence when negotiating abroad and should remember that it is extremely difficult to outwit a foreign negotiating team that has developed well-honed negotiating skills as a result of their cultural heritage.

U.S. and Chinese Negotiating Styles: An Instructive Contrast

It is impossible to give an encyclopedic analysis of the world's different negotiating styles in one chapter. Fortunately, we have another approach that will provide both an understanding of potential hazards of negotiating abroad and some examples of proven techniques for avoiding these hazards.

The U.S. and China represent two poles of negotiating behaviors. U.S. negotiators tend to take a more task-focused approach favored to some degree by many westerners. Chinese negotiating styles often resemble those of other relationship-oriented cultures in Asia, the Middle East, and Latin America. Although negotiators from some countries may already be more skillful at balancing tasks and relationships than either side of a U.S.–China negotiation, the comparison offered here can still be useful in learning to calibrate our approach to working with a different culture. This chapter offers recommendations on the following topics:

- Understanding the negotiating context
- Effective openings—presenting the team's position
- Maintaining a continuous negotiation record
- Knowing your bottom line
- Making concessions
- The importance of discipline
- Patience and control of the time element
- Negotiating "after hours"
- Postcontract negotiations[1]

Understanding the Negotiating Context

U.S. negotiators frequently assume that the context in which negotiations are conducted in China is the same as that in the U.S. Important features of the U.S. commercial negotiating context include freedom from governmental interference, a high degree of confidentiality, and well-established, efficient markets and supply chain infrastructures. Without experience or sufficient research, it is understandable how a U.S. team might conclude that these features would be present in China as well. But, the fact is that the Chinese negotiating context is very different from that in the U.S., and to base a negotiating strategy on an assumption of similarity is to commit a grave mistake.

Government influence.

Perhaps the most surprising, and often the most frustrating, difference for U.S. negotiators in China is the high degree of governmental interference in the negotiating process. Although the central government has been steadily granting greater freedom in the economy over the last two decades, China's communist legacy of economic control by the state has not disappeared completely, particularly in the so-called state-owned enterprises, or SOEs, as distinct from private or collective enterprises that are much freer from government intervention.

Governmental or political interference in Chinese negotiations frequently appears in the form of demands or conditions that have very little apparent connection to the underlying commercial or economic terms of the negotiation. For example, in a negotiation for a manufacturing operation joint venture between a Chinese SOE and a U.S. firm, the lead member of the Chinese team might make the following comments with regard to a senior Chinese officer of the SOE whose actual responsibilities are somewhat unclear and who does not appear to offer much value to the prospective joint venture.

> **Chinese team leader:** *We understand why you would prefer to have seasoned individuals with operational experience on the management team, but for us it is very important that Vice President Chen be included, even though he does not have a technical background and his actual business experience is limited. We feel that Vice President Chen will bring valuable perspective to our joint venture, particularly with respect to the unique characteristics of the Chinese market and economic situation.*

This somewhat cryptic message is in fact a kind of code intended to signal that Vice President Chen is a member of the Communist Party with a great deal of power over the fate of the joint venture. He or she (many senior Communist officials are women) may indeed be an influential player in local, provincial, or even national politics. And, although party officials will indeed not add much to the operational management of the joint venture, their role can be critical when it comes to securing official support for the project, obtaining necessary licenses, and avoiding the many bureaucratic entanglements that can easily undermine a commercial venture in China.

U.S. negotiators with little understanding of the Chinese political context will frequently push back against Chinese demands such as these, insisting that in order for a venture to be economically competitive and "efficiently" run, only experienced businesspeople or individuals with technical knowledge should be part of management. By failing to understand and accommodate the Chinese request, the U.S. team may not only give offense, but also rob the venture of precisely the politically connected Chinese officials it will need to succeed.

Confidentiality.

A second element of the Chinese negotiating context that is very different from that in the U.S. is the issue of confidentiality. U.S. business professionals generally maintain very high standards with respect to handling sensitive information and maintaining confidentiality. For example, a U.S. firm will not share information about a confidential negotiation with its suppliers, vendors, or business partners, even though the information might be enormously valuable to them. U.S. negotiators are therefore surprised, and often angered, when they learn that the Chinese do not view confidentiality the same way they do. The following is a typical exchange that illustrates this problem:

> **U.S. team leader:** *Subassembly pricing is of course a major factor. And we want to be sure that our components division will supply the subassemblies to our joint venture at a fair price—one that enables us to control our JV's costs, while at the same time allowing our components division to make some profit. That's why we feel that a price of $1,500 per subassembly is reasonable. Our senior management at headquarters will, I am afraid, have great difficulty supporting a price any lower than this.*
>
> **Chinese team leader:** *We appreciate your need to ensure that your components division operates profitably—we are realists about this.*

And your willingness to ensure a lower price for our joint venture is acknowledged. All we are asking is that you match the price of $1,300 per subassembly that you offered the Ministry of Machine Industry's plant in Tianjin last year.

U.S. team leader: [Angry silence.]

As this example illustrates, many Chinese negotiators have an extremely effective information network that operates with sometimes astonishing speed. In this case, the Chinese have obtained an important piece of confidential information about a negotiation with a different ministry, in a different city, and at a different time. The U.S. team may at this point feel a number of emotions ranging from anger to betrayal to shock.

In dealing with the problem of confidentiality in China, it is important first to understand that the Chinese view information as a commodity to be used for whatever commercial advantage it can bring. Sensitive information is thus shared widely in a kind of information barter economy, where a holder of valuable information trades it in return for new information of equal value. Central to this practice is the idea that nothing is really confidential. Information is simply too valuable to be kept secret.

Moreover, many Chinese negotiators still harbor a historical suspicion of foreigners and their willingness to treat China and Chinese counterparts fairly. Unfortunately, their suspicions have a well-established historical foundation. From 1850 to the end of World War II, a succession of foreign governments and the commercial enterprises they supported took advantage of China's weakness, forcing many a "deal" on the country that contained extremely unfair terms agreed to only under duress. It is therefore no surprise that today most Chinese negotiators are wary about being taken advantage of, and they feel that using any information they can get their hands on to ensure a fair deal is simply being prudent.

The rule for U.S. and any other Western negotiators in China is therefore simple: never assume that any statement will be kept confidential. We must approach our business in China with the assumption that details of every negotiation we engage in will be widely known, and we must expect that any favorable terms from past negotiations will appear as a demand from our Chinese counterparts in future negotiations. This means that it is essential to take a strategic approach to negotiating in China—to view a negotiation today as an isolated tactical move in the absence of a carefully considered overall strategy is to guarantee a weakened negotiating stance tomorrow.

Market and supply chain infrastructure.

The third aspect of the Chinese negotiating context that is likely to cause headaches for U.S. negotiators is the nature of the Chinese market and supply chain infrastructure. Most U.S. negotiators are used to extremely efficient markets for supplies such as electricity, water, and key components, along with equally efficient relationships with their suppliers. Consequently, when a U.S. team must evaluate whether it will be able to follow through on a supply commitment in a negotiation, this typically does not require a lot of time or work. Provided there are no unresolved technical issues, the team usually only has to look at its experience with supply and demand for the key components it needs and then evaluate the costs and reliability of its own supply chain. It can then make a supply commitment with a high degree of confidence that it will be able to follow through and uphold its end of the bargain.

The situation in China is very different, however, as the following conversation illustrates.

> **U.S. team leader:** *So, it looks like all that's left is for your team to ensure that you can secure the electric power and the transformer equipment we'll need to power the plant, and we will be able to conclude our discussions about operations. This is really good news, since this means that our negotiations are essentially complete. I would hope that we could sign our final JV agreement as early as next month and look at beginning manufacturing test runs sometime within the next sixty days.*
>
> **Chinese team leader:** *It is indeed good news that we have made rapid progress, and we look forward as you do to an early signing of our*

agreement and the all-important startup of operations. But, it may take us some time to handle the power supply issue. I think it would be prudent to discuss how we might begin worker training in anticipation of signing a final JV document three months from now…

U.S. team leader: *Three months from now? I guess I am a bit puzzled… Why do we have to wait so long?*

What the U.S. team has failed to realize here is that markets for important supplies such as power and water in China are not particularly efficient and may involve complex subnegotiations between their counterparts and a wide array of Chinese political and economic entities that the U.S. team will never see. Furthermore, suppliers and supply chains are frequently neither clearly defined nor highly reliable in China; consequently, the Chinese team may have to invest a great deal of time to create contingency arrangements to be sure that once they commit to certain terms for supplying power and associated power supply equipment to the joint venture, they will be able to follow through.

The U.S. team will be wise in this case not to show their frustration, but instead allow their Chinese counterparts the time they will need to complete the required subnegotiations. A well-prepared U.S. negotiating team will have allowed substantial extra time for these Chinese subnegotiations *before* making any commitments to their own management back home regarding when manufacturing operations can begin.

Thus, a U.S. negotiating team in China must remember that the Chinese negotiating context is very different from that encountered in the West. There are great perils in neglecting to research the additional risks that are involved. Additional time will usually be required for negotiations to run their course and yield an agreement that is realistic from the Chinese perspective. The U.S. team must also protect itself by managing the expectations of its own executives at home. Otherwise, it could inadvertently commit to wrap up negotiations and begin operations in China sooner than is either realistic or prudent given the circumstances of its business partners and the Chinese economic system.

Effective Openings: Presenting the Team's Position

Most U.S. representatives will begin a negotiation in China by "getting down to business" and presenting a list of the key items they wish to discuss. In preparing for a joint venture negotiation, for example, their team will typically list each of its major negotiable items and calculate a broad negotiating range for each. Items on the list might include the following:

- Ownership percentage
- Profit split
- Management representation
- Salaries and benefits
- Monthly rents
- Imported component pricing
- Rates for electricity and water
- Building costs

Following are possible opening remarks exchanged between the lead U.S. negotiator and his or her Chinese counterpart at the start of the two teams' first negotiating session.

> **Lead U.S. negotiator (with the above list in hand):** *It's a pleasure for us to be here today in Beijing, and I'd like to express our gratitude for all of the arrangements you have made for our visit. We are really looking forward to our discussions over the next several days.*
>
> *I thought I would begin by reviewing a list of the key items that we feel we should discuss, arranged in order of importance. Our feeling is that if we can come to agreement on the first three-to-five major items on this visit, then we will have made good progress and can likely complete negotiations when we return next month.*

For all of its clarity and precision, this opening is likely to be met by a long silence from the Chinese, after which the lead Chinese negotiator might respond as follows:

> **Lead Chinese negotiator:** *We are delighted to have you here and are pleased to hear that your accommodations are comfortable. It is clear that you have made very detailed preparations for our talks, which we really appreciate. We thought it might be valuable to hear first what you think are the principles that should guide our relationship and the main benefits of our proposed joint venture…*

At this point the U.S. negotiating team is likely to be caught completely off-guard. Some will wonder what on earth the Chinese really want. Others will feel annoyance at having to waste time discussing benefits when they should be obvious to everyone—after all, the Chinese would not be at the meeting if they did not have a clear understanding of the potential benefits to them. Still others may be suspecting that this is some devious opening gambit designed to distract and confuse the U.S. team. The risk is that from its outset the negotiation is in danger of going off track; the U.S. and Chinese teams may quickly begin to distrust each other, reducing or even eliminating the possibility of a productive outcome.

The U.S. team's opening strategy is a common one. Because they are under pressure to produce results quickly, and because there is indeed a long list of items to cover in the negotiations, they have followed their task-oriented instincts and started by "working the list" with the Chinese. While this approach may make perfect sense from the U.S. perspective, it is a mistake in China. The Chinese are relationship-based negotiators and turn to the details only after they have established a trusting relationship and a clear conceptual framework for the partnership.

Consequently, a list of opening items for discussion from the Chinese perspective might look like this:

- Essential interests of both parties
- Potential areas of conflict
- Principles that will govern both the negotiation and the partnership

- Track record of the other company and outcomes of prior partnerships
- Commitment of top management in the other firm to the joint venture
- Level of urgency to complete the negotiation

Note the striking contrast between this list and that of the U.S. team. The U.S. list focuses exclusively on the "to-do's" for the project, taking the relationship as a given. The Chinese list focuses on the parties involved and the manner in which they will work together, with the aim of establishing a relationship where none exists now. With this list in mind, the lead Chinese negotiator might make the following opening comments:

> **Lead Chinese negotiator:** *It is our pleasure to have you here in Beijing, and we are looking forward to a productive several days with you. As a way to get to know one another better, we'd like to suggest that we start by agreeing on some principles that will guide our relationship and negotiation, before we get to the details. It would also be helpful if you could outline broadly what you feel are the main benefits of our potential joint venture and what you feel are the key requirements for it to be a success. Of course, any information you can share based on your past experience with similar joint venture projects will be very helpful.*

The Chinese will then listen very carefully to the response. If the U.S. team seems unable to articulate principles of fairness, trust, and friendship, or if it is unable to clearly spell out potential benefits to its prospective joint venture partners, the Chinese are likely to have misgivings about the partnership and suspect that their U.S. counterparts are only looking after their own interests.

If, on the other hand, the U.S. team shows it has given careful thought to the principles on which a partnership should be based, the benefits to the Chinese side, and its company's positive track record with other joint ventures, the Chinese will be much more inclined to move on to a discussion of the details with the feeling that a basis for trust has indeed been established.

The following examples illustrate two possible U.S. responses to the Chinese introduction above, the first flawed and the second much more effective.

> **Lead U.S. negotiator (flawed response):** *Actually, we feel that since this joint venture is quite complex, and since we have a lot of issues to discuss, it is probably most efficient to begin with the top items, namely, ownership representation and profit split. I am sure you will agree that these are extremely important. And I am sure that the operating principles and benefits you mentioned will become quite clear as our discussion develops.*

This response reflects no sensitivity to the Chinese preference—an error compounded by the fact that the U.S. team is the "guest" in China and therefore behaving rudely by insisting that its preference comes first. This response is therefore bound to cause a negative reaction.

Now note the following much more effective response:

> **Lead U.S. negotiator (recommended response):** *We are happy to share with you our thoughts and look forward to hearing your thoughts as well. As for principles, we feel strongly that our discussion and our partnership, if we reach agreement, should be based on trust, friendship, and mutual benefit. We understand that this project represents significant risk for you, both as a Chinese firm and as individuals. So, we want to be sure also that our agreement minimizes that risk while at the same time assuring that we can realize our desired return. I'd like now to describe for you a joint venture project we began last year in Brazil that shares many similarities with the project we are discussing with you. It has brought a number of benefits to our Brazilian partners, including technology transfer and comprehensive training of their employees.*

Note how this response incorporates the principles of "trust, friendship, and mutual benefit" that the Chinese value as the framework for a partnership. Note, too, that it astutely addresses a major concern for the Chinese in any joint venture—namely, the risk of serious consequences should it fail. Finally, the response highlights precisely those aspects of a Brazilian joint venture that are most appealing to the Chinese—technology transfer and training—and cleverly steers the opening away from price, where negotiations tend to be most contentious.

In sum, the lesson for Western negotiators is simple: the ticket to getting down to details in a Chinese negotiation is to present your position first in terms of broad principles that foster a relationship based on trust while at the same time showing concern for the Chinese interests. Without investing in the relationship first, no amount of pressure or tactical skill on the Western side can move discussions forward.

Maintaining a Continuous Negotiation Record

Maintenance and control of the negotiating record is an extremely important part of any successful negotiation in China. This means simply that a Western negotiation team must maintain a clear and continuous record of: (1) the positions and principles of both sides, (2) the agreements reached, and (3) the issues that may have led to an impasse or have been postponed for later discussion. This is important because it is impossible to create a completely unbiased record; the members of each team will interpret the negotiation process in a way that confers maximum benefit to them. Without its own record, the Western team is entirely at the mercy of the Chinese version of events.

This discipline is particularly troublesome for U.S. teams for three reasons. First, U.S. negotiators tend to be extremely future oriented. For them, the past is largely irrelevant; what counts is the unrealized potential of what lies ahead. Taking careful notes to serve as a record of the past is thus not a natural instinct for most U.S. negotiators. By contrast, the Chinese, with their four-thousand-year history, have a strong sense of the value of the past and are therefore meticulous note takers in almost any negotiation.

Second, because of frequent organizational changes and associated turnover, the tenure of U.S. team members tends to be brief. It is very difficult for a team to rely on oral history and collective memory to reconstruct the record when team members change frequently. Chinese teams, however, tend to remain intact for as long as a negotiation takes; this makes it very easy for them to maintain not only a formal written record, but also a team memory of the entire negotiation.

Third, senior U.S. executives love to "fly in" and lend their wisdom at key moments of major negotiations. But because their appearance is ephemeral, often no one bothers to note exactly what they say, and they themselves almost never make a point of remembering. Thus, when there is a sticking point in the negotiation, it is all too easy for the Chinese side to look back at their notes—very dramatically and solemnly—and declare flatly that the question at hand must be decided in their favor, "because your VP of Asia-Pacific promised us." Without its own written record, the U.S. team has no way to counter the Chinese claim.

The following exchange illustrates how damaging this failure to have a clear record can be:

> **Lead U.S. negotiator:** *We realize that the training of your work force is a key concern for you, as it is for us. But it will be very difficult for us to include more than one-half of your factory workers within the scope of our agreement. This will be very expensive for us, and we are depending on you to help us choose the best workers so that we can train them to train the remaining workers.*
>
> **Lead Chinese negotiator:** *Of course it is understandable that you are concerned about expense. Effective training is always expensive, and that is why it is so valuable. But we'd like to remind you that at our banquet at the Shangri-la Hotel on November 15 last year, your VP of Asia-Pacific, Mr. Rogers, said,...* [motions for note taker to give him their record] *"Training is the key element of success for this joint venture, and I am happy to commit to you that we will do whatever is necessary to ensure that your workers have the skills they need to be productive."*
>
> **U.S. team leader:** [Stunned silence.]

Foreign negotiators are thus well advised to keep a careful record of all negotiation proceedings and to create a database where this record can be stored safely. This will be of great benefit not only to them, but also to future members of the team and to other company teams doing business in China.

Knowing Your Bottom Line

Knowing your bottom line is an essential part of any negotiation; it is the only way to protect yourself against the relentless pressure to make concessions, which in China can take many forms. And yet, it is striking how often U.S. negotiators overlook this key step, both in China and elsewhere.

This problem has a number of causes. The first is haste: all too often U.S. negotiating teams operate under pressure from headquarters or the executive "China champion" to produce results in a hurry. As a result, they do not have time to think carefully about their "walk-away" position for each of the major areas in the deal. Teams may decide simply to "wing it"—surely the most foolish decision one can make in any negotiation.

Another cause is "China intoxication." This refers to the problem of otherwise sensible negotiators becoming starry-eyed at the prospect of 1.2 billion new customers. Urged on by promises of vast wealth by their Chinese counterparts, negotiators often completely forget to think carefully about the limits of what they are willing to give in exchange for an appealing promise with no guarantee.

A further cause for neglecting to set a bottom line is the insidious "China charm." Chinese negotiators can be infectiously charming as the negotiating relationship develops and deepens. Once a sense of trust and goodwill has developed, the Chinese are masters at coaxing additional and substantial concessions out of U.S. negotiators by appealing to the spirit of "friendship and mutual cooperation." Often, the implied threat is that if the concession is not forthcoming, the friendship will be put in jeopardy. The Chinese use this technique with spectacular results time and time again.

It is thus essential that a foreign negotiating team devote the time it needs to think carefully about its bottom-line position for each element of the deal before the negotiation starts. And, the team must not worry about appearing overly forceful in signaling that it has reached its bottom line. While the Chinese may feign disappointment that a U.S. team is unable to make further concessions, they in fact will respect a firm push-back. Chinese negotiators typically want to assess exactly where their interlocutors' interests really lie before coming to agreement; they see a "hard stop" as an important signal in this assessment.

By way of illustration, note the difference between two possible U.S. responses to a Chinese request for a shorter time period for transfer of key technology in a joint venture.

> **U.S. negotiator (flawed response):** *Well, we have tried hard to make it clear that transferring our process technology to you within thirty months is really an aggressive timetable. And, we'd hoped that the examples of technology transfer schedules in our Brazil and Thailand joint ventures would give you a sense of how generous the thirty-month schedule really is. But, if it is truly a key issue for you, I suppose that we could consider accelerating the schedule even further, although we can't make any promises right now—we'll get back to you tomorrow on this.*

The U.S. negotiator makes a number of mistakes here. First, he signals to the Chinese that the team itself is able to make the decision about a concession of strategic importance without resorting to higher authority; this will likely embolden the Chinese to press for more concessions later in the negotiation. Second, he suggests strongly that they will make some kind of concession—the "no promises" disclaimer is meaningless. Even if the U.S. teams responds with, "we've thought about it, but can't do it," the Chinese will press again and again until something gives.

Now note the more effective response below:

> **U.S. negotiator (recommended response):** *We have tried hard to make it clear that transferring our process technology to you within thirty months is really an aggressive timetable. And, we'd hoped that the examples of technology transfer schedules in our Brazil and Thailand joint ventures would give you a sense of how generous the thirty-month schedule really is. I'm afraid that our management at home will simply not support a timetable shorter than this. We sincerely hope that you understand the effort we have made to secure a thirty-month timetable for you, but if this is still not acceptable to you, then we must regrettably end our negotiations.*

This recommended response is powerful for several reasons. As in the flawed response above it, the negotiator emphasizes that the timetable is better than those in any other location. Then he makes clear that the team does not have decision-making authority to shorten the timetable; instead it must defer to management back home. This response is smart because it signals to the Chinese something that they understand and respect only too well—namely, that for major decisions, someone higher up in the organization must decide. The U.S. team is thus cleverly positioning its problem as one of hierarchy, a characteristic built into all Chinese organizations. Finally, the team suggests that there will be damage to the relationship if the Chinese continue to press. The U.S. team has clearly looked after its end of the relationship by doing everything it can to get a good deal for the Chinese; now the Chinese must reciprocate by being reasonable and backing off or risk being seen as negotiating in bad faith.

Knowing your bottom line is an essential negotiating discipline. The promise of fabulous wealth in untapped markets or the allure of exotic surroundings should never be allowed to get in the way.

Making Concessions

When it comes to making concessions, the U.S. approach is fairly predictable. In keeping with linear, logical thinking, a negotiation team will first decide its best-case position, then determine its walk-away position, then structure a set of concessions that lie in between the two extremes. For example, let's assume that a team is negotiating the price of a component to be sold to the Chinese as part of a larger joint venture agreement. It determines that $10 per component is the optimum price and that $6 is its bottom-line price. It then structures a series of concessions at $8, $7, $6.50, and finally $6. The strategy is to give these concessions one at a time as required, while attempting to give as few as possible.

Such an approach to concessions is often called positional bargaining—former Secretary of State Henry Kissinger uses the term "salami slicing" in his well-known memoirs regarding negotiations on the opening of U.S.–China relations in 1971. While this approach has the advantage of being simple and straightforward, it also has serious drawbacks, particularly when negotiating with the Chinese. First, once the team gives its first "slice"—that is, it moves from $10 to $8—it sends a clear signal to the Chinese that the first price is meaningless and that there is probably a lot of negotiating room left. This will motivate the Chinese, who are extremely price-sensitive negotiators, to focus relentlessly on discovering the U.S. team's true bottom-line price. They will apply tremendous pressure for more concessions, and will take whatever time is necessary to extract them.

As a result it often becomes impossible to broaden the discussion to other areas; the U.S. team is effectively trapped in a "sinking floor" discussion about price alone. Worse yet, when the U.S. team finally hits its bottom-line price of $6, it is likely to be tired and exasperated; it is therefore likely to send its "hard stop" message in a harsh, unfriendly way. This can offend or anger the Chinese who, from their perspective, are only engaged in a perfectly normal round of haggling over price. In this situation, feeling worn out and annoyed, a U.S. negotiator may respond as follows:

> **U.S. negotiator:** *Look, we have been discussing this component price issue now for the entire morning and, frankly, we are feeling very frustrated. We have made no progress on any of the other issues we have to cover, despite multiple suggestions that we move on. If price is all you care about, then we suggest perhaps this partnership is not as promising as we initially thought. We feel we have been exceptionally generous in moving from our initial price of $10 per component to $6.50. We can make one final offer at $6 per component; take it or leave it.*

At this point an additional problem surfaces that can be quite dangerous. As a negotiating ploy, the Chinese will themselves occasionally shift from a friendly, engaging tone to a cooler, sometimes even confrontational, one. The risk now is that the Chinese may suspect the U.S. team is using the harder tone of the "take it or leave it" line as only a ploy; as a result, they make one more attempt to extract another price concession. Not realizing that the U.S. team is truly at the end of its rope, they may inadvertently cause irreparable damage, as the now angry U.S. team suspects that they are negotiating in bad faith.

The "salami-slicing" approach to concessions thus incurs considerable risks, in spite of its appealing simplicity. There is, however, another approach that is far more effective with the Chinese and many other cultures that do not share the U.S. view that events occur in a linear progression. This approach is based on the fact that some cultures view time as circular—that is, that human events tend to repeat themselves in predictable, circular patterns. This view is prevalent in countries with ancient traditions such as China and India, where people have observed repeating themes of history for thousands of years, including the rise and fall of imperial dynasties.

Those cultures tend to view the progression of events in what could be described as a spiral. Though there is forward motion, it is not strictly linear, and events are not linked strictly within one progression of cause and effect, but rather through multiple, related sets of events. People from these cultures thus tend to think associatively: when confronted with a problem, they will not think solely in terms of the "next logical step," as in a mathematical proof; instead, they will look to other areas for perspective and insight that may only be distantly related to the problem at hand.

A skilled U.S. negotiating team can use this fact to deal with concessions in a more effective way. The U.S. team can shift to other elements of the negotiation in response to the Chinese request for a lower component price:

> **U.S. negotiator:** *We understand your concern about the component price and appreciate the economic constraints that require you to obtain the lowest price possible. At the same time, we'd like to emphasize what we shared with you two days ago—namely, that we are responsible to our senior executives and ultimately to our shareholders to ensure that our project generates an acceptable return. The component price of $10 we have quoted you is both fair and takes this requirement into account; a lower price will make it very difficult for us to fulfill our financial obligations.*
>
> *However, there are a number of other areas in which we have flexibility, and we would like to discuss these with you. You've mentioned your*

concerns about ensuring that factory operations begin smoothly and about the ongoing costs of operations. We are willing to consider increasing the number of our on-site technical personnel for the first twelve months, as well as substituting a newer generation of electric motors on the production line that will reduce power consumption. But we would request that you increase the size of the factory's warehouse in return.

Advantages of this response are that it

- **Deflects the request for a price concession when it first comes up.** This sends a strong signal that the component price is not negotiable and eliminates the problem of the "sinking floor" discussed above.
- **Reminds the Chinese team of the U.S. team's responsibilities in a way the Chinese easily understand.** The emphasis on fulfilling obligations to senior executives and shareholders personalizes the U.S. team's problem and implies strongly that there will be damage both to relationships and careers if those obligations are not fulfilled.
- **Opens two appealing avenues to resolve the Chinese need for a concession.** The Chinese have asked for a lower price on the components, and the U.S. must make a good-faith response or cause the Chinese to lose face. Since risk of failure is always a big concern for the Chinese, the U.S. offer of more technical personnel to help with supervision and training has tremendous value as a risk-reducing measure. And, since electric power remains expensive and in short supply in China, substituting newer motors that consume less electricity will likely have far greater value as a concession than the incremental cost of the motors themselves.
- **Observes the most important rule of all—which is never to give a concession without asking for one in return.** It is astonishing how often U.S. teams forget this simple rule and end up with agreements in China that are much less favorable than they might otherwise have been. And, observing this rule confers an additional benefit:

the Chinese respect tough negotiators and view concessions given without a reciprocal demand as a sign of weakness. By asking for a larger warehouse, the U.S. team makes a good choice. It stays away from price, which was the original point of contention, and wisely asks the Chinese for a concession that will be easy for them to grant and that will have considerable value to the project.

Taking this kind of creative, nonlinear approach to concessions can help a negotiating team to accelerate the pace of negotiations, increase the likelihood of a beneficial outcome to both parties, and reduce the risk and irritation of ceaseless wrangling over price.

The Importance of Discipline

U.S. negotiators are by nature highly individualistic, and team leaders typically allow the members of their team a great deal of latitude to express their opinions and interact freely and creatively with other members. This egalitarian, flexible notion of a team is what gives U.S. teams much of their creative energy. But at the same time, it exposes U.S. negotiators to a lack of discipline that can have serious consequences.

By contrast, the Chinese are far more collectivist and hierarchical in their orientation; they share this characteristic with many other Asian cultures. A Chinese team leader will encourage input from team members, but this input is given thoughtfully, deliberately, and with great respect for the leader's position. Moreover, Chinese team members will view their leader as a superior whose orders they must obey, and once the team has decided a position, it is expected that all team members will speak with a single voice. This combination of group orientation and hierarchy imparts an inherent discipline to a Chinese team that frequently gives them an advantage in negotiating with westerners.

The first mistake a U.S. team is likely to make is to fail to appoint an individual who will consistently speak on behalf of the entire team. Reflecting their preference to give each person his or her own voice, U.S. team leaders will often encourage members of the team to give their opinion as they see fit. This habit stems as well from U.S. Americans' love of unstructured, creative "brainstorming" as a way to solve problems.

As individual members of the U.S. team speak up, the Chinese team will very quickly figure out who is more generously disposed toward their interests and who is more cautious, skeptical, or reserved. The more that individual members of the U.S. team give voice to their own opinions during the negotiation, the easier it is for the Chinese to accurately assess their personalities, attitudes, likes, and dislikes. This assessment comes very naturally to the Chinese, as theirs is a relationship-based culture.

Let's now suppose that the Chinese side has determined who on the U.S. team appears to be most friendly to their interests. What comes next is a clever set of strategies intended to deepen a sense of friendship with that person and to maneuver him or her into feeling a sense of obligation to the Chinese. For example, the Chinese side may go out of their way to praise the "wisdom" or "sensitivity to Chinese feelings" of this person's remarks. Or, at a banquet, the Chinese team leader may make a toast and specifically thank the individual for his or her contributions that day. And, on a sightseeing trip that occurs on a weekend during an extended negotiation, the Chinese team may assign their smoothest English speaker to accompany this individual and interpret the trip's sights with great humor and charm.

If the U.S. team is unsuspecting—and it usually is—the Chinese before long will have developed an advocate for their interests on the U.S. side. The power of this strategy lies in its manipulation of emotions: the individual who is their "friend" now feels genuine discomfort when taking a stance that is unsupportive of the Chinese position. This person hesitates to risk damaging the new and special "friendship" by appearing unsympathetic to the interests of his or her new Chinese "friends."

It is hard to overstate how skilled the Chinese are at this game. They are masters at the art of managing human relationships, and this strategy is executed so subtly that the person may be entirely unaware that his or her feelings and perspective have been manipulated. It is worthwhile to point out, too, that negotiators who consider themselves to be more culturally sensitive than their other U.S. colleagues or who have a strong need for affirmation and validation are particularly susceptible to this "friendship" strategy.

Once they have developed a "friend," the Chinese now are in a position to "call in their chips" when there is a contentious issue and they need support. Here is an example of how this might sound as the Chinese play their "friend" Kevin Moore against U.S. team leader Leslie Rogers:

> **Chinese team leader:** *It appears as if we have a significant disagreement on the amount of your investment in our service centers. We have tried our best to show you that given our other commitments to the joint venture, one-third is a very generous amount for us to pay and that asking you to pay the remaining two-thirds is really quite reasonable.*
>
> *I know that you, Ms. Rogers, have spoken very clearly about how this will be difficult for you. But I wonder if we can ask Mr. Moore what his view is. We have all benefited from his thoughtful input on past issues, and I am sure we will benefit as much from his wisdom on this one…*
>
> **Kevin Moore:** [Thinking very hard!] *Well, there is no question that what Leslie said is true about the difficulty of our going beyond one-third of the total investment. But I also see very clearly your point about the other substantial commitments you have made…* [turning to Leslie] *Leslie, this may be worth our taking a second look at… It might be possible to look at the numbers again and see if there is a way we can find a little extra room on this one…*

Note that the Chinese invitation to Kevin to share his thoughts is accompanied with a lovely bit of flattery, making it even more difficult for him to stick rigidly to the U.S. point of view. Kevin makes a game try at supporting his leader, Leslie Rogers, but he completely undermines his team's position by suggesting "it might be possible to look at the numbers again." This is the thin edge of the negotiating wedge that the Chinese are looking for, and in the ensuing discussion they will drive the wedge home with all the force they can muster.

To minimize their exposure to China's artful exploitation of relationships, the visiting negotiating team must maintain a discipline that is, thankfully, not particularly difficult to cultivate. The main requirement is some planning before negotiations begin. By deciding who will serve as the team's official spokesperson (usually the team leader), by agreeing to speak with one voice, and by being careful never to reveal unresolved disagreements among one another, even the most individualistic and free-wheeling Western team can shield itself from this powerful Chinese negotiating technique.

Patience and Control of the Time Element

As indicated previously, the world's cultures view time from a variety of perspectives. Another major difference is the degree to which people from different backgrounds feel a sense of urgency in concluding negotiations. People from nations with relationship-based cultures and long histories such as China and India tend to be less hurried than their counterparts from younger, task-oriented cultures like those of the U.S. and Australia. This is because they see today's concerns as but a brief point in a history that stretches back thousands of years.

Because they tend to be impatient, U.S. negotiators often yield control of the time element to their counterparts—and control of timing is one of the most potent weapons in the arsenal of a skilled negotiator. The following case study illustrates how this can work.

Three Days in Beijing

John Sullivan has just returned home from three days in Beijing, upset and bewildered. What was to have been a triumphant success has turned into a disaster.

John was in Beijing with his VP of Operations, Elaine Martinez, for the final round of negotiations with his counterpart, Mr. Chen Bei-ming, CEO of Guang Hua Cosmetics. John's firm, Electra Cosmetics, manufactures a line of high-end cosmetics that John believes will have huge appeal to China's newly affluent female professionals. John and Mr. Chen have been negotiating a packaging and distribution joint venture between Electra and Guang Hua. Under the terms of the joint venture, Electra will manufacture and ship a line of its premium cosmetics to Guang Hua, which in turn will package the products and distribute them to retail shops in the greater Beijing area.

Just three weeks ago, John e-mailed Mr. Chen to propose that he arrive on Tuesday, May 7, and return home the afternoon of Friday, May 10. This would allow John and Mr. Chen a comfortable three days to come to agreement on the last remaining issue to be settled—namely, how Electra and Guang Hua would split sales revenues.

In the same e-mail, John thanked Mr. Chen for his hospitality and hard work during their past discussions. He also shared with Mr. Chen the news that his CEO, Dave Nicholson, was looking forward to John and Mr. Chen concluding the agreement and to beginning shipments within sixty days.

In past discussions, John had said that a 65/35 split in favor of Electra was fair because of Electra's high manufacturing, shipping, and insurance costs. Mr. Chen had favored a 50/50 split based on his repackaging costs and the principle of "friendship and equality" that he felt should be the basis for the joint venture. While they had not come to agreement yet, John had the clear feeling that Mr. Chen was willing to be flexible and that after some haggling they could arrive at a 60/40 split without much effort. As a precaution, John had based all his financial projections to his CEO on a worst-case scenario of 55/45; the 60/40 split that he anticipated as a likely outcome was thus going to be extra money in the bank.

John arrived at Mr. Chen's office on Wednesday at 9:00 a.m. as agreed, but was surprised to find an agenda for the meeting that had a long list of items on which he and Mr. Chen had already reached agreement. Mr. Chen greeted him warmly and then proceeded to tell him that he wanted to review "each of the items they had discussed before and make sure there were no misunderstandings."

What ensued was a long, tedious review of their negotiations to date, sprinkled liberally with requests from Mr. Chen to make minor adjustments here and there. On a number of occasions John reminded Mr. Chen that the chief purpose of their meeting was to address the revenue split issue; each time Mr. Chen replied that while the revenue split was indeed important, it was also essential to be clear about what they had already agreed to, now that they were so close to signing a deal.

To John's further dismay, Thursday was devoted entirely to a similar review, this time between Elaine Martinez and Mr. Chen's director for packaging and distribution, Mr. Zhang. Elaine and Mr. Zhang reviewed a long list of logistical and technical concerns; whenever Elaine reminded Mr. Zhang of the urgency of addressing the revenue issue, Mr. Zhang replied that it was critical that Electra and Guang Hua be sure that the packaging and distribution logistics work be in place before signing a final agreement.

Finally, on Friday morning Mr. Chen was ready to discuss the revenue split. To John's great surprise, Mr. Chen was adamant that the only fair split was an even 50/50; he showed none of his previous flexibility on the issue. With a growing sense of anxiety, John did his best to recall a number of occasions on which Mr. Chen had signaled his flexibility. In response, Mr. Chen asked Mr. Zhang to look in his notes and confirm the specific dates on which Mr. Chen had insisted that a 50/50 split was the only acceptable arrangement.

When they returned from an agonizingly long lunch at 1:30 p.m., John began to feel a sense of panic. He had promised that he would return with a deal, and was depending on a worst-case split of 55/45. Now he was looking at a hard choice: to take 50/50 and hope he could find a way to adjust the numbers or to return home empty-handed and face the anger and disappointment of his CEO.

At 2:00 p.m. John made his final, forceful appeal to Mr. Chen to see the huge benefit to Guang Hua of a 60/40 split. But Mr. Chen would not budge—if they were truly going to be partners going forward, the only acceptable deal was 50/50.

Faced with the toughest business decision of his career, John reluctantly agreed to accept 50/50, at which point Mr. Chen's assistant quickly brought two copies of the joint venture agreement. With only ten minutes left before having to leave for the airport, John signed each copy, at which point Mr. Chen and Mr. Zhang both shook his hand and thanked him warmly. Feeling stunned, John placed his copy in his briefcase, said a perfunctory good-bye to Mr. Chen and Mr. Zhang, and headed for the door.

Comments

One of the most common mistakes that U.S. negotiators make is revealing their own negotiating deadline. In some cases this is simply an unintended oversight. In other cases a U.S. negotiator will reveal his deadline in the belief that it will help spur his interlocutor to move more quickly to agreement. In the case above, John has unwittingly put himself in a vise, as Mr. Chen delays discussion of the critical revenue split issue until just hours before John has to catch a plane home. John realizes too late that he has made a very serious blunder.

As mentioned earlier, many cultures simply do not put a premium on getting things done in a hurry, and negotiators from these cultures always gain the upper hand if they know their interlocutor's deadline. Because they are under little time pressure themselves, skilled negotiators from less hurried countries such as China, Mexico, and Saudi Arabia can manipulate the agenda and the tempo of a negotiation so that the key issues are deferred until the last minute. Faced with the choice of making a major concession or returning home empty-handed, many impatient Western negotiators will prefer making a concession, even if it is a very expensive one, and this is exactly what their more patient interlocutors are counting on.

But, revealing his own deadline is not the only serious mistake that John makes. In the naïve hope that it will entice Mr. Chen to move quickly to a favorable agreement, John also reveals his CEO's wish to begin shipments in sixty days. To Mr. Chen, who clearly has planned to use the time element to his advantage, this additional news is like a gift from heaven—for he knows now that John must satisfy not only his own expectation to close the deal, but also his boss's expectations. John has in fact put himself in a double vise.

To avoid the kind of difficulties encountered by the hapless Mr. Sullivan, Western negotiators should take a few precautionary steps to ensure that the time element is not turned against them, as follows:

- Avoid revealing your return departure date when negotiating abroad; if asked, say something like, "I've left my return open-ended…"

- Never reveal internal operating deadlines under any circumstances
- Build in plenty of time between the expected end of negotiations and your internal deadline; this allows time both for adjusting your business plan and for additional discussions should the negotiation not proceed as planned
- Never reveal superiors' expectations unless they position you to gain concessions or avoid giving them
- Avoid negotiating with only one potential partner; simultaneous negotiation with multiple potential partners provides tremendous leverage

Negotiating "After Hours"

Two additional aspects of negotiating in China are likely to catch many U.S. and other Western negotiators off-guard. The first is negotiating "after hours," and the second is negotiating after the contract.

Many an unwary U.S. negotiator has accepted an invitation to a Chinese banquet after a long day of arduous negotiation only to be completely blindsided when many of the unresolved issues of the day's discussion appear again during the course of the banquet. The U.S. team may be at a further disadvantage if they have accepted their Chinese hosts' many invitations to drink a hearty toast to the future success of their partnership and consumed a large amount of beer or various forms of hard liquor, the most notorious of which is *mao tai,* a fiery concoction sometimes referred to by unaccustomed westerners as "a mixture of jet fuel and lighter fluid."

Seasoned Western negotiators know there is nothing quite as difficult as having to focus one's mind on a complex negotiating issue when half-drunk and unprepared. And they know it is all too easy to give away important concessions in the atmosphere created by good food, plenty of alcohol, and effusive expressions of "friendship"—an atmosphere that their Chinese counterparts are masters at creating.

Frequently, Chinese negotiators will use banquets as an opportunity to make lengthy toasts in which they signal negotiating demands, intents, or possible solutions to roadblocks in the negotiation. These toasts often make use of traditional Chinese stories, allegories, and metaphors to deliver their intended message; they can be highly coded and difficult for westerners to understand. It is therefore a good idea to have a skilled interpreter whom you trust and who can explain both the literal and the intended meanings to you. It is also a good idea to prepare your own toast in which you not only thank your hosts, but also signal either a response to their coded demand or present a demand of your own. This "ceremonial" form of negotiation at banquets and formal occasions should not be overlooked, especially at critical junctures in the negotiating process.

The Chinese toast.

Following is an example of a typical Chinese toast that contains a number of coded messages:

> **Chinese negotiator:** *Friends, and esteemed members of the Company X negotiating team, please let me take a moment to share a few words. First of all, I'd like to thank everyone for their hard work over the past couple of days in creating a framework for our mutual cooperation. If we continue to work hard together, I am sure we will create a final agreement that is fair and based on friendship and one that brings substantial benefits to both sides.*
>
> *On the part of Laoshan Medical Instruments, we are delighted to be working with you at Company X, for you are truly world leaders in your field. We often say that we feel we are students in the presence of the best teachers, and we look forward to learning a great deal from you as our partnership matures.*
>
> *I also want to say that since we lack your experience with manufacturing and testing advanced medical equipment, it is inevitable that we will make some mistakes in the beginning. But, we trust you will*

understand that these mistakes are a natural and inevitable part of our journey toward mastery of some critical new technologies.

Finally, although I probably don't need to say this, we all know that China today is under very great economic stress, particularly where budgets are concerned. Since we at Laoshan are part of the traditional, state-owned economy, we feel this pressure in everything we do. We hope that soon our joint venture will be a shining example of the competitive, profitable, dynamic new economy that China is building. But in the meantime, we are so pleased to be working with a Company X team that understands our financial constraints and is willing to be flexible.

*Once again, let me thank everyone for their hard work...to future success, to mutual benefit, and to friendship...*gan bei...*bottoms up!*

Analyzing the toast.

Although on the surface this toast may sound innocuous, there are some important points that an astute Western team will not fail to pick up:

- Paragraph 1 suggests strongly that the Chinese team will want an even split of revenues; this is what "fair" means
- Paragraph 2 is a signal that the Chinese expect a great deal of training to bring their technical skills up to Company X's level, and it is likely that they will expect Company X to pay for it
- Paragraph 3 says that implementation is likely to be very rough at first, with a lot of quality problems; the Chinese know that their work force has a long way to go before they arrive at Company X's world-class standards
- Paragraph 4 says that whatever the financial concerns were in the day's negotiations, Laoshan will not foot the bill; the Chinese expect Company X to find a way to solve the financial problems without additional contributions from the Chinese side

The responding toast.

A well-prepared U.S. negotiator might respond with a toast like this:

> **U.S. negotiator:** *President Wang and esteemed friends, I'd like to say a few words. First of all, thank you so much for the superb banquet we have enjoyed as your guests tonight. You have shown yet another example of China's wonderful hospitality that we will not forget.*
>
> *We, too, look forward to a partnership based on friendship and mutual respect and are very pleased that you have shown such willingness to understand our perspective and the need we have to satisfy our management and stockholders back home.*
>
> *I am flattered that you view us as teachers. In fact, we view you very much the same way—as our teachers in understanding a very complex Chinese commercial environment. We often say that we must continue to depend on you to understand many things we would overlook in arriving at an agreement that is truly beneficial to both sides.*
>
> *As for mistakes, they of course are inevitable. And, we know ourselves how challenging a new direction can be for any company or organization. That is why we are so happy with your willingness to understand the risks a venture in China presents to us and to help us minimize those risks so that we can remain a long-term partner with you.*
>
> *Finally, I am well aware of China's financial constraints. All of us on the Company X team are great admirers of the bold new path you are taking. We have felt from the beginning that you understand the many financial constraints that we must live with back home. This mutual understanding and respect is what gives us such confidence that our partnership will be a success.*

Analyzing the response.

Notice how our clever U.S. negotiator parries each of his Chinese hosts' negotiating points gently and politely, while at the same time sending a message of his own that protects Company X's interests and serves notice that there will be no concessions for free. More specifically, note the following:

- Paragraph 1 establishes the U.S. team as grateful guests, a necessary point of protocol before getting to the negotiating points to follow
- Paragraph 2 sends a clear message that the Chinese interests are not the only interests in play; the U.S. team has its own constituencies to satisfy, too
- Paragraph 3 neutralizes the "train us—ideally for free" point of the Chinese by pointing out that the U.S. team has much to learn as well, and suggests that there may be hidden costs to doing business in China that the U.S. team has yet to uncover
- Paragraph 4 deftly turns the idea of Chinese mistakes into a reminder that the U.S. team is at risk and that the Chinese have a vested interest in helping them reduce that risk
- Paragraph 5 deflects the Chinese concerns about costs by reminding them that in spite of their impression to the contrary, Company X does not have boundless resources and in fact it, too, must manage its own financial constraints

By taking some time to prepare for the toasting ritual at Chinese banquets, a U.S. team can pick up vital signals from their Chinese counterparts while at the same time using the occasion to send their own negotiating messages in a manner that the Chinese respect and appreciate.

After-hours precautions.

U.S. and Western negotiators are therefore advised to take a few precautions before accepting any after-hours invitations by their Chinese counterparts, be they banquets, gatherings at karaoke bars, or sightseeing trips on weekends:

- Be aware that the Chinese will not hesitate to resume negotiations at any time "after hours" if they see an advantage in doing so

- Understand that Chinese negotiators are masters at creating a feeling of ceremony, warmth, and "friendship," especially at banquets, during which they can apply psychological pressure on their Western counterparts to make concessions "in the spirit of friendship"
- Always have a "designated drinker" as part of an "alcohol management plan," in which one member of your team can participate in toasts while other key team members can either drink less or abstain in order to maintain a clear head
- Be prepared to decline to negotiate if you are unprepared by saying something like this: "After such a long and productive day, we'd prefer to focus on the marvelous food and drink you have prepared for us and resume discussions tomorrow. We certainly hope we will cause no offense with this request. Now, please tell us more about the delicacies you are serving us...they are spectacular!"
- Be prepared to take advantage of after-hours negotiating opportunities with your own agenda and a carefully prepared plan for who will speak for your team. Skilled negotiators know that some of the most productive negotiating in China is done after hours; they don't want to overlook this opportunity, so they prepare accordingly.

The trick, in the end, is to maintain a clear head and be prepared for after-hours negotiations when they occur to defend your interests and even turn the negotiations to your advantage.

Postcontract Negotiations

Western business professionals often complain that Chinese negotiators like to negotiate after a contract is signed, a practice that westerners sometimes view as negotiating in bad faith. While it is true that the Chinese do on many occasions ask to continue negotiations after the ink is dry on a contract's signatures, it is better to understand the cultural background behind this practice and prepare accordingly, rather than being surprised or upset by it when it occurs.

As previously mentioned, the Chinese are a highly relationship-based people; they organize their lives and work around complex networks of human relationships that are critical to getting things done in China. These relationships, or *guanxi,* are so important that they are like a form of currency in China.

Consequently, during a negotiation the Chinese are primarily interested in assessing the possibility of developing a productive working relationship with their Western counterparts based on trust and mutual respect. When both sides agree to the terms of a contract after extended discussions, the Chinese tend to view the contract signing as a symbolic mutual acceptance of a new relationship based on trust and the contract itself as a kind of snapshot of that relationship at a particular point in time.

For the Chinese, the contract is thus secondary in importance to relationships, and it is the relationships, not the contract, that the Chinese see as the vehicle by which the project will be carried forward. This means that when unexpected problems arise after the contract is signed, as they inevitably will, the Chinese naturally look to the flexibility of the new relationship they have established to solve them. Their behavior when they raise these problems and ask their partners to solve them together is quite similar to that during negotiations before the contract is signed, but the intent is very different. During negotiations, the relationship is still being tested, and the two parties are still to some degree adversaries; after the contract has been signed, the two parties are partners solving problems together.

In contrast to the Chinese, U.S. or Western negotiating teams tend to be far more task focused. For them the key concern is working through a list of operational issues and placing the outcome into a tightly structured contract that will govern both parties going forward. This reliance on a contract and the legal machinery that surrounds it as the operational vehicle for executing the work of the business venture means that a U.S. team is not that interested in building human relationships at first. Usually, the feeling is that if such relationships develop in the course of business, so much the better; but even if they don't, business is still possible.

This focus on task accompanied by a more legalistic outlook means that for the U.S. side the contract takes on enormous importance. Far more than a mere symbol of a new relationship, the contract is in fact a new entity whose importance supersedes either negotiating party and which contains in it all the stipulations and conditions that will ensure a successful business outcome for both parties. A U.S. team will thus turn immediately to the contract if problems arise after it is signed, and it will typically deem a good contract one that will specify what each party is supposed to do when major problems occur.

Consequently, U.S. representatives often get angry and upset when the Chinese seem to ignore the contract and ask to work flexibly outside its specifications to solve problems. Most westerners see this as a profound failure to understand the fundamental meaning of a contract in the first place. In addition, since they usually lack an understanding of the Chinese perspective, they assume the Chinese are deliberately evading the contract's terms in a late and unfair ploy to gain the upper hand. This inevitably leads to a severe erosion of trust that can culminate in complete destruction of the business relationship.

The unfortunate fact is that no area in U.S./Western–Chinese negotiations leads to more misunderstandings than this problem of two interpretations of what a contract really means. The Chinese actually have a saying for a situation like this; it goes "tong chuang yi meng," and means, "sleeping in the same bed but dreaming different dreams." And until China, following its accession to the WTO, gradually builds up its own legal infrastructure and recognizes greater value in abiding by the legal rules for creating and honoring business contracts according to "international" standards established by the West, these misunderstandings are likely to continue.

The best advice for U.S. and Western business professionals is therefore simply to recognize first that contracts are a highly problematic area of doing business with China, and the situation won't change overnight. That said, there are a few sensible things you can do to minimize the impact and frustration of problems with contracts and their execution, as follows:

- **Don't assume that a signed contract means negotiations have stopped.** For the Chinese a contract is only a snapshot of your relationship and a guide to implementation; problem solving outside the contract terms that feels like negotiating is to be expected.

- **Build an extra measure of flexibility into your postsigning plans for implementation.** If you do not assume that the contract will be followed exactly and plan accordingly, there will be fewer nasty surprises.
- **Don't hesitate to approach your Chinese partners with your own requests for flexibility outside the terms of the contract if you need to.** Though this may feel awkward and unfamiliar at first, it is a way to turn the Chinese way of doing things to your advantage.
- **Avoid taking legal action against a Chinese partner or entity that you feel has violated the terms of a contract unless you deem it absolutely essential.** Though you may be tempted by your Western instincts to take an issue to court, remember that the legal infrastructure in China is still weak and stacked in favor of the Chinese. It is much better to creatively leverage your "relationship resources" to find individuals whom you can enlist to help solve your problem.
- **Don't assume your Chinese counterparts are acting in bad faith if they wish to operate outside the terms of the contract after it is signed.** Recognize that in most cases the culprit is two vastly different perceptions of what a contract stands for and not a deliberate desire by the Chinese to act in an unethical or devious way.

Culture and Negotiating Behaviors

As mentioned at the beginning of this chapter, negotiating styles are deeply rooted in cultural behaviors, which differ widely among the world's peoples, regions, and nations. Table 23 lists key cultural dimensions and the behaviors that are at divergent ends of the cultural spectrum. This comparison can be a useful guide in creating an effective strategy when negotiating across cultures in any direction. It should also serve as a reminder that there are grave risks in assuming that our counterparts from another country view negotiation the same way we do.

Table 23. **Negotiating: Comparative Styles**

Cultural Orientation	← Expectations and Behaviors for Negotiating	→	Cultural Orientation
Individual	Individual members of the negotiating team can all speak; diversity of opinion is valued during negotiation; the preference is to leave negotiation less structured, with a tendency to "wing it"	Team members speak with a uniform "voice"; the preference is for a structured negotiation process—responses are made only after careful consultation	**Group**
Task	Focus is on the content of the negotiation, i.e., the specific issues; approach to negotiation is sequential, linear; legal contracts are highly regarded, and time is money	Focus is on the process of the negotiation, i.e., building trust first; approach to negotiation is associative, nonlinear; one's word is one's bond; contracts are not that important; building trust takes time	**Relationship**
Direct	Vigorous debate and discussion on key issues are expected; emotions are expressed openly; important messages are delivered as clearly and succinctly as possible	Debate may occur quietly off line; emotions are controlled; key points of interest or potential concessions may be transmitted through coded messages or back channels	**Indirect**
Equality	Team leader is often "first among equals"; creative input from all members is encouraged; preference is for the brainstorming model in dealing with problems	Team leader speaks for whole group; senior members are asked for their opinions before junior members; the team is uncomfortable with brainstorming—problems are often solved off line	**Hierarchy**

Table 23. **Negotiating: Comparative Styles (continued)**

Cultural Orientation	← Expectations and Behaviors for Negotiating	→	Cultural Orientation
Future	Negotiation is viewed as a fresh, new opportunity; decisions are based on future promise; need for note taking is limited—what lies ahead is what matters	Negotiation is viewed as an extension of the past; decisions are based on lessons of the past; note taking is essential, a link to the past	**Past**
Universal	Fair standards across the board are to be maintained; preference is for terms that maintain consistency across all negotiations; concessions are made according to objective factors, e.g., purchase volume	Special circumstances naturally influence the terms of a final agreement—each negotiation is different; concessions are made according to subjective factors, e.g., reputation and family	**Situational**

Negotiating

SUMMARY AND REVIEW QUESTIONS

1. Do you understand the contextual factors—e.g., government influence, information sharing, commercial infrastructure—that shape your counterparts' behavior and thinking?

2. What is your usual approach to opening negotiations? How might the other side respond to this approach? How should you modify your approach to take the other culture's point of view into account?

3. What is the current practice in your firm with regard to note taking and ongoing documentation of negotiation proceedings? How will you match or exceed your counterparts' skills in this area?

4. Is your negotiating team aware of its bottom line and prepared to walk away if this is not met? Do you have a concession strategy that will deter endless haggling over price while providing your counterparts with benefits they will perceive as being valuable?

5. Who is the spokesperson for your team? Are all team members prepared to speak with one voice? Are you alert to possible attempts to split off members of your team and turn them into sympathizers for the other side?

6. What is your firm's approach to the timing of cross-border negotiations? How much in-country time is generally allowed for the team? In your experience, has this been adequate? If your firm's guidelines permit only limited flexibility, what can you do or say during negotiations if necessary to create a greater sense of open-endedness?

7. In cultural settings that you are familiar with, how do after-hours negotiations differ from the official negotiation process? Do you feel equally skilled at both? Why or why not? What steps could you take during the planning process to take advantage of the differences? Are you ready to present a formal toast or to interpret the meaning behind a toast offered by someone else?

8. What is the status of contractual agreements in the countries in which your firm currently has operations? What factors appear to affect the weight given to the contract by your negotiation counterparts? If a contract is not an accepted signal for the end of negotiations, how can you best plan for what follows?

Part III

Organizational Skills

CHAPTER NINE

Strategic Planning

The term *global strategy* has a nice ring to it. Strategy making is often seen as a refined and somewhat abstract art that focuses on marketplace and competitor analysis, ways to differentiate one's products or services, and the allocation of limited corporate resources to create the maximum possible return on investment.

Global strategies often go wrong, however, because the basic assumptions that underlie them are flawed. In a cross-border context, the most critical strategic act is "frame shifting": moving from a plan of action that makes sense within one market environment to another that is better suited to a different context. Strategic planning as a global people skill means having a management team that can systematically question basic assumptions held by its own members while entertaining multiple perspectives suited to the requirements of various markets. Consider again the U.S. executive mentioned in chapter 1.

The Whirlwind Tour

A U.S. executive, newly appointed as the head of International for his company, made his first trip to the European region. He carefully analyzed the state of the company's operations in each subsidiary location, listening to presentations and recommendations by the country management teams. He then instructed the top leadership of each subsidiary on strategic positioning of the company's products in local markets and on next steps to address key issues and to generate more revenue.

After a rugged two-week trip to six countries, the Western executive returned home tired but satisfied. Based on his own extensive experience and strategic savvy, he was confident that the business was on the right track. Other pressing matters at headquarters and with different regions quickly began to demand his attention, although he continued to track the progress of initiatives in the six European countries through periodic conference calls and e-mail. Six months passed before he was able to return to the region. There he was surprised and concerned to find that, upbeat reports to the contrary, no real progress had been made on any of the instructions he had left.

Skill #9: Strategic Planning

The Western executive above must first revise his schedule and his approach to establish his credibility and create better teamwork with the subsidiary management personnel in each location. Beyond these fundamental people skills, however, he has also failed on the level of organizational strategy—he has not even begun to question his own assumptions about how to do business based on fresh information from different country environments. More critically, he has made little progress in creating a climate of engagement with subsidiary leaders that would enable participants to shift more nimbly between their established assumptive frameworks and a fresh set of possibilities. Without such engagement, even apparent agreements will ultimately deteriorate and implementation will falter as decision makers revert to their original assumptions when conflicts arise.

Challenging Assumptions

Original, ground-breaking strategy comes from a management discipline of conscious frame shifting that can question and potentially overturn the basic assumptions of any participant in a strategic discussion, taking the debate in a direction that is new to everyone involved. Strategic thinking about the business environment and even about one's own organizational capabilities must grasp the core features of radically different foreign markets; it also needs to anticipate future global market changes that no one has yet experienced.

For businesspeople who are new to global business and about to embark on a strategic-planning venture, it may be helpful to start with an exercise like the one on the following page, which can be used to practice questioning one's assumptions vis-à-vis the perspectives of foreign counterparts. This can also serve to stretch the mind and prepare one for the unexpected scenarios that another country may present.

Mistaken strategic assumptions and the problems that they bring are often much more subtle than the statements used in the exercise and are grounded in the circumstances of a particular industry. An organization must build: (1) methods for obtaining key intelligence from customers and employees and conveying it to decision makers without excessive alteration; and (2) the capacity to respond flexibly when unexpected information is presented. (See chapter 4 for more on obtaining information.)

As an organization's global strategic-planning process becomes more sophisticated, its participants are less likely to be surprised by local market assumptions. They learn to supplement their increasing store of specific local market knowledge with a deeper understanding of the values and history of a country's residents. Based on such knowledge, they may even become able to accurately predict the behavior of local business counterparts.

There are four different ways of building frame-shifting capabilities among global strategists that could help to turn the case of the U.S. executive from a dismal failure into a more inspiring set of accomplishments:

Exercise: Western Assumptions and Possible Alternative Perspectives

Instructions: Examine the items below—each of which incorporates a fairly standard Western business assumption—and consider alternative perspectives that people in another country may hold.*

1. Serving customer needs is the foundation of our business.
   Alternative perspective: ______________________________

2. The product with the best quality and price will win out.
   Alternative perspective: ______________________________

3. Time is money; we must get things done quickly and efficiently.
   Alternative perspective: ______________________________

4. Alternative viewpoints are good.
   Alternative perspective: ______________________________

5. Each country has an official government to deal with.
   Alternative perspective: ______________________________

6. This is a win-win situation, an expanding pie.
   Alternative perspective: ______________________________

7. The written contract is the final word.
   Alternative perspective: ______________________________

8. We have come to be helpful, to teach; business is a positive, democratic force.
   Alternative perspective: ______________________________

*For examples of possible alternative perspectives from various foreign markets, see appendix C.

- Emphasizing the "what," "who," and "how" of strategic planning
- Achieving a global/local balance in the positioning of products and support activities across borders
- Linking business and relationship strategies
- Developing global leaders

Figure 13. **Strategic Planning Cycle**

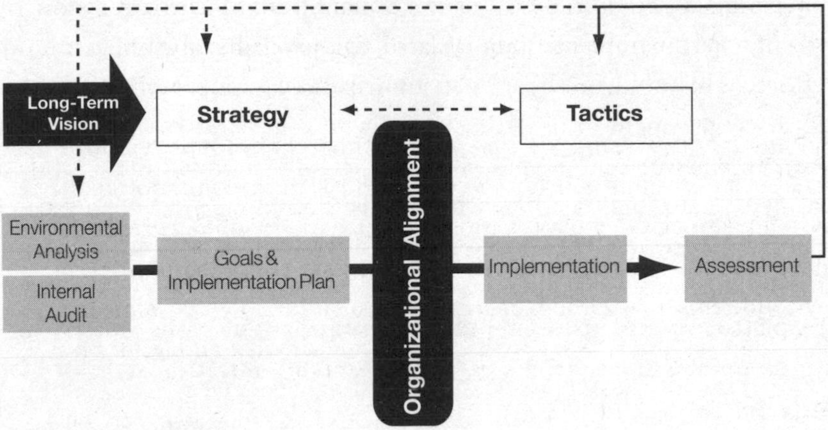

What, Who, and How

Strategic planning begins with an analysis of the external business environment and the internal capabilities of one's own organization. Based on such information as well as the company's long-term vision of where it wants to go, the planning team formulates strategic goals and then translates them into an action plan. Organizational resources are aligned, and the implementation process is begun, with tactical adjustments made as needed. The team then assesses implementation results and incorporates them back into the system as rapidly as possible to permit rapid tactical shifts or more fundamental strategic adjustments. A model of the way in which global strategy is commonly crafted might look something like the sequence depicted in figure 13.[1]

What could possibly go wrong with this type of strategic-planning model in a global business context? Experienced observers might suggest, for example, that the initial environmental analysis must be broad enough to incorporate accurate information about local markets and customers, even though these may be both distant and different from the company's home market. It is easy to think you know more about foreign markets than you actually do. Upon further reflection, you might also see that it would be important to engage people in the planning process who could provide such information—not only about the local business environment, but also regarding the capabilities of the organization, the strength of the implementation plan, and the results of implementation efforts. This kind of engagement is naturally a step toward enabling local management to think strategically and properly execute the plan. Finally, an issue that people who have actually attended these kinds of strategic-planning meetings will raise is the manner in which participants interact with one another. Unfortunately, it is possible to invite all the right people yet still have a meeting dominated by a few. Vocal participants may fail to draw out vital information, while others don't speak up due to differences in language, communication style, or hierarchical status.

So the success of strategic-planning efforts depends on *what* is examined, *who* participates, and *how* the planning events themselves are organized.[2] When the what, who, and how of the strategic-planning process are not carefully addressed, a host of common issues such as the following can appear:

- Home-market products or services do not appeal to customers in new environments
- Local capabilities are inadequate to implement strategy
- Local employee agendas run counter to headquarters' goals and directives
- Lack of commitment to implementation produces unsatisfactory results
- Limited assessment systems do not provide accurate feedback on strategy outcomes

The three variables of what, who, and how should in fact be considered at every phase of the strategic-planning process: environmental analysis, goal setting, implementation planning, and the assessment of results (see figure 14).

Although similar pitfalls exist even in coordinating strategy between two cities in the same country, it is particularly easy to get these elements

Figure 14. **Strategy: Integrating the What, Who, and How**

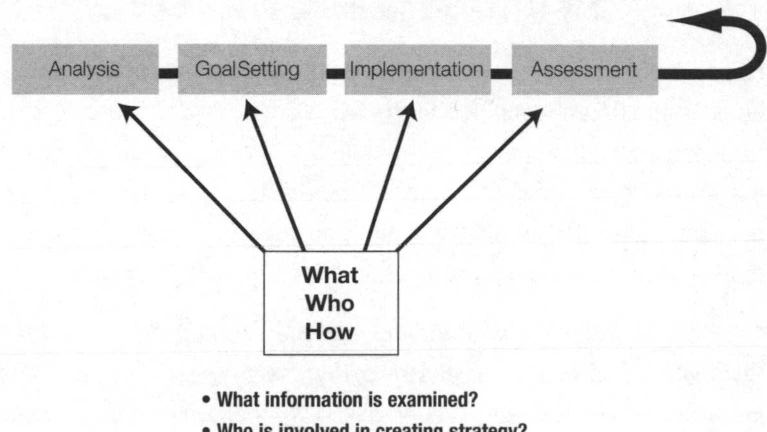

- **What information is examined?**
- **Who is involved in creating strategy?**
- **How is the process structured?**

wrong in a cross-border business context. Critical information is neglected because it is not available through the usual market research channels available in the headquarters country. A key person may not be invited or informed because he or she is located in an office that is literally on the other side of the world and therefore out of sight and out of mind. Meeting participants from different countries each bring their own expectations about how the meeting should be held and wind up blaming others for "not contributing" or for "dominating without asking." An approach to global business that regards strategic planning as a people skill will constantly keep the what, who, and how in the forefront of each strategic activity.

Cross-Border Positioning

Successful strategic positioning requires a vision that is both global and indigenous—melding what is best for the global organization with what works in the local business environment. Vision in this sense means both a perspective—a way of seeing things—and a sense of direction. It entails clarity about what parts of a company's home-market strategy appeals to local customers, plus a willingness to create new products and support activities that will enhance the firm's global network. Employees in every country where a firm does business can thus justifiably find inspiration

My Mistake: Strategic Planning

I was participating in a strategic-planning meeting with people from a number of different countries in the Asia-Pacific region. The subject of the company's approach to the market in Thailand came up, and a lively discussion ensued. Several people, including myself, expressed opinions about the current situation and future direction of the Thai market for the company's products, and the tastes of Thai consumers.

As I was speaking I had the feeling that something was wrong. Suddenly it occurred to me that two Thais were present at the meeting, and that neither had yet been asked for their opinion or managed to get a word in edgewise. Here was a team of "strategic" planners pontificating about their country, their markets, and their operations, and we hadn't yet even tried to include them in the conversation. They were polite about it, kept smiling, and did offer some very useful information when we finally asked them, but I felt like a fool for not asking them sooner—they were probably thinking the same thing.

and take pride in their contribution to a global enterprise along with the distinctive services they provide to local customers.

Management guru Michael Porter defines *strategy* as the creation of a unique and valuable market position supported by a system of activities that fit together in a complementary way. This combination produces sustainable competitive advantage. Porter cites the example of Southwest Airlines, which supports its market position as a low-cost, efficient carrier with an activity system that includes lean ground crews, high levels of employee stock ownership, flexible union contracts, short-haul flights, no seat assignments, no baggage transfers or meals, a standardized aircraft fleet, high aircraft utilization, and so on.[3]

Potential problems and advantages both arise when this definition of strategy is considered in a global context, as illustrated in table 24. In other words, both the distinctiveness of products or services and the fit between supporting activities may be either compromised or enhanced

Table 24. **Implications of Cross-Border Strategy**

Problems	**Advantages**
Distinctive products or services may not be as good a fit in some global markets as in the home country	Distinctive products or services may have equal or greater appeal and face only limited competition from local firms
Organizational support systems cannot be easily duplicated in every market	Organizational support systems can be leveraged across different markets
Adaptation of products or services to meet local customer needs often creates the need to adapt support activities	Adaptation of products or services can result in innovations that appeal not only to local customers, but also to customers elsewhere
Cross-border fit between different sets of support activities is not guaranteed	Cross-border fit between support activities produces competitive advantage on a global scale

when companies expand across borders. The positive urge to adapt one's offerings to the needs of overseas customers can undermine or enhance long-term competitive advantage. Product adaptation often means modifying methods of procurement, sales, or delivery in ways that incur substantial new expenses or strain home-market support systems. Yet such adaptation could also produce strategic advantages on a global scale.

To address global strategy issues in their full complexity requires a clear, shared understanding of a company's unique home-market advantages, and a readiness to map those to other environments to look for areas of similarity and difference. Here are some questions that strategic-planning groups must ask themselves in the quest for the optimum global/local balance:[4]

- "What is our unique home-country market position?"
- "How does it fit or not fit with the market in Country X?"
- "What set of activities supports our market position domestically?"

- "Do we have the capability to provide the same level of support in Country X? If not, is it worth the investment to generate such a capability? Will this enhance our overall strategic position or divert resources?"
- "Will the support for our market position in this country be local, regional, or based in our firm's home country?"
- "Are there other distinctive products or services that we should be offering in this local market?"
- "Is it worth the investment locally to create and support these new offerings? Will new local products, services, or support activities be useful outside the country of origin? Will they support or undermine our unique market position?"
- "How does our whole global network fit together? Do we have one global strategy, an integrated set of global/local strategies, or a conflicting mix?"
- "What are we not willing to do because it would dilute our strategic position?"
- "Where is there room in the global system for greater leverage and knowledge transfer across national boundaries?"

Strategic positioning is ultimately a people skill because it depends on the interactions of employees with key leadership and interface roles. Just a few managers in important positions who are not able to shift between different frames of reference and instead stick to old patterns of behavior—favoring, for instance, a so-called global solution without local buy-in—can sabotage a new organizational structure designed with careful strategic intent. Christopher Bartlett and Sumantra Ghoshal point out that the project of building a transnational enterprise should begin with the modification of individual perspectives and interpersonal relationships that lead key participants to resist change. They propose creating not a new and more intricate matrix structure for the organization, but a "matrix in the minds of managers" that balances the tensions between different strategic considerations: local responsiveness, global efficiency, and knowledge transfer.[5] This is another way to describe frame-shifting behavior—both headquarters and subsidiary employees must have the mental agility to consider global issues one moment and local customer needs the next. Such a fluid mental matrix needs to be both the mind-set of each individual and the joint behavioral pattern of the strategic planning team.

The way that overseas operations are positioned relative to a company's core strengths frequently spells the difference between squandered resources and synergistic growth across multiple country markets, as illustrated by the divergent paths taken by the two companies in the cases below.

Lack of Cross-Border Fit

A U.S.-based software firm made a major investment to establish a new subsidiary in Germany. It entered the market by purchasing a local enterprise that also specialized in software development. The company's leaders rationalized their investment on the grounds that Germany, with its central location and economic status as the largest market in the European Union, was the best place to expand their European business beyond its existing base in the U.K.

Unfortunately, a number of difficulties soon began to crop up. The acquired firm's software was sold through distributors to trade professionals rather than to a mass retail market. Its users were accustomed to paying a higher price and receiving a rich array of features and a high level of ongoing service and support in return. The U.S. firm attempted to broaden its new subsidiary's offerings by introducing a mass-market product that had been extremely successful in the U.S. But even though selling to a broad consumer base was a core strength of the U.S. firm, it quickly encountered resistance from German consumers who were suspicious of the low price and still demanded meticulous service rather than a "do-it-yourself" approach.

In the meantime, the German operation's preexisting products languished without receiving the attention necessary to keep them current. Government regulations, established industry practices, and language issues required ongoing local software development that had little application in other markets. As investments in these former flagship products were pared back to shift more money into building the consumer business, they began to lose their status as market leaders. Competitors started snatching away distributor-based business by offering features better suited to unique local requirements. Distributors were not as eager to sell the U.S. firm's products because they feared that its consumer products would gradually take on new features that would undercut their own lucrative business.

A factor that complicated the U.S. firm's efforts in Germany was the presence of hard-working expatriates who had seen the U.S. software model win explosive sales in the home market and were convinced that the same success could be achieved in Europe. They were encouraged in this way of thinking by the German managing director and his top team. These local executives, who had been hired from outside the company to replace the departing founder and president, made confident pronouncements that the U.S. approach would succeed and that the company could have the best of both worlds—a successful consumer product line and a high-end specialty business. It turned out that these executives were relatively inexperienced in the software industry and were telling their superiors in the U.S. what they wanted to hear.

Facing decreasing revenues in its established products and lower-than-anticipated sales in the consumer market, the U.S. firm finally decided to exit the German market altogether, swallowing a loss of tens of millions of dollars. Instead of the fit its leaders had hoped for, they found that the introduction of successful U.S. products and support activities not only failed to gain traction with customers but also backfired, damaging the business they had purchased and ultimately causing the whole country operation to fail.

Mistakes

The U.S. firm made three crucial mistakes that led to failure:

- Purchasing a foreign firm with a unique value proposition and supporting activities that were too different from those of the acquirer

- Misreading the applicability of a U.S. marketing formula to the German market
- Attempting to straddle two incompatible product lines and not doing either well, while actually damaging the acquired franchise

Frame-Shifting Failures:

- ***Differences between the German and U.S. markets and the best ways to satisfy German customers were not fully understood***
- ***U.S. expatriates and German executives combined to engage in wishful thinking about how a U.S. formula could be applied in Germany while losing touch with established customers***

Cross-Border Fit Using Global Leverage

A Canadian maker of industrial equipment had received numerous requests from customers in Germany and the U.K. to add a new compact, high-performance machine to its product line. From the customer standpoint, this would reduce costly energy consumption and give the machine a smaller footprint on the factory floor. Customers noted that they did not require all the power and advanced features of the company's larger products.

The Canadian firm assembled a design team that included several leading members of its European design center located near Frankfurt, two representatives from Japan, and two Canadians based in Europe. All the team members had experience in engineering previous product models for European and Asian markets that were more compact than the company's most popular flagship product in North America.

Over the course of the next year, the design team created an attractive prototype that was compact and yet included the performance characteristics most in demand from customers in Europe and Asia. The product was then rolled out simultaneously in both Europe and Asia, meeting with a very positive response and winning market share in both regions. It strengthened the

Canadian firm's reputation as a responsive, full-line global business partner with established customers and even earned new business from medium-sized European firms. Substantial purchasing economies were obtained from global parts suppliers by combining orders from different countries.

A further significant benefit of the team's work was that several of its design innovations were incorporated in larger product models built in Canada and supplied primarily to North American customers. These innovations enabled the Canadian firm to reduce the energy consumption, space requirements, and manufacturing costs of larger machines as well, while still providing high-end features.

Successful Decisions

The Canadian firm made three decisions that led to success:

- Understanding and responding to European customer needs with a product suited to the requirements they express
- Rolling out the new product simultaneously in multiple markets that have similar customer needs
- Incorporating design innovations from overseas markets into home-country products to enhance customer benefits and cut costs

Frame-Shifting Successes:

- ***The Canadian firm assembled a team of people from different countries who were able to simultaneously respond to the demands of local European customers and plan wider global applications***
- ***Their investment in product development for one region led to global economies of scale with suppliers as well as design innovations that were incorporated into other product lines***

Relationship Strategy

Creating a deliberate relationship strategy is another way to comprehend and work within a radically different cultural framework for mutual business advantage. As discussed in chapters 1 and 7, relationships are the foundation for doing business effectively across borders. In many regions of the world—in Latin America, Asia, or Africa, for instance—relationships are commonly valued in the decision-making process above specific tasks or impartial product data. This is particularly true where business is still dominated by family-owned enterprises and/or close-knit elites.

Strategy in such places is often defined first and foremost in terms of relationships: "Here are the connections we have, and this is how we are going to use them to grow our business." Relationships may be the best available source for gaining access to key customers, collecting market intelligence, protecting intellectual property, or winning government support. In many countries, personal relationships are indeed the single most valuable form of business capital—far more important even than money in the bank. People define themselves as part of a group; family and school contacts may be mixed in together with professional ones. In fact, each individual is a point or a node in a whole galaxy of human relationships, and this network may be something that has been built up painstakingly over several generations.

The cultivation and sharing of these personal networks is a critical factor in grasping indigenous frames of reference and making the adjustments to a strategic plan that will bring success. Full entry into a strong network of relationships makes almost anything open and available, and gives us a whole new perspective on what is actually going on in a particular business environment. But, access to this type of network is granted only cautiously, step by step, to those who demonstrate that they can contribute lasting value to the whole group. The following example shows how causing even inadvertent damage to another person's network can lead to exclusion from it.

Network Abuse

Elena Ivanova, a Russian working in the U.S., received an inquiry from a former colleague, Mark Stevens. Mark was a manager she had worked together with on a project team before he moved on to his current employer. He told Elena that he was trying to find a Russian technical expert in a certain discipline to speak at an upcoming industry conference in Chicago. Mark mentioned that he thought there were several world-class researchers doing work at Russian institutions and asked for Elena's assistance in locating them.

Elena replied that she thought she could help. She proceeded to contact a family friend in Moscow with connections at one of the most prestigious universities. This friend provided the name of a university professor with strong research credentials in the right specialty as well as good English presentation skills. Elena in turn passed the name on to Mark, who sounded enthusiastic. Because the Russian professor wanted to find out more about the conference, Elena also spoke with him directly over the phone and gave him some background information. The professor, although very busy with his research, was pleased to hear more about the conference and said that he could probably attend if invited.

In the meantime, Mark had also asked several other contacts for help. Through another acquaintance he received an e-mail address for a different person in Moscow who seemed to be the perfect fit. He corresponded with this individual, who on paper looked a little better than the one introduced by Elena. With the deadline coming up for finalizing the speaker, he decided to go ahead and send this second person a formal invitation to speak. He quickly became absorbed in other conference details.

A week later, Elena called Mark back to check on what progress had been made in determining the conference speaker. Mark reported that he had found the right person, thanked her for what she had done, and apologized that he had not gotten back to her sooner or contacted the Russian professor she had recommended. When Elena heard from Mark about the person who had been selected, she realized that he was from a rival institution and that her own university contact would probably not be very pleased to discover this. She immediately became concerned about the reaction not only of the Russian professor but also of the family friend who introduced her. Elena vowed that she would be more careful the next time Mark asked her for help.

Businesspeople from highly mobile societies such as the U.S. tend to underestimate the value of a good introduction, seeing it as an opportunity to create a functional contract between individuals rather than as a potential lifetime asset—the doorway to a much wider world. In many countries, if one is perceived to abuse a contact when it is made available, then the sound that one does not hear is the sound of all the other unseen doors in that network silently closing. On the other hand, the outsider who proves his or her trustworthiness and willingness to add value stage after stage as each new level of contacts is offered will have an entirely different experience. Ultimately, that rich constellation of relationships and all the combined information, resources, and opportunities present within it become open and accessible. This is a tremendously significant strategic proposition.

Companies that are trying to enter or expand their presence in an overseas market would do well to ask themselves what their relationship strategy is. Here are some questions that can guide that inquiry:

- "What relationships do we currently have?"
- "What are the key networks in this business environment that we need to access?"
- "How do people with influence in our industry regard our current employees (local and headquarters)?"
- "Is our company perceived as a short-term or a long-term player, as a localized institution or a foreign enterprise?"
- "What further relationships do we have to build, and how can we build them?"
- "Do we know the right people in government and have good relations with them?"
- "How can we best work through this network to grow our business?"
- "How can we systematically integrate the information and resources that our local relationships make available into our strategic-planning process?"
- "In what way can we add value to the relationships that we have or seek? What do others want that they do not currently have?"

Relationships do not come free. Gradual integration into another party's network is naturally based on mutual benefits, and the ultimate level of access that is granted is determined by how much lasting value one can contribute to the whole group. A relationship strategy must therefore consider both "what we want to get" and "what we can offer." Personal networks are enhanced not only by specific actions, but also by factors such as the association with a prestigious partner and by the ability to provide access to someone else.

Different boundaries between personal and professional lives in other countries can lead to requests that might sound jarring: "Could you help my son get into college?" "Please tell me what kind of gift I should take to the first meeting with your government contact." The foreign guest in another country may need to spend time to learn what to ask for and what to give in return. Yet the principle of mutual benefit remains the same, even if mutual education is necessary to determine how this is best accomplished.

A solid relationship strategy and what that makes possible can be enormously useful within every phase of the strategic-planning process: environmental and internal analysis, goal setting, implementation, and assessment. It helps to recruit and retain the right people, set the appropriate direction in the marketplace, obtain the cooperation of government officials, and get unvarnished customer feedback. In order to be able to shift one's frame of reference to fully take into account local perspectives, such deep and candid relationships are invaluable.

I once asked a friend in Latin America about the best strategy for entering the local market. He replied without hesitation, "Find the right local person to head up the operation. It is worth spending months or even years to find or develop this person. Someone with the right capabilities and connections can accomplish almost anything, while the wrong choice will be the cause of endless frustration and waste."

While every market offers its own complexities, and a single hire is seldom a complete solution, finding local talent that can build an effective network of relationships produces a myriad of advantages, including:

- Government access
- Ties to potential customers
- Timely market intelligence

- Sources of people and ideas
- Ways to solve problems

Beware, however, of the local executive who claims to have terrific relationships with key customers or people in government but has a hard time getting anything done while passing time with an "old boy" network of loafers. "I've got the relationships" is sometimes code for "I don't expect to do any real work."

Global Leadership Development

Strategic planning should have a regenerative dimension focused on global leadership development. Grooming successor candidates for top leadership roles is arguably the most critical long-term priority of any company, and this ought to include nurturing the frame-shifting capabilities of future leaders. High-potential employees must learn to: (1) plan with the proper what, who, and how; (2) consider cross-border positioning and global/local balance; (3) build key relationships with customers and employees in other countries; and (4) develop future leaders who work for them. These points are summarized in table 25.

Strategic planning as a people skill thus becomes a self-renewing organizational asset. The best way to raise the people skills quotient in an organization over time is to foster the development of capable leaders who will themselves raise future leaders. At the same time, putting future leaders in a position to contribute strategic ideas not only helps them to learn, but also gives senior executives the chance to have their own thinking challenged by promising managers from around the world.

Leaders who have developed the capabilities listed in table 25 combine the analytical skills and the personal qualities needed to direct and engage with employees around the world. They have both sufficient cognitive flexibility to comprehend unexpected information from different markets and the empathic agility to put themselves in the shoes of an employee far away from corporate headquarters. A sad and bitter expression used by some subsidiary employees is, "I am just a messenger boy." In the messenger boy culture there is little engagement, enthusiasm, or accountability. The leadership qualities outlined here are intended to

Table 25. **Stategic Planning: Global Competencies**

Core Capability: Frame Shifting	*Able to digest and respond nimbly to new information from global markets; willing to overturn basic assumptions*
What, who, and how	Brings the right information, people, and processes together to create and implement effective strategies
Cross-border positioning	Adapts product distinctiveness and fit of support activities across borders for maximum global and local benefit
Relationship network	Achieves goals through creating and deploying strategic networks that provide fresh insights
Future leader development	Spreads global competencies by cultivating leaders with frame-shifting skills

achieve the opposite outcome: every employee in every location committed to making a real contribution. Figure 15 provides a graphic summary of the key strategic-planning capabilities and how future leader development can become part of all of them.

Factors that can contribute to the development of strategic competencies include

- Genetics and upbringing
- Varied job experience
- International business travel
- Multicultural teamwork
- Contact with executive role models
- Global account management
- Training and development: action learning

Figure 15. **Global Leadership: Strategic Competencies**

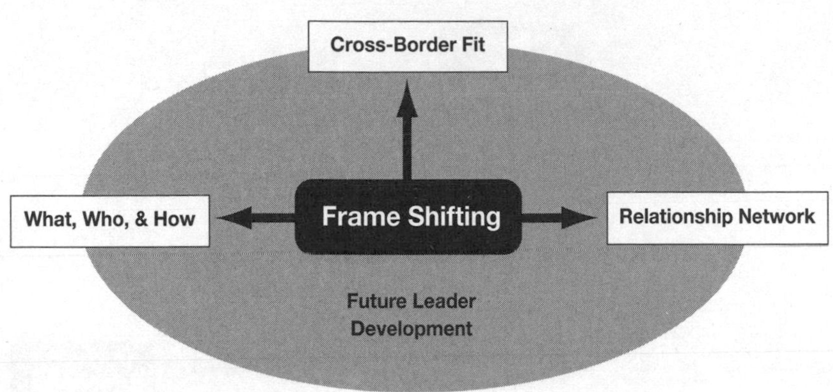

- Expatriate assignments
- Global business responsibility

Companies cannot control factors such as genetics or family upbringing. Among the options that they do shape, the best developmental formula for any employee of course depends on the nature of the organization and its business priorities, the background of the individual being assigned, and the types of opportunities available. Every firm has certain functional slots that it must fill to achieve its global business objectives. A deliberate developmental approach will try to both meet this imperative and match the characteristics and desires of job candidates themselves with the nature of the assignment. From a leadership development standpoint, there is always the same twofold goal: to get the job done and to gain experience in adjusting to new circumstances.

There are many possible development opportunities. For example, individuals who are designated as future corporate leaders may be first exposed to global business through activities such as travel or participation in a global or multicultural team. They might also be assigned to assist a current leader who models key competencies. A more challenging job at the next career phase could be running a global sales account from one's own country (e.g., a Korean manager who has worldwide responsibility for coordinating sales to a major Korean enterprise). A mentor relationship with a foreign executive might also be useful at this point.

Figure 16. **Developing Global Leadership Competencies**

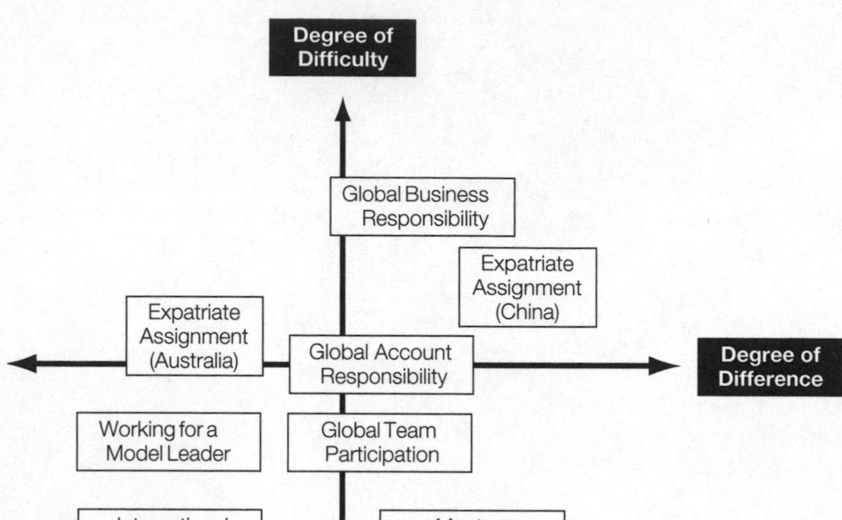

For the person who performs well under these kinds of circumstances, the most radical exposure to other ways of thinking and acting still usually comes through a full-scale expatriate assignment. However, expatriate positions can pose very different challenges based on the location, the objectives, and the degree of support one receives.[6] The most sophisticated global corporations have a large percentage of top executives who have successfully completed assignments abroad and have moved on to positions in which they are responsible for global business lines or regions.[7] Figure 16 illustrates a number of these growth opportunities along with their degree of difficulty and potential level of exposure to different ways of working and living.

So corporate strategy should include plans for cultivating future strategists. Leaders who have undergone developmental experiences that entail increasing exposure to foreign markets become adept at viewing their enterprises from the edges as well as the center. They are often the first to detect places where the core value propositions of their business may be questioned, or to spot new forms of competition. Subjecting leadership candidates to "fish out of water" experiences abroad makes the survivors stronger, more flexible, and more resourceful—able to mediate between divergent viewpoints and turn conflicts into productive outcomes.

Strategic Planning

SUMMARY AND REVIEW QUESTIONS

1. What assumptions will your organization need to question to establish a more effective presence in foreign markets? Are there any assumptions about products, business processes, or customers that are valid domestically but may be dysfunctional abroad?

2. Consider a time when your firm introduced a product or service into a foreign market but failed to meet expected targets for sales or profits. In this case, can you attribute any part of the outcome to mishandling the "what," "who," or "how" elements of strategic planning? Are there better ways to engage overseas employees in strategic planning so that you have the full benefit of their contribution?

3. Is there a good fit across borders between the products and/or services that your firm offers in different countries? Are features created for one market used in other markets as well? Are there markets in which you are poorly positioned in terms of cross-border fit? If so, how will you address this situation?

4. What long-term relationships has your firm developed over time? How are these relationships maintained, developed, and integrated into current strategic thinking? Do your friends and customers abroad trust you enough to share their own most prized circle of key contacts with you?

5. Think of a situation in your own work history where you or a colleague demonstrated an ability to shift perspectives between a local and a global viewpoint and truly consider the best interests of the company. In what ways does your organization currently recognize and take steps to develop this ability in its leaders?

6. Among the various kinds of experiences that can help to cultivate global leadership competencies, which is your organization currently using? Are there other possible ways to develop future leaders who have the "frame-shifting" capability so crucial to strategic planning?

CHAPTER TEN

Transferring Knowledge

The ability to transfer knowledge smoothly and efficiently across borders has become an important competitive differentiator. As firms move away from semiautonomous operations in foreign countries and attempt to build global networks with multiple centers of expertise, knowledge transfer systems become an increasingly pivotal success factor worldwide.

A key people skills aspect of knowledge transfer is creating "pull," or demand for the knowledge that is to be transmitted. If employees in a particular location have a strong desire to incorporate new skills or information and are active agents in seeking it out, the likelihood that it will take root and grow is far greater. How to generate and enhance this pull factor thus becomes a critical puzzle for organizations that place a priority on leveraging knowledge globally.

Skill #10: Transferring Knowledge

Among the major drivers accelerating the pace of global knowledge transfer are trends ranging from sales prospects abroad to the availability of human resources:

- Business opportunities to leverage existing knowledge in new markets
- Global product development strategies
- Relocation of production facilities to lower-cost labor sites
- Requirements for a better flow of market intelligence between different countries
- Host government demands for a policy of proactive technology transfer
- Projected knowledge and skill gaps as core technical employees leave the company
- Turnover of high-potential subsidiary employees due to limited chances for advancement
- High costs of expatriate packages

Typical venues for knowledge transfer include new factory startups, moves to expand subsidiary functions, joint ventures, licensing or sales agreements, global teams, formal training and development programs, and corporate intranets. The maquiladora case described in chapter 1 is an example of a factory expansion project where knowledge transfer was essential to achieve the objectives of simultaneously lowering labor costs while also improving product quality and worker productivity. As usual, cultural differences are present as part of a complex mixture of ingredients. In this chapter we examine the case, repeated below, in greater detail.

Cross-Border Knowledge Transfer

"Joaquin, why is this machine still running?" the foreign manager asked the senior shift mechanic during his regular rounds

to monitor the process. "This process measurement recorded by Hernando is far below what it should be!" "I have been too busy to check up on it," Joaquin replied. Next, the manager called over to the machine operator who recorded the measurement. "Hernando, do you know that this measurement is out of tolerance?" "No," Hernando replied. "No one told me what the spec was." In reality, the specification was clearly posted on the wall over his machine.

A maquiladora operation in Mexico sought to install a quality system that would allow factory workers to make continuous improvements in the manufacturing process. The new system generated a constant stream of precise data about whether or not each piece of factory machinery was operating within acceptable tolerances. Using the new system, workers had the capability to monitor product quality and take corrective action. The next stage planned for the Mexican factory, beyond simply running the manufacturing process it received, was to use the accumulated data and improvements to take the operation to higher levels of quality and productivity. But the key hurdle, as it turned out, was to persuade the Mexican factory workers to actually use the system. Considerable time was lost while the factory struggled to put a team of people in place that was both able and willing to develop along with the manufacturing process itself; high rates of maquiladora employee turnover made it difficult to establish lasting solutions.

Knowledge Transfer: Four Phases

This quality system transfer was part of a larger project that involved moving an entire production line into a new factory in a Mexican town near the U.S. border. The plan was to examine the quality control system in the existing factory, seek out ways to make improvements, and introduce the revised procedures into the new factory environment. Advanced measuring and testing equipment would be installed to support the system upgrades. The knowledge transfer process consisted of four overlapping phases:

- Gathering the knowledge
- Conveying the knowledge
- Getting the knowledge to stick
- Generating new knowledge

Important lessons were learned during each phase.

Gathering the knowledge.

Much of the knowledge related to quality control in the parent factory was tacit rather than explicit. It existed in the minds and the hands of the factory workers but was not fully documented. An initial hurdle for the knowledge transfer project was to identify and record the vital experience they possessed. But workers who face the prospect of losing their jobs to foreign counterparts, as was the case in this situation, are not necessarily eager to share what they know. Early attempts to film them working on the product assembly line resulted in resentment and protests.

Outsiders tasked with collecting information only began to make progress when workers recognized that the decision to move the production line had already been made at the executive level and that the visitors simply had a job to do. After the workers had the chance to air their grievances, they even began to take some enjoyment in sharing what they knew. Another key turning point for the knowledge transfer effort was identifying key individuals in the existing factory who were holding operations together with their accumulated experience and intuition—not only to debrief them, but also to create contractual arrangements that brought them into the Mexican factory as trainers.

Lessons learned:

- ***Anticipate and handle in a straightforward manner worker anxiety or resentment related to knowledge transfer to a foreign location***
- ***Identify key individuals with tacit knowledge and get them into the new production site abroad***

Conveying the knowledge.

A fresh obstacle to transplanting valuable knowledge gleaned from the old factory was the attitude of the receiving organization. A rumor passed between Mexican managers and workers early in the knowledge transfer process that the factory up north was being shut down due to poor-quality products and lack of worker skills. This negative perception was reinforced by the fact that some of the first worker exchange programs that brought Mexicans to the U.S. were not well organized. A related problem, both at the original factory and at the new one, was that task-focused U.S. instructors would rush through their materials and then head back to work—they were already putting in long hours just to run the factory. The Mexican trainees, on the other hand, found it awkward to learn from someone they did not know and who was not available to offer follow-up advice or answer questions. And many who returned to Mexico did not even share whatever knowledge they acquired with others due to hierarchical and horizontal boundaries in the organization there.

The Mexicans only became more ready to learn once they saw first hand the skills of the expert workers from the U.S. factory and began to taste the difficulties of running the production line themselves. This created a pull factor on the part of the knowledge transfer recipients that greatly accelerated the learning process. Reprioritization of the knowledge transfer function helped to free up more time for U.S. experts to spend with the Mexicans. And when the trainers from the U.S. also began to attend Mexican social events such as outdoor barbecues and weddings, personal connections were made that enhanced mutual trust and finally began to lead to real learning. Not surprisingly, the U.S. trainers who had become well acquainted with Mexican trainees before arriving at their factory found it far easier to become effective in Mexico—even with trainees who were new to them. They began to spend much more time on the line providing hands-on instruction to Mexican workers. Another contribution they made was to assist their Mexican colleagues in establishing new standards and expectations for information sharing, allowing learnings to be disseminated more broadly across organizational lines.

Lessons learned:

- ***Look for ways to create a "pull" factor in the receiving organization for the acquisition of new knowledge***
- ***Ensure that information is shared across horizontal and vertical lines, even in hierarchical work environments***
- ***Build cross-cultural social ties and opportunities for hands-on instruction***

Getting the knowledge to stick.

The process of drawing in fresh knowledge from outside must ultimately be localized in the form of an autonomous knowledge-gathering process. For the quality program at the Mexican factory to be successful, workers would have to take on the accountability for linking quality data with machinery adjustments in a closed, traceable loop. The new process management system at the heart of the manufacturing operation had to shift, in other words, from an auditor-centered system to one that was instead operator centered. Machine operators themselves needed to assume responsibility for the quality of the product they made, not auditors or supervisors looking over their shoulder.

This philosophy of personal accountability did not come naturally to the Mexican factory workers, many of whom were more accustomed to being told specifically what to do and then letting their boss take both the credit and the responsibility for results. Getting them to accept this new set of responsibilities proved to be a far more arduous task than was originally anticipated—the advice and input of the first foreign technicians who came to Mexico on short-term assignments was received politely but often ignored. The factory's management met with the most success by putting in place local and foreign managers who could forge strong personal ties with individual workers while also asking them to demonstrate greater accountability. They rewarded and promoted employees—often those with a hard-working farming background—who proved able to respond to this approach. Some caution was necessary, however, to avoid promoting employees who sought to ingratiate themselves with managers as a way of enhancing their pay and status even when they lacked critical skills.

Driving individual accountability through to every level required supplementing the initial worker training and instruction from managers with regular, ongoing evaluation of skills and knowledge regarding the quality process. Daily meetings between supervisors and technicians and periodic meetings among supervisors were instituted to track quality data and corrective actions. Reduction of cycle time for the testing process used for product quality analysis made it easier to provide meaningful, short-term feedback to machine operators; this in turn allowed them to take more timely corrective action.

Based on the general group orientation of Mexican culture, a team-based accountability system might appear to be more appropriate than trying to enforce accountability on an individual level. However, this has not been the case so far. In the distinctive border environment of the maquiladoras, the worker population is a patchwork of numerous subgroups that do not easily bond with one another: local-area natives, bicultural Mexicans who relate more readily with U.S. managers, peasants directly off the farm from other regions of the country, and young middle-class engineers who have graduated from technical institutes. These groups are separated by boundaries of regional identification, status, skills sets, and the fact that most have come to work at a maquiladora for harsh personal and family economic reasons—there are few inherent community ties. High work force turnover in border factories, with employees quick to move elsewhere for better pay, makes it even more difficult to establish consistent teamwork practices, although these might indeed be effective elsewhere.

Lessons learned:

- *Expect problems in establishing individual accountability for applying fresh knowledge in more hierarchical and group-oriented environments*
- *Look for ways to strengthen accountability through personal relationships between managers and subordinates*
- *Reinforce accountability when necessary through concrete systems for data collection, individual evaluation, and performance-based rewards*

Generating new knowledge.

An additional key step for taking advantage of opportunities for quality improvement was finding Mexican management personnel who would take it upon themselves to aggressively enhance the link between testing and production. Many Mexican managers hesitated to assume such an assertive leadership stance, particularly when foreigners were present, unless they knew the technical details and felt comfortable with the people they were managing. As they gained in confidence, they also turned into more effective managers. At the same time, there were some who talked a good game but demonstrated over the long term that they were not really committed to implementing improvements. It was necessary to penetrate the cultural and linguistic smokescreens that several people put out and make personnel changes that either promoted or brought in managers who were more capable of getting things done.

As new knowledge is generated, it can lead the system beyond what it inherited from abroad and produce fresh practices that are of value to other locations worldwide. The next stage for the Mexican operation is to further raise its quality levels, which already equal those of the U.S. factory at one-third the cost. Explicit systems for generating quality data and tracing problems will furnish regular opportunities for continuous improvement as new knowledge is gained. Further documentation of processes such as equipment setup and operation procedures, preventive maintenance, reaction plans for typical quality problems, toolmaker knowledge, and so forth will support the accumulation and updating of critical knowledge.

Lessons learned:

- *Cultivate local leaders who have fully bought into new practices based on acquired knowledge and are willing to drive them to the next level by generating new knowledge locally*
- *Accommodate cultural differences but do not allow them to be used as a smokescreen to conceal poor performance*[1]

Knowledge Transfer: Other Key Issues

Besides the challenges encountered in the four phases mentioned earlier, there are other issues that tend to crop up repeatedly during knowledge transfer efforts and are crucial to creating the pull among recipients that will drive the process.[2] Among these are

- Organizational vision and strategy
- Politics and community relations
- Definitions of knowledge
- Subsidiary capacity
- Personal trust and relationships
- Information technology systems
- Performance evaluation and rewards
- Protecting intellectual property

The form that these issues take naturally varies from country to country. One of the greatest transfers of knowledge in human history—an event that dwarfs even the sizeable U.S.–Mexico relationship—is now taking place between the world's most advanced economies (including Europe, Japan, and the U.S.) and China. Thousands of joint ventures or new wholly owned subsidiaries are bringing vast quantities of technical and managerial expertise to a country that has in past eras been a source of learning for other civilizations. The sheer magnitude of this endeavor and the fact that China encompasses a fifth of the world's population makes it a prime example in the sections to follow.

Organizational vision and strategy.

Do the organization and its leadership support the dissemination of vital knowledge beyond the home country?

Many firms are global or transnational in theory but far more parochial in practice. Executives sometimes extol the virtues of being "boundaryless" and of worldwide knowledge exchange while neglecting to back them up with the authority and the resources at their disposal. Unless an organization has a clear vision that embraces cross-border knowledge transfer, coupled with specific strategies for making it happen, obstacles are likely to surface that make fine words appear to be so much empty rhetoric. Employees at various locations around the world are not likely to be enthusiastic about drawing in knowledge from other locations if they sense that there is no real organizational commitment or strategic focus.

People working at corporate headquarters are preoccupied with the work in front of them, and often simply forget about their colleagues abroad—neglecting to send them useful information or to include them in important discussions. And business unit or R&D personnel based at corporate headquarters or elsewhere in the company's home environment may hesitate to share leading-edge technologies or sensitive information with colleagues in places such as China, where there is a history of intellectual property violations and product piracy. Overseas employees whom they do not know well or have never met are naturally treated with suspicion when they ask probing questions about proprietary or confidential matters, a posture that deflates their morale and leads them to believe they are second-class corporate citizens.

Part of the strategic challenge that companies face in determining the appropriate degree of knowledge transfer is to realistically define the role of their subsidiary operations. Are employees in locations abroad supposed to be implementers of ideas and products invented at headquarters, or are they true partners who require ready access to all of the firm's knowledge to accomplish their goals? Exactly what kinds of knowledge should be shared, and to what degree? The most suitable formula for knowledge transfer naturally varies industry by industry and country by country.

One Asian executive in the U.S. described the local employees of his company as the "hands and feet" of the corporate parent—in his view it was only necessary to provide them with the small quantity of knowledge necessary to carry out their particular tasks. Meanwhile he expected them to convey large volumes of market intelligence back to corporate headquarters. In this case, the only pull factor that the company strategy supported was the centripetal flow of knowledge from overseas markets back to the home office. Such a strategy may or may not be the best one for the company, but it certainly does not encourage local employees to be active assimilators of knowledge for use in their own environment.

Politics and community relations.

What are the goals of the national government and local communities? How are they reflected in employee attitudes? Are foreign capital companies associated with the threat of external control, resource depletion, or unwanted cultural features?

The degree of fit between corporate strategies and the goals of the host country can either foster or inhibit knowledge transfer. Organizations headquartered outside the host country will find it far easier to expand their operations if they are seen as supporting national and community goals. On the other hand, the types of support valued by the government could require them to transfer sensitive information and to place vital intellectual property at risk. National priorities are frequently reflected in individual employee attitudes. Employees who perceive their company—even a foreign firm—as a champion for the introduction of much-needed products and services will be eager to acquire and apply new knowledge. In this situation, their personal interests and the priorities of the country as a whole can both be served.

In the case of China, as with other developing economies, technology is regarded as the best way to catch up with the rest of the world and the key to national success within the global economy. As suggested in chapter 8, the country's overriding national objective is to erase the historical humiliations it has suffered over the past 150 years as a result of its technological inferiority. The Chinese have learned the hard way—for instance, through the sudden withdrawal of foreign expertise at the time of the Sino-Soviet split in the 1950s—that they need to avoid dependence on outside forces who may manipulate this kind of vulnerability for their own political purposes. China's national political agenda not only includes a drive to gain control over vital technology, but also targets particular industrial sectors such as telecommunications or electronics in which it is determined to make rapid progress. Foreign capital company employees in China are well aware of this as well as the fact that inefficient and outmoded state enterprises are not the best place to learn the skills that will help the country to develop.

In an environment of this kind, foreign companies that are willing to transfer advanced knowledge and to train and develop local employees are most likely to receive favorable treatment from the government. There is an unofficial quid pro quo arrangement whereby the government holds out the prospect of increased local market access in exchange for significant transfer projects. In addition, these companies attract bright and motivated workers who aggressively seek out knowledge from other locations.

Governments of course have multiple levels: national, state, regional, and local. Political clout with the national or state government may not translate into cooperation from local politicians. "Heaven is high, and the Emperor is far away" is a well-known maxim in China. Companies with a large-scale presence in various parts of the nation must also create successful partnerships with local government officials to finalize business agreements, receive essential services, or gain legal permits or protections. With local governments as well it is vital to be positioned as an organization that supports governmental priorities rather than one that exploits weakness.

Local government or community resistance to corporate actions can inflame employee opposition to bringing in products or ideas that they view as harmful. For instance, workers in many countries might resist importation of proprietary technologies that are unrealistically priced for local buyers, or cultural imports such as movies or fashions that do not conform to local moral standards. And community members or employees who feel that a company is exploiting their natural resources or taking unfair advantage of workers instead of introducing new knowledge and skills sometimes resort to even more drastic forms of protest. Pilfering, sabotage, kidnapping, and other guerrilla tactics are commonplace events in many parts of the world.

Definitions of knowledge.

Do both contributors and recipients in the knowledge transfer process define what is to be conveyed in the same way? Is the knowledge that is being shared what the recipients want?

Knowledge is defined in different ways depending on one's background. Those who seek to transfer a body of knowledge to another location may take for granted sophisticated concepts that are not understood or shared by the prospective recipients. Knowledge that is seen by the transferring party as involving technical and managerial skills, integration with other factory production systems, and long-term preventive maintenance could be regarded more narrowly by the people on the receiving end as a piece of equipment and the instructions for running it. Here, for example, is how a Western executive describes the notion of technology he has encountered in China:

> *The definition of technology is different here. Technology means equipment in people's minds. "I'm going to buy this machine." So the difficulty in transferring is that it's not just the machine. It's the process. It's the people. It's the product. All of that falls into the realm of technology, whereas here it's almost clinical. It's a piece of equipment. That's technology. So when we came here, people seemed to be waiting for someone to bring the box of technology.*[3]

State-run Chinese enterprises did not customarily define technology as part of a package that included, for instance, quality control and preventive maintenance. They previously had a captive market in which they could sell whatever they made, regardless of product quality. When such firms partner with Western companies it can be hard for their employees to grasp immediately why quality control is essential. Attitudes toward maintaining equipment were similar to those regarding quality—preventive maintenance was not seen as a source of competitive advantage.

Effective knowledge transfer can only take place through building common definitions of the whole range of knowledge to be shared, including factors such as

- Worker attitudes and behaviors
- Machinery and equipment
- Core technical skills

- Factory processes and systems (e.g., quality control or preventive maintenance)
- Supplier relations
- Physical infrastructure requirements

There must also be sense of urgency on the part of the knowledge recipients to acquire not just the machinery, but the full array of knowledge needed to run it efficiently.

Subsidiary capacity.

Are local employees and infrastructure ready and able to absorb new knowledge effectively? Is what they want realistic?

The varied education and experience levels of workers make it necessary for organizations to consider their capacity to acquire new knowledge. In some cases they are well qualified, while in others they are not; there may be significant variations among employees of the same nationality at the same site.

A European executive in China remarked that his technical work force could be divided into two groups. The first group consists of workers who have received little technical education. They have learned to maintain one kind of pump, for instance, but cannot maintain a different kind without further training because they lack basic knowledge of pump technology. The second group includes workers who have strong technical backgrounds—having received an education as good or better than their counterparts in the West—but who arrive at the factory with little practical experience.[4]

Any knowledge transfer effort must take a different approach to each of these two groups, with the first receiving more basic education and training and the second focused on practical application. Inexperienced foreign technicians or trainers who are not fully aware of the background of their audience may gear their presentation in the wrong way. Rather than beginning with a discussion of pump maintenance, for instance, they might need to begin with the more basic question of "What is a pump?" Or, instead of an overview of marketing techniques, asking the question "Why do marketing?" might be a better place to start in order to create the same foundation of assumptions. (See chapter 6 for more on training and development.)

The local organization's appetite for knowledge, distorted by narrow definitions of technology, may simply be bigger than the digestive capacity of its workers. A "more is always better" attitude is understandable for people who are driving toward self-sufficiency and feel that they have been held back in the past, but it can also lead to wasted investments in hi-tech equipment that local employees cannot adequately maintain, or enormous plants to which foreign technicians have to be called back in to run. George Renwick describes an example of this that he witnessed:

> *They built a very sophisticated processing plant in northeastern China, importing the very finest equipment—state-of-the-art equipment from Germany, from England, from the United States. Everything was in place and ready to go, and it sat for more than two years, virtually idle. The reason was that the "know-how" and the "know-why" were not also transferred and put in place. So what they had to do was call in another Western company and bring in fourteen seasoned Western engineers and managers, who then moved to the city with their families, with the express purpose of transferring capability in order that the technology could be fully used.*[5]

In the case of foreign capital companies, subsidiary operations are generally targeted to fulfill a specific set of objectives—for example, local sales, manufacturing, and/or technical service. When planning a knowledge transfer project it is advisable to consider the current purpose of these operations and the infrastructure, both human and technical, that is in place to support them. Knowledge transfer that aims to increase subsidiary capabilities by a notch or two is generally feasible; too great a leap may be unsustainable for local personnel. Although subsidiary development takes multiple forms and is not necessarily linear, a sample progression beginning with the representative sales office could be formulated as follows:

1. Representative sales office
2. Product adaptation
3. Local design
4. Local manufacturing
5. Pricing authority
6. Profit-and-loss responsibility
7. Global account management
8. Global product management

It is imperative to be aware of the subsidiary's current circumstances at each stage. Members of a representative sales office—one of the initial functions that companies tend to install in an overseas operation—may heartily endorse the idea that they should be able to take on global account management for key customers that are headquartered locally. However, in the absence of other functions higher on the organizational development ladder such as product design or manufacturing and without prior experience in handling pricing, such a proposal could be quite premature. This sort of gap between knowledge transfer aspirations and local capabilities can become the recipe for fiascoes of almost comical proportions.

Personal trust and relationships.

Is there sufficient trust and respect to enable rapid cross-border dissemination of knowledge and skills? How can personal relationships be leveraged to enhance pull?

Potential knowledge recipients, especially those who are from countries where a high priority is placed on relationships, are most comfortable asking for knowledge from people they know and trust. Much has been said about the subject of relationship building in other chapters, and it is relevant for cross-border knowledge transfer as well. Personal relationships have a tremendous effect on speeding up and ensuring the accurate transmission of information.

Companies with a long history of personnel exchanges between different locations around the world possess a network of global contacts that crisscross the official organizational structure and supplement its functions. When a question emerges that another company employee somewhere in the world knows the answer to, having a network of contacts abroad can serve as a powerful personal search engine. Such links save the time and trouble of long background checks, speed the exchange of vital news or best practices, and ensure that the employee abroad not only dares to ask, but also finds the knowledge that he or she needs. In this way the initial tentative pull of an inquiry from abroad is rewarded and reinforced, while in another corporate environment the same type of request might fall on deaf ears.

Employees in remote locations typically view the ocean of knowledge held by the organization as a whole with awe and trepidation. Without personal contacts who can help them to sort through what is available, the experience is similar to looking into a huge library through a window—the resources are there, but they cannot be easily accessed. Online company catalogs of information are often bewilderingly complex and hard to decipher. Personal relationships open the door to various forms of assistance that make this knowledge available in practical ways. Having personal ties to corporate headquarters might help an employee at an overseas site to

- Locate individuals with the expertise to assist with a specific issue or technical problem
- Open backdoor channels for obtaining product samples or resources
- Understand future strategic directions that have not yet been formally announced
- Discover new technologies or products that would fit the local company's markets[6]

Most important, however, when the person who holds the keys to a desired piece of knowledge is a trusted friend or acquaintance, that person can significantly lower real or perceived barriers to knowledge acquisition. Pull from prospective knowledge recipients is increased over time through the special touch a friend provides: a bit of encouragement, an explanation or demonstration of how a piece of knowledge is used, a resource to turn to with questions, and even someone who will just respond in a timely way to messages. Companies that take a strategic approach to human resources development utilize a combination of experiences—business travel and informal social contacts, global teamwork, regional conferences, leadership training programs, short-term project work abroad, overseas assignments, and so on—to build these personal networks across borders.

Information technology systems.

Is information technology designed to supplement and enhance personal interaction, or to replace it?

IT solutions by themselves seldom create a pull factor for new knowledge, and yet they are often the center of knowledge transfer packages. The problem with such systems, whether they are domestic or global, is that they don't work unless people use them. Building usage requires a complex set of conditions such as ease of access, compelling content, regular updates to information, and ways of recognizing contributors. As if this were not already complicated enough, the obstacles are much greater in a far-flung global operation. Some overseas facilities have modem speed so slow that business travelers have to adjust their laptops just to make a connection, or else they simply give up trying to link to the Web through creaky phone systems. Employees in these places might check e-mail just a few times a week, if that.[7] Even voicemail, with its daunting array of menu options, can be a vexing obstacle for non-native-language speakers.

One leading American firm recently took the opportunity to invest in the installation of a set of videoconferencing facilities in Thailand. In addition to enabling communication with other sites around the world, the new videoconferencing capability was intended to increase the productivity of the firm's Thai subsidiary employees. Many of these employees would spend an entire day on the crowded roads between the company's local Bangkok headquarters and its factory in the suburbs in order to attend a single meeting. Videoconferencing would make such travel unnecessary and facilitate easier knowledge transfer between the two sites.

Things didn't quite turn out as planned, however, as the Thais had trouble getting used to the new technology. The former managing director of the Thai subsidiary, a U.S. expatriate, remembers ruefully, "I soon found out that the local managers were conducting the videoconference for my benefit, and then arranging in their own language to have an additional face-to-face meeting after the videoconference was finished. They still wanted to be able to meet in person to gauge the reaction of the other side." So instead of creating greater efficiencies, the new videoconferencing facility was resulting in extra meetings as well as extra costs.[8] The impact on knowledge transfer was doubtful because the employees were using the technology to please their boss rather than because it was giving them the information they most wanted.

Mapping out a new communications system based on the assumption that people in one country will use it as others do elsewhere can be a mistake. A significant investment in orientation and training with respect to the new technology may be essential to ensure that there is a real return on the investment. Asking for input and gaining buy-in from overseas partners before installation is an even better way to ensure mutual commitment to using the system—this includes being clear about both what it will and will not be used to accomplish.

The best global IT systems make the expertise of the entire company available through the laptop of a frontline salesperson anywhere in the world, or help employees to solve customer problems by drawing on the knowledge of colleagues they may never have met face-to-face. Many admirable technical solutions tap into and facilitate the practices of an existing community of knowledge exchange, making it easier for people to accomplish what they have been doing already. And when the goal is to introduce new work processes, the change should not be technology centered, but rather grounded in the evolving culture of the firm. Employees have to do more than learn how to access and operate an IT system; they must cultivate new work habits that include utilizing the system regularly and discover for themselves the benefits of sharing knowledge rather than hoarding it. For companies that seek to transform themselves, an IT solution serves best when it is used as a tool that supports corporate culture renovation rather than being expected to function as a change agent itself.

Performance evaluation and rewards.

Are business travelers, expatriates, and local employees rewarded for knowledge transfer? Are there disincentives to sharing or acquiring vital learnings?

Creating and sustaining pull from potential knowledge recipients requires meaningful measurement systems and incentives for both the transmitters and the receivers of knowledge. Performance management systems and rewards must be structured to support knowledge transfer.

A surprising number of companies somehow expect employees to happily share knowledge with people in other countries who will soon be performing their jobs in another location at a lower cost. In the maquiladora case cited earlier, the U.S. factory workers who possessed vital operational knowledge were on the verge of being laid off, a fact that hardly made them eager to share what they knew—particularly when training activities were treated as an added responsibility on top of their regular jobs. A lack of motivation on the part of knowledge transmitters is quickly perceived by those who ought to be actively seeking out what they have to offer: Mexican visitors to the U.S. factory who were eager to learn at first returned to their country with stories about poor U.S. worker morale and lack of hospitality and openness.

After the flaws in these practices became apparent, the company discovered partial solutions such as officially dedicating more employee time to training Mexican counterparts and bringing key employees into the Mexico facility while paying them as consultants. Both changes involved modifications in the reward structure. This process also enabled the most skilled U.S. workers to demonstrate their skills in a hands-on fashion, earning the respect of Mexican colleagues and rekindling their desire to learn from the U.S. factory veterans.

The maquiladora management in the Mexican example found it necessary to revise the performance evaluation and reward system for knowledge recipients as well. They began to conduct regular evaluations of worker skill and knowledge of the new quality process to drive home the principle of individual accountability. Pay and promotions for the knowledge recipients were ultimately tied to skill acquisition and implementation of the new quality system.

Expatriates and local employees, whether in a maquiladora or a Western company's operations in China, commonly face conflicting corporate mandates. As a human resources executive based in China put it,

> *Expatriates are told, "Charlie, you have two jobs. One is to develop local employees and the other is to get business results. And, by the way, your performance will be evaluated entirely on the basis of the second job..." So Charlie responds, "Got it." And then two years later you have to replace Charlie with Ed, another expatriate, because no one has been trained up to replace Charlie.*[9]

Local employees, too, often discover that the pressure to produce immediate results takes precedence over training and development objectives. A more farsighted approach to goal setting and rewards that significantly lowers costs in the long run is to set specific objectives and timelines for the development of local successors and to incorporate these into performance evaluations for both expatriates and their replacement candidates.

A Success Story: Knowledge Transfer at Buckman Labs

Buckman Laboratories, based in Memphis, Tennessee, has been recognized twice in recent years with the top ranking among Global Most Admired Knowledge Enterprises (MAKE) Winners. It is the only organization to ever win this award twice, and it is joined in the top echelon by other renowned firms such as Toyota, Nokia, and Unilever. It has also been ranked among the world's top knowledge enterprises for five consecutive years, not to mention receiving environmental awards on three different continents. The Buckman case exemplifies the role of corporate vision and strategy driven by executive modeling, personal trust and relationships, a properly positioned IT system, and the use of rewards in promoting global knowledge exchange.[10]

How could a small, privately held specialty chemicals company come to rub shoulders with such global giants in the knowledge transfer area? Having only a fraction the size of competitors within its own industry, Buckman Laboratories differentiates itself by promising to apply knowledge more creatively. It seeks to make the accumulated knowledge and wisdom of the entire organization available worldwide at the point of sale to resolve the operational challenges of customers: "Our resources effectively place all of the company's knowledge and talent at our associates' fingertips."[11]

Buckman's knowledge transfer system is not a recent fad or the product of some information technology miracle. It is rooted in the management philosophy and business experience of former CEO Bob Buckman, son of the company's founder. He first established a corporate Knowledge Transfer department in the early 1990s and focused consistently on knowledge transfer in shaping the Buckman Laboratories' mission, values, and business strategies. The firm's official pronouncements, which clearly go much further than being encased in a plaque on the wall, are replete with references to the strategic application of knowledge: "Since its founding, Buckman Laboratories has worked toward becoming a true global organization.... We are leveraging the world-class knowledge-sharing culture of our organization to the benefit of global customers."[12]

Starting in 1992, the company built a Web-based knowledge transfer network that came to be known as K'Netix, but it was not an immediate hit with employees. Through several years of experimentation, Buckman found that the system could only succeed if it were closely linked with the everyday practices of his enterprise, and he developed a variety of measures to support and reinforce its use. First, top executives, including Buckman himself, set the example by using the K'Netix IT platform regularly to answer employee queries on behalf of customers. They also shaped a reward system that carefully measures and tracks customer contacts while providing both direct and indirect incentives to employees who use the company's network to share knowledge that will help resolve customer problems. Participation is easily assessed by a CEO who is constantly using the system (he has also been known to review weekly lists of people who use the company's TechForum). Those who contribute are rewarded with special events such as a celebration held at a resort to recognize top knowledge sharers, whereas those who do not are told that their opportunities within the company will diminish.

Over time, use of K'Netix has become an integral part of Buckman's global culture of knowledge exchange, encompassing a broad range of activities that include private forums tailored to particular customers, a customer information center with complete files on each customer, a number of special technical forums, and even free-flowing online discussions with the CEO about sensitive subjects such as compensation. Buckman himself has reportedly attributed the success of the system to trust among employees.

A further illustration of how Buckman's global knowledge management system works is the case of Dennis Dalton, a managing director for Asia based in Singapore. Seeking to respond to a request from a customer in nearby Indonesia, Dalton sent out a call for help on K'Netix, asking for updates on successful pitch-control strategies in pulp mills elsewhere in the world. Within a few hours he had a response from Memphis with a specific chemical recommendation and a reference to a master's thesis written on this subject by an Indonesian studying in the U.S. But that was just the beginning:

> *Michael Sund logged on from Canada and offered his experience in solving the pitch problem in British Columbia. Then Nils Hallberg chimed in with examples from Sweden; Wendy Biijker offered details from a New Zealand paper mill; Jose Vallcorba gave two examples from Spain and France; Chin Hill in Memphis contributed scientific advice from the company's R&D team; Javier Del Rosal sent a detailed chemical formula and specific applications from Mexico; and Lionel Hughes weighed in with two types of pitch-control programs in use in South Africa.*[13]

Dalton's request for help from Singapore produced answers from eleven different countries along with several ongoing conversations between respondents. Using the knowledge he had just gleaned through this process, Dalton was well positioned to receive a $6 million order from his Indonesian customer. Overall, the company calculates that new product sales increased 50 percent within a few years of introducing its online knowledge transfer system.[14]

Thus, in the case of Buckman Laboratories, there appears to be not only pull from people around the world who are seeking vital knowledge, but a fluid, self-reinforcing network in which the person who sends out an appeal for help one day could be offering it up the next. This knowledge exchange function, far from being esoteric or for researchers only, is applied directly to meet the challenges of global customers.

Protecting intellectual property.

Will proprietary information or technology be safe from misuse by others? Is there sometimes a need to guard against too much knowledge pull?

While creating an attraction factor that enhances the transfer of knowledge is generally a good thing, companies must prevent overly enthusiastic or illicit pull from leading to the spread of proprietary knowledge beyond its intended business purpose. A make-or-break issue for many knowledge transfer projects is protecting vital intellectual property, and no matter how much a company's vision and business strategy may support a free and open flow of information, such a flow is not sustainable if others outside the company can take advantage of it as well. This is a special conundrum in countries where the legal system provides only limited and inconsistent recourse.

The prevailing attitude in a number of developing-country markets is that there is no point in further enriching wealthy foreign firms through strict enforcement of intellectual property laws. Such an attitude may be shared by the company's own business partners. Copying foreign technology is both profitable and patriotic according to some arguments. Countries and workers with a communist legacy also have limited experience with the privatization of knowledge. Intellectual property protections often only really begin to take hold when domestically headquartered firms begin to complain that other countries are abusing *their* property rights.

There are several tactics for protecting valuable knowledge that have proved to be successful in developing markets. The best place to start is to create a strong, mutually beneficial relationship with a well-connected local partner. Profitable business ties with a foreign firm provide the local partner with a major incentive to monitor the use of proprietary information or technologies so that these do not become available to their domestic competition. As William Fischer, an experienced China hand, puts it,

> *The most logical and attractive way to protect technology is to develop a relationship that is so rewarding for your Chinese partner that they would never think to infringe upon your intellectual property. I believe in building a partnership rather than a supply or a customer relation. Partnership is a better answer than just trying to control everything because that, I believe, is not so easy.*[15]

Even well-meaning employees or partners sometimes accidentally share valuable company knowledge when they are not clear about what is proprietary and what is not. This can occur through the swapping of information with customers, government officials, and so on that takes place in restaurants and bars after work in most countries. It may be necessary to work closely with those who have numerous outside contacts to help them understand not only the yes or no, black or white of information sharing, but also potential shades of gray in between where it is permissible to offer something to another person in exchange for a meaningful piece of knowledge in return.

Knowledge Transfer: A Comprehensive Approach

The successful approaches that leading firms have developed for transferring knowledge are comprehensive rather than piecemeal, addressing the entire context of the transfer. This means keeping in mind the four phases and the eight transfer issues discussed in this chapter, which are summarized in figure 17. Knowledge transfer ideally begins with a corporate vision that meshes with indigenous aspirations for learning and development. A steady commitment to developing subsidiary organizations raises the motivation of local knowledge transfer recipients to draw in knowledge at a rapid rate, and ensures that what they acquire will be properly digested and put to work. "The important signal we want to send to employees is that they're good enough to take the top jobs," says Jason Lum, a Motorola executive in China.[16]

Figure 17. **Cross-Border Knowledge Transfer: Creating "Pull"**

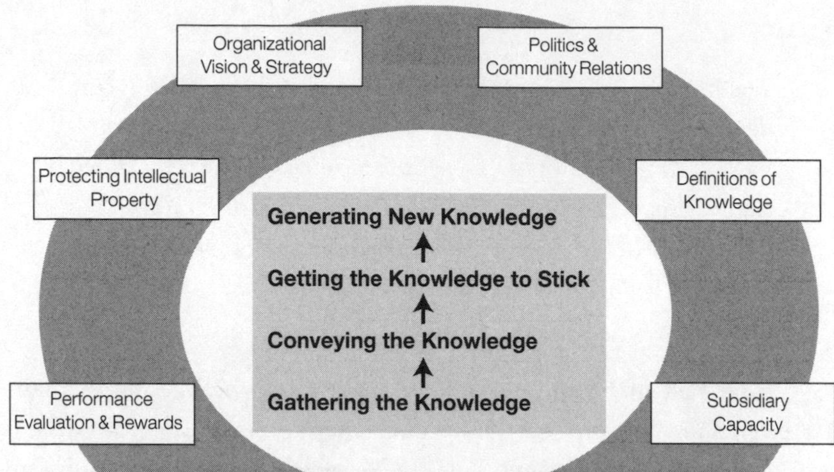

Employees who are inspired to learn and then to generate new knowledge themselves will soon find ways to contribute to the company as a whole. There should be a willingness to allow fresh knowledge to flow in all directions—from any country to other locations. In this way, global organizations can be continually renewed and enriched by the exchange of ideas, information, and enthusiasm between their people around the world.

Transferring Knowledge

SUMMARY AND REVIEW QUESTIONS

1. For each of the countries in which your organization has a presence, what form does your company's knowledge transfer process take? What adjustments, if any, are made to accommodate local priorities and cultural values?

2. In your experience, what is the impact of host-country attitudes toward knowledge brought in from outside their own country? Do these attitudes constitute an advantage or a disadvantage to knowledge transfer in the situations that you're familiar with?

3. What approach would you take to deal with the anxiety that can arise among workers when they are aware that their knowledge is being transferred from them to a new location?

4. In what way do you go about fostering accountability for growing new knowledge within your organization? What steps would you take to strengthen employees' sense of responsibility and ownership if the cultural setting of a subsidiary does not appear to support it?

5. How does your organization leverage the areas listed below to create "pull" from locations abroad for new information and ways of doing things?

    - Organizational vision and strategy
    - Politics and community relations
    - Definitions of knowledge
    - Subsidiary capacity
    - Personal trust and relationships
    - Information technology systems
    - Performance evaluation and rewards

6. Does knowledge in your company flow mainly from headquarters to subsidiaries, or are employees able and willing to contribute their knowledge to the global organization regardless of their location?

CHAPTER ELEVEN

Innovating

To succeed at innovating, managers and employees must successfully carry out a sequence of actions that begins with the generation of ideas, turns these ideas into substantive products, services, or workplace improvements, and culminates with their implementation or commercialization. *Growing ideas* means bringing together a variety of contributing factors across borders of all kinds, including national boundaries.

Skill #11: Innovating

The Korean case introduced briefly in chapter 1 illustrates the difficulties involved in creating a full-blown innovation system. Here is a more complete description of the company's innovation effort.

Organizing for Innovation

A Korean electronics enterprise was determined to grow beyond its traditional status as a "fast follower," or copier of other companies' innovations, and become a breakthrough innovator itself. It engaged expensive foreign consulting firms and examined overseas benchmark organizations. Based on this input, the company created a new set of values that emphasized innovation. It also modified its organizational structure to move away from the traditional, pyramid-shaped hierarchy to focus more on flexible, egalitarian project teams. Former divisional heads were freshly anointed as team leaders, and all managers were encouraged to work with their employees in a way that enabled innovative ideas to "bubble up" from the lower levels of the organization.

Entrenched management habits, however, refuse to die easily. Team leaders did not change their stripes overnight and still frequently resorted to a top-down, command-and-control style of leadership focused on short-term results. The new "coaching" practices that the company was encouraging managers to adopt in order to elicit more active employee participation did not take root immediately either. Managers were accustomed to telling employees what to do and found it difficult to draw out employee thinking and encourage subordinates to make their own choices.

High-potential employees who could potentially become spark plugs for innovative activity noted that the new structure still offered very limited support for people to shoulder the risks involved in promoting new technologies. There were also severe career consequences for those who participated in unsuccessful projects, however creative the original idea might have been. Opportunities for foreign employees in overseas subsidiaries were even more restricted—they typically noted that managers dispatched from headquarters used an autocratic management style incompatible with innovation. The result was high turnover among the most ambitious and assertive overseas R&D and manufacturing personnel.

The more fluid organizational structure that the company envisioned turned out to be very difficult to put into practice. A number of people, both at headquarters and overseas, began to take a skeptical view about the commitment of top leadership to the new structure, calling the supposed transformation a change in name only.

This company's innovation drive is admirable and undertaken with the best of intentions. Its prospects for real success in growing ideas are questionable, however, without further changes; company leaders have not yet orchestrated a complete alignment of the major factors that contribute to innovation.

Official corporate values and managerial titles have been altered, and top executives extol the virtues of innovation, but company-wide management practices that embody a more traditional set of hierarchical values remain in place. It is easier to tell subordinates what to do than to acquire new skills for drawing out their ideas, especially when a manager's entire career and prior military experience (all Korean men serve an obligatory term in the military) have been based on a command-and-control model. A major investment of resources and energy is still required to transform the mind-set of middle managers and to provide them with a concrete set of skills for promoting innovation.

Another aspect of the case described above is that individuals are being encouraged to take risks, but the company's organizational systems do not yet reward innovative risk-taking behaviors. In fact, the failure even of well-conceived projects continues to result in career derailment and other forms of punishment. Without new organizational systems that both provide incentives and minimize disincentives, it is hard to imagine that employees will push for promising but untested ideas or volunteer for risky projects. Foreign employees are even less enamored with the company's innovation drive than workers at headquarters, pointing to what they see as blatant contradictions between rhetoric touting innovation and their own degree of decision-making latitude or the kinds of directives that come from headquarters.

Innovation and Alignment

Factors that affect innovation include individual behaviors, teamwork, management practices, organizational systems, and organizational culture, along with methods for partnering effectively with customers. The more these different factors are orchestrated or aligned to foster innovation, the better the chances that a good idea will be transformed into reality. And each level of activity must be able to support any step in the innovation sequence from invention to product development to commercialization. An environment in which innovation is cultivated at all levels and at every stage acts like a greenhouse—new ideas germinate and bear fruit far more quickly than they would in a location where even fertile seeds fall on dry ground. Figure 18 displays key features of an innovative climate.

Meaningful results will emerge for the Korean firm only when it aligns management practices, organizational systems, and other key forms of support at every level and every stage of the innovation process to support its new emphasis on breakthrough innovation. So long as

Figure 18. **Innovation: Growing Ideas**

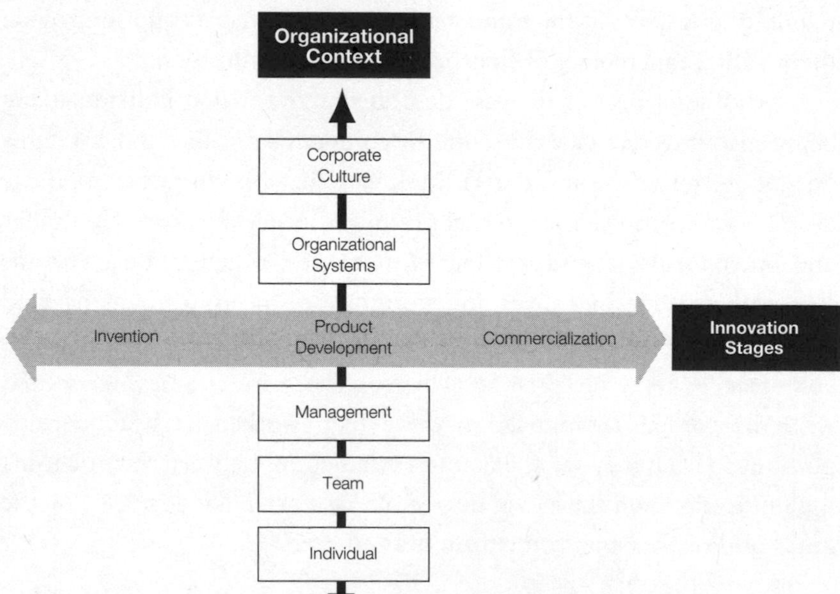

executive pronouncements are perceived as being in conflict with what occurs on an everyday basis, there is a danger that increasing employee skepticism will overwhelm the attempts of top executives to bring about such a change.

Translating Alignment Across Borders

How can a supportive alignment achieved in one environment be transmitted effectively across borders? When innovation actually does begin to flourish, conveying this delicate balance to other environments becomes a new challenge. Each feature of the diagram in figure 18 has a cross-border dimension to it. Individuals may find themselves more or less free to contribute to innovation based on their location in one cultural setting or another. Teamwork, management practices, and organizational systems vary between countries. Likewise, an innovative corporate culture will permeate a company's operations around the world to varying degrees. Successive steps in the innovative process—invention, product development, and commercialization—must often be implemented across cultural and national boundary lines. And customer relations of all kinds are influenced by national culture as well.

The paradoxes inherent in innovative activities become even harder to manage when employees are working across multiple cultures and sets of capabilities. For example, it is not easy to balance the simultaneous need for the freedom to generate new ideas as well as discipline and structure to ensure that the best ideas are selected and implemented. A state of balance achieved in one environment may be dysfunctional in another. And an organization that is trying to move upstream from copycat activities to breakthrough innovation naturally has to shift in the direction of generating more ideas internally and turning them into new products. This in turn may make it necessary to change the roles of some overseas employees from implementers to creative partners.

The Korean company above is struggling in part because of its very effort to import a model of innovative activity based on overseas benchmarks. A foreign recipe for innovation will not necessarily fit its own particular history and circumstances. Indeed, the drive for greater "innovation" might ironically become a subtler and less productive version of the company's established pattern of reengineering overseas technologies. A fresh state of alignment must be achieved that takes into account past practices (including previous successes) while also drawing out future potential. It may be necessary to create brand-new innovative practices along the way that work within its distinctive context. Breakthrough innovation is not a copycat activity, but rather must come from the guts and life experience of the innovators themselves.

Western firms have as much trouble as companies from Korea or anywhere else in finding a formula for innovation that works well in different environments. Table 26 lists behaviors that Western companies commonly associate with innovation and problems that come up as they seek to transplant these into their subsidiaries abroad.[1]

The social values that underlie obstacles such as those listed in the table's right-hand column are not always antithetical to innovative activity. In some cases they could in fact be conducive to types of innovation that are less well known or celebrated in Western business literature. For example, even though hierarchical distance is viewed as an obstacle to innovation in places where employees come to work in T-shirts and address each other on a first-name basis, breakthrough inventions have occurred through the actions of farsighted senior executives in more hierarchical environments. A respected manager might actually order subordinates to invent a new product—even when they at first believe it to be impossible—and commit both the resources and a voice of authority that make a breakthrough innovation possible.[2]

Innovation: Key Cross-Border Issues

In addition to the obstacles described above, there are several basic organizational issues that are at the core of almost any effort to grow ideas across borders. These issues, too, are exacerbated by cultural differences and must be addressed before effective global innovation can take place.

- **Incorporating requirements of global customers into new products and services.** When the starting point of innovation is a company's home country, there is a natural tendency to place the interests and concerns of domestic customers above those of customers abroad.

Table 26. **Global Innovation: Common Obstacles**

Innovative Behaviors	Possible Cultural Obstacles
Individual Innovation • Employees readily generate and contribute new ideas • Employees are open to innovative ideas from others • Employees actively seek out fresh information, input, or approaches to stimulate creativity	• A junior employee with a good idea finds it difficult to speak up in the presence of his or her elders • Senior employees or managers are not receptive to new ideas from younger workers, who must serve long apprenticeships before their ideas are taken seriously • Foreign sources of information are disregarded due to national pride or perceived value conflicts
Team Innovation • Team members are able to think and brainstorm together to generate a rich supply of new ideas • Teams move new concepts forward through rapid creation of prototype versions and learning through trial and error • Teams effectively utilize the diverse skill sets of different members	• Brainstorming is viewed as irresponsible speculation • Rapid prototyping is avoided in favor of meticulous planning to minimize the risk of failure • A majority group on the team ostracizes other team members who violate the group's cultural norms
Management Practices • Managers support employees who take reasonable and informed risks to generate new business • Managers utilize setbacks constructively to promote individual and organizational learning • Managers challenge employees to stretch their innovative capabilities	• Managers who have been trained to value stability and security actively discourage risk taking by their subordinates • Failures or setbacks are punished and held up as examples of why risks should be avoided • Future goals are determined by past performance; employees who conform to existing norms are rewarded

Table 26. **Global Innovation: Common Obstacles (continued)**

Innovative Behaviors	Possible Culture Obstacles
Organizational Systems • The company deliberately seeks to hire individuals on the basis of their potential as innovators • The contribution to innovation made by an employee or manager is an important criterion in evaluating overall performance • The company is able to introduce new innovations even when they threaten established business lines	• Employees are recruited based on family connections, social status, or personal character traits unrelated to innovation • Performance evaluation and compensation are based on seniority or political affiliation • Collectivist thought and behavior strongly support established business lines and punish maverick behaviors; religious beliefs reinforce a fatalistic acceptance of existing circumstances
Innovation Culture • The organization's basic values encourage innovative activity • The actions of organizational leaders make it clear that innovation is a priority • Informal contacts between individuals across organizational lines help to bring innovative solutions to customer issues	• Company values stress employment security, national service, or other values not necessarily related to innovation • Organizational leaders ignore innovation and focus on maximizing their personal wealth or political connections; business is won through corruption rather than through innovation • A professional "guild" mentality or militant union activity makes cooperation difficult
Customer Relations • Innovation is based on careful listening and analysis of customer requirements • Innovation is based on observation and insight into unarticulated customer needs • Product development groups partner with customers who are lead users to observe and identify fresh marketplace trends	• Vendors cater to relatively minor or piecemeal customer requests while failing to focus resources on breakthrough technologies • Employees who are reluctant to question customer statements take their demands at face value and miss important opportunities • Customers make one-way demands on vendors and lose chances for more synergistic partnerships

Such an arrangement may be effective so long as the percentage of overseas sales is small or in cases where a company provides products or services that customers in other locations accept with little modification. However, as foreign markets become more important, it becomes increasingly necessary to incorporate the requirements of nondomestic customers early in the design process.

- **Enabling employees from any location to push back when they believe that new ideas or initiatives will not work in their business environment.** Employees abroad frequently do not feel they have the option to reject a new product or service that is unsuited to their business environment. Their reluctance to oppose headquarters' directives is reinforced by language gaps or culturally based differences in persuasion methods. The result can be a tremendous waste of resources when a new product is introduced to local consumers who find it undesirable or even insulting.

- **Helping co-workers of other nationalities to build their own innovation capabilities.** Employees working at newer operations abroad normally have limited technical depth or experience, which makes it difficult for them to create ground-breaking inventions or convert these into commercial products. Moreover, R&D personnel based at headquarters or in the home country of an organization face a natural conflict of interest. The more they help their counterparts abroad to build their innovative capabilities, the greater the likelihood that the company will transfer vital functions and resources to those locations.

- **Balancing global and local innovation priorities.** As employees around the world become more capable, an organization can face a chaotic innovation bazaar where everyone struggles to acquire limited investment resources to fund the development of products or services for their own local markets. Cross-border integration of innovative projects is vital to identify and implement common strategic priorities. Just as headquarters personnel need to open their eyes to the requirements and potential of markets around the world, employees elsewhere must be able to both champion the cause of local customers and look for ways to create innovative solutions that are applicable to multiple markets. In some cases, subsidiary employees should be prepared to take the lead on global projects when they have the appropriate skills and experience.

Global Innovation: Recommendations

Although there is no silver bullet that suddenly makes innovation happen smoothly, there are a number of useful ways to upgrade the quality and tempo of cross-border collaboration in order to nourish new ideas on a global scale.

Improving communication and personal networks.

Headquarters employees must learn skills for drawing out the views of others, while overseas personnel must acquire the skills, confidence, and sense of empowerment that emboldens them to represent local customer needs. These measures are easier to describe than to implement. For people located at headquarters, pride and attachment to assumptions and behaviors that have been successful at home make it difficult to really hear the voices of counterparts abroad. For those counterparts, ingrained patterns of deferring to authority and the departure of frustrated rebels stunt the potential of subsidiaries to become full-fledged innovators. Only companies that make a conscious, systematic practice of cultivating and utilizing input from many locations are able to overcome these barriers.

A broad range of measures is usually necessary to increase cross-border communication and to generate a network of personal contacts that encourages the rapid flow of ideas and information. For instance, companies may choose to

- Send headquarters researchers out to visit or live near overseas customers

- Bring overseas technical personnel to headquarters research facilities to incorporate their perspectives and to help them learn what technical resources are available

- Tap former expatriates with strong networks abroad to coordinate global projects
- Relocate or build research and development facilities closer to key global customers
- Upgrade technical capabilities to enable more effective and regular exchanges of information through videoconferences, computer networks, and other forms of virtual communication

The cumulative effect of these actions is to create a global web of innovative employees whose contacts are enhanced by personal trust and friendship, common awareness of available resources, readiness to share new information, and eager exchanges of ideas that grow quickly beyond the value brought by any individual contributor.

Building a shared culture of innovation.

Many of the obstacles to innovation noted in table 26 are due in part to familiar cultural value contrasts: individual/group, equality/hierarchy, security/risk taking, and so on. When employees are repeatedly exposed over time to a consistent set of corporate culture values, they gradually take on new perspectives that modify or depart from local norms. The acculturation process for subsidiary employees begins with recruiting, in which only a small subset of the local population applies for jobs with a foreign employer and an even smaller group is selected. Training and development opportunities shape their behaviors, values, and assumptions, as do organizational systems such as compensation or promotion practices. Global and local executives serve as role models on a day-to-day basis, providing employees with cues as to how they should behave. Each of these conditioning methods can be utilized for the purpose of instilling a distinctive set of innovative practices that company members share with their colleagues around the world.

There are hazards to the acculturation process as well. Subsidiary workers might become so far removed from the needs of local customers that they become ineffective in their own country. Polarizing conflicts that pit the national interests of one subsidiary against another or against headquarters also undermine common corporate culture values and

Figure 19. **Five Steps to Innovation**

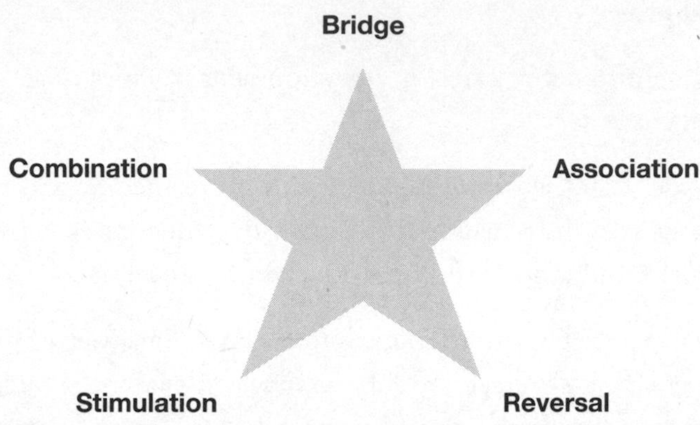

reinforce differences. This is most likely to happen when the acculturation process is rushed or turns out to mean a one-sided imposition of headquarters values on other countries. The ideal outcome of a more gradual process of mutual accommodation, on the other hand, is a growing population of employees who are conscious of both corporate and national values and are able to mediate effectively between them, serving as innovators themselves and introducing innovations from abroad.

Embracing the "Other."

Contact with other people, ideas, markets, and customers provides fertile soil for innovative leaps, and companies can benefit from instilling this principle in the minds of their employees. A range of actions is required to make the embrace of strange and unusual sources of innovation a corporate habit. These include symbolic events, well-publicized revisions of corporate values, and the creation of formal and informal systems that bring a diverse range of individuals together.

Figure 19 depicts some of the ways that innovative ideas are born. Such ideas might appear through the building of a "bridge," or an extension of previous ideas (e.g., an existing laptop is made even smaller and lighter through miniaturization). Innovation also occurs by "association" when a practice in one area is applied productively to a different area (e.g., flat computer screen technology is modified to create flat television screens). "Reversal" means that a problem is solved by viewing it from a completely different perspective (e.g., the problem of increasing computer battery life is solved not by higher-powered batteries but through inventing a film that enables a better-quality display with less power). "Stimulation" is the exploration of ideas from a seemingly different technical discipline that may nonetheless prove helpful (e.g., using materials science to investigate potential ingredients for lighter-weight laptop casing). "Combination" takes place when ideas from such different fields are brought together in the same product.[3]

Every one of these steps toward innovation is facilitated when one has access to a global assortment of colleagues and ideas. "Stimulation" and "combination" in particular occur naturally through contact with foreign technologies and markets. The concept of leveraging diversity is often interpreted narrowly as the inclusion of underprivileged ethnic groups in decision making or management. On a global scale, however, it can be expanded to mean that every possible perspective is brought to bear in creating breakthrough products and services suited to a variety of markets.

Targeting subsidiary activities.

It is important to focus the innovative energies of each subsidiary in a way that is suited to its current capabilities and also leaves it room to grow. Subsidiaries naturally have different degrees of innovative potential according to their size, employee mix, and business objectives. An operation that has been created primarily as a sales outpost is naturally less likely to make a major scientific breakthrough than one that has a substantial R&D facility. But innovation need not be limited to product invention—contributing to the development or commercialization of a product or service could be equally significant in helping a company to meet its business objectives. Depending on the type of subsidiary and its stage of development (see page 260 for an outline of development stages), any of the forms of innovation listed below may be an appropriate place to focus.[4]

Invention.

- **Original inventions.** As companies decentralize their R&D operations and relocate technical resources closer to global customers in key markets, original inventions begin to come from places quite distant from headquarters. Subsidiary researchers might not have all the equipment or the breadth of technical expertise available to headquarters colleagues, but their relative freedom from bureaucratic constraints and the stifling weight of preexisting practices gives them a fresh starting point.

- **Co-design.** When employees in different places have the ability to contribute to a particular new product or service, they may be assigned to work together on a global design team. Providing that the team can overcome communication challenges presented by virtual teamwork, the inclusion of subsidiary employees is typically a source of fresh thinking and better knowledge of global customer needs.
- **Acquisition of technical information.** A number of companies make a very deliberate practice of placing offices in locations where they can gather new technical information and channel it rapidly back to researchers elsewhere. Major benefits also accrue from the actions of individual employees who are sufficiently alert and assertive to notice technical advances and share them with colleagues.

Product development.

- **Concurrent development.** Even when products are invented at headquarters, involving employees abroad in product development efforts from a relatively early stage can enable better fit with local needs, more rapid product introduction, faster local regulatory approval, and a greater return on investment. A simultaneous product introduction in several global markets is more likely to catch competitors off guard and make it more difficult and costly for them to respond.
- **Use of existing technologies.** There are often technologies sitting on the shelf at headquarters than could be turned into viable commercial products in other markets. Subsidiary personnel who have both knowledge of local customer needs and the ability to assess technologies in headquarters laboratories are better positioned than

anyone else in the company to develop these technologies for their own markets. In the best-case scenario, applications of technologies first introduced in foreign markets are then brought back to the firm's domestic-market customers.

- **Product adaptation.** Sometimes relatively small changes in the shape or function of a product based on the input of subsidiary employees suddenly make it far more attractive. Variations of size, weight, or color, for example, may also increase a product's appeal. Subsidiaries with limited technical capabilities can still conceive and implement such changes.

Commercialization.

- **Product packaging.** A new package of products and/or services that incorporates a local language message along with a trusted symbol or logo will probably sell better than one that does not. Several offerings combined in an attractive way may induce consumers to buy a package deal that appears more desirable than the individual items by themselves. Such packaging not only increases the total value but also provides greater protection against imitators, thereby making possible greater profitability over time.

- **Sales and marketing techniques.** Local customers tend to be most responsive to products and sales approaches that incorporate their values, customs, and unique requirements. At the same time, there are sometimes opportunities to introduce foreign products that have appeal precisely because of their foreign image. The difficult task of bringing a new product to market offers ample room for innovative activity. Sales and marketing are worthy areas for innovation because finding the right mix of commercialization methods will garner better results.

Innovating by Globalizing

State-of-the-art innovation leverages globalization to make further innovation possible. The complete package for achieving global competitive advantage is to provide attractive products or services in the world's most profitable markets at the lowest possible cost in a socially responsible way. There are, in fact, a few companies that have managed to do this, achieving the corporate equivalent of hockey's "hat trick" or basketball's "triple double."

One of the best historical illustrations of success at growing ideas through globalization is the Honda Motor Company. Soichiro Honda, the company's founder, was a maverick from the start. In a country known for obedience to authority and conformity, he beat his own path. Japan's all-powerful Ministry of Trade and Industry (MITI) told Mr. Honda to stick to motorcycles and stay out of the automobile business. His indignant reply to the ministry official was, "Why must we do things according to government commands? If MITI officials want us to do as they decree, then they should buy our stock and voice their opinions at the stockholder meetings."[5] Throughout the 1960s and 1970s bland colors were favored by Japanese automakers and many consumers—half or more of all automobiles were white. Fire engine red in particular was considered off limits because of its use by emergency vehicles. Honda again protested: "Among First World nations, not a single one controls the use of color among its citizens.... We'll never be able to produce world-class vehicles unless this ridiculous tradition is repealed." Honda Motor's first automobile was offered in both red and white, and Mr. Honda himself seemed to be obsessed with red clothing.[6]

Honda sidestepped Japanese government control and eventually built his modest motorcycle firm into an automotive power that could compete with domestic giants such as Toyota and Nissan by achieving a string of successes in foreign markets. At first his company exported motorbikes, beginning with the SuperCub. There was talk of concentrating on exports to nearby Southeast Asia first, but the ambitious firm deliberately selected the American market because its executives reasoned that goods accepted there would find markets elsewhere. The SuperCub motorbike, with its light, carefree image and step-through configuration was highly innovative from a technical standpoint, but it did not sell at first due to the public perception at the time that motorbikes were for juvenile delinquents. Through innovative marketing, Honda Motor was able to create a new image and wide consumer acceptance for its products with the advertising slogan "You meet the nicest people on a Honda" and a new chain of dealers that it established rather than going through existing motorcycle dealers.[7]

A further series of daring moves established Honda Motor's pattern of innovation through leveraging global sources of challenge and opportunity. The company entered its cars in Formula I automotive Grand Prix races to build its worldwide reputation and to learn from the act of competition. Mr. Honda was willing to pay high fees to foreign drivers because "They were so eager to win that they made many demands, telling us, for example, that the machine wobbled or the brakes were not effective enough. And such demands raised our own technical standards. Japanese racers were not like that." After numerous failures, the company finally won its first Grand Prix race in 1965 in Mexico City.[8]

On the organizational side, Honda Motor founded American Honda, the first successful Japanese motor vehicle subsidiary in the U.S. It shunned the traditional trading company channel for selling its products because, while less risky, this arrangement would not allow it to provide direct service to American consumers and also learn from them in the process. Honda was the first Japanese company after the war to set up a manufacturing facility in the West, doing so in Belgium as early as 1962. It later led the other Japanese automakers into the U.S., opening a motorcycle factory in Ohio in 1979 and building an automobile plant nearby shortly thereafter.[9]

These pioneering steps in the U.S. market enabled Honda to build an operation that was insulated from so-called voluntary import restrictions and the hazards of shifting exchange rates. The U.S. manufacturing facility was not only successful from a quality standpoint, but also enabled the company to build cars at a lower cost than U.S. rivals because it hired and trained a young, rural workforce. Honda vehicles gradually acquired a reputation among customers in the U.S. and other markets for offering excellent value at a reasonable price.

Rapid growth and competitive experience in the U.S. market have stimulated Honda's expansion elsewhere around the world, including an enviable position throughout Asia. The edge that the firm gained in for-

Figure 20. **Honda Motor: Innovation Through Globalization**

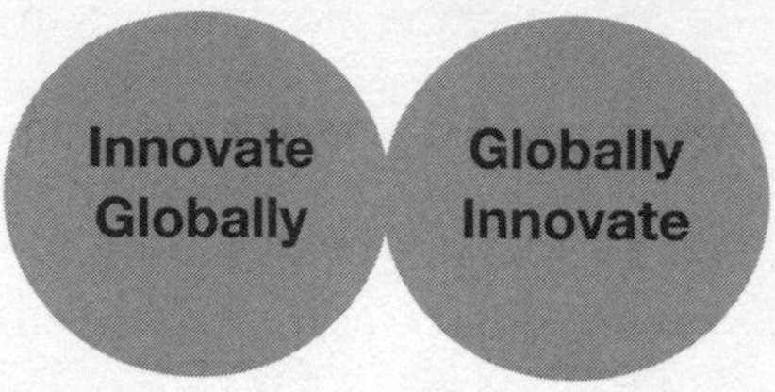

Use Globalization to Spur Innovative Thinking

- Hire foreign race car drivers to learn from their demands
- Learn to compete in the world's toughest markets

Leverage Innovative Products and Services Across Global Markets

- Use the competitive edge gained in tough markets to win around the world
- Import innovations from overseas to surpass domestic competitors

eign markets has also been parlayed into an increasingly formidable domestic position, a far cry from the days when MITI sought to keep Honda from making automobiles on the grounds that the country could not support any additional car companies. Honda has since passed other less adventurous competitors in Japan to become second only to Toyota. It is an extremely lucrative enterprise, with global profits in a recent year that were four times those of GM, the most profitable of the U.S. manufacturers, even though its overall revenues are still much smaller. Figure 20 depicts Honda Motor's dual strategy for growing ideas on a global scale: (1) pushing itself to innovate through exposure to demanding foreign influences; and (2) leveraging innovations rapidly across world markets for profit and competitive advantage.

With respect to environmental issues such as fuel economy that are becoming increasingly prominent, Honda has looked into the future and turned the tables again, taking lessons learned from building fuel-efficient vehicles in energy-poor Japan into other global markets. As early as 1975, Honda's CVCC engine was given top marks by the U.S. National Academy of Sciences. It was reportedly the first engine that met the standards set by the U.S. Clean Air Act.[10] Honda has continued to gain considerable goodwill among consumers and environmentalists over the years for its dedication to high mileage and low emissions. Recently it was the only automobile manufacturer that chose not to oppose a legislative drive in the U.S. to set tougher fuel economy and emission standards. A representative of the Sierra Club, a group not generally inclined to praise automakers, said of Honda, "They have repeatedly led the way on technology.... They started the race for hybrids. They put on vehicles fuel-saving technologies that Detroit only keeps on the shelves."[11]

This innovative combination of globally competitive products built at relatively low cost while providing positive social benefits has allowed the company to move from strength to strength. At the present time Honda Motor is once again turning up the heat on its competitors through a major drive into China. It not only builds more vehicles there than its Japanese rivals, but is also taking the lead in establishing low-cost, high-quality Chinese sources of supply. Honda's China presence has been a major contributing factor in allowing it to introduce new vehicle models at lower cost while actually adding more valuable features, catching many competitors by surprise. Meanwhile, it is investing heavily in research and development, introducing a hybrid version of its popular Civic model, and experimenting with other areas related to energy conservation and environmental protection.

Honda Motor is not the only firm to innovate through globalization combined with deliberate attention to social benefits. Infosys, the Indian provider of IT services, provides another example outlined in the case below.

The Infosys Success Story: Innovation for the Future

Infosys, incorporated in 1981, now has offices in sixteen countries, yearly revenues of over half a billion dollars, and approximately ten thousand employees worldwide. Headquartered in Bangalore, India, it provides low-cost IT outsourcing services to global customers.[12]

While Infosys describes itself as an innovator in "solution definition and engagement delivery,"[13] perhaps its most compelling innovation has been to package an almost irresistible business proposition for customers located overseas:

- Well-trained English-speaking software talent

- The ability to manage large-scale software projects
- Supportive government policies
- Round-the-clock service provided by operations in different time zones
- Costs that are a fraction of those of in-house services or competing outsourcing operations based in the U.S. or Europe[14]

Indeed, Infosys has been a pioneer in the outsourcing revolution that has turned Bangalore into a global business center and has begun to transform India itself. The company's business formula has enabled it to grow rapidly and to convince a large number of customers on the other side of the world to purchase its services—70 percent of its business comes from U.S.-based clients. Narayana Murthy, founder of Infosys, describes his firm as a company built on globalization and claims that even as Infosys expands into other countries such as Japan, the U.S. will remain a primary focus because it is the world's most competitive market and is open to outsiders.[15]

Since the time of its founding Infosys has faced the same twin demands encountered by other firms based in the developing world. On the one hand, it must prove to skeptical corporate buyers, mostly based in the West, that it can provide high-quality, reliable services that will not be subject to political interference or corruption. At the same time, it has to demonstrate to local residents and institutions that it is not simply part of a prosperous elite that exploits cheap labor, but rather a positive force for national development and addressing the gap between rich and poor.

Infosys has done remarkably well on both counts, collecting an impressive array of honors along the way. Part of the company's genius has been to turn potential negatives into attributes that draw new supporters. Infosys has been ranked as "India's Most Respected Company" and as the number-one India-based firm. It has also received high marks for corporate governance among emerging market companies. Another significant award for Infosys is its top ranking in the list of the "Best Employers in India." In the meantime, Infosys Foundation is providing medical facilities in rural areas and programs for orphans. It sponsors a large-scale rural education program that has set up 5,500 libraries in government schools scattered across many villages. Other initiatives include setting up rural science centers and support for traditional Indian art and culture.[16]

It is interesting to see how Mr. Murthy, now chairman of the board at Infosys, positions the use of technology. He is clearly seeking to address questions of international competitiveness and Indian economic development while positioning his own organization as a new sort of global leader. "An export orientation helps Indian enterprises benchmark their products and services on a global scale," he says. "If you succeed in the highly competitive global market, you are likely to provide high-quality products at the best prices even for the domestic market. The tragedy of the Indian consumer is that he has been forced to put up with shoddy quality." Murthy also notes,

> *Technology is a great leveler. It does not distinguish between the rich and the poor. For example, one of my younger colleagues, who is a janitor at Infosys, is extremely happy to use an ATM because it does not discriminate against him—unlike the clerk at the manned bank counter. Further, technology makes services cheaper.... The use of the e-governance paradigm for deployment of inexpensive, efficient, quick, and corruption-free community and public services is another case in point. Information technology can enhance transparency in decision making and, thus, improve the confidence of people in government.*[17]

Infosys, like Honda before it, has prospered through finding innovative ways to enter and prosper in the global marketplace, thereby laying the foundation for further innovation.

Figure 21 depicts the combination of world-class product offerings and tangible social contributions that both Honda and Infosys have been able to forge. Organizations that can make this formula work are the most likely to attract customers, employees, and a well-deserved reputation for global citizenship that will enhance their future prospects in

Figure 21. **Innovation for the Future: The New Global Standard**

World-Class Product

- High quality
- Low price
- Reliable delivery
- Strong corporate governance

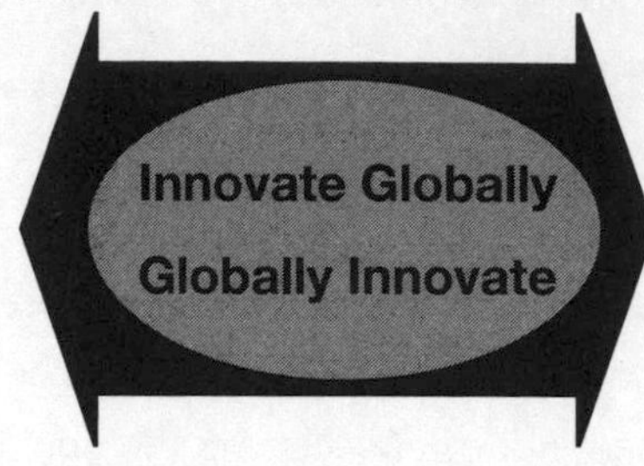

Social Contribution

- Superior employment conditions
- Commitment to develop third-world education and medical facilities
- Anti-corruption measures
- Environmentally friendly products

world markets. In an age of ever more alarming human and environmental crises, the task of growing ideas increasingly means that companies must address universal human issues at the same time they furnish products or services that customers are ready to buy.

Innovating

SUMMARY AND REVIEW QUESTIONS

1. In your opinion, what factors are most crucial to establishing a climate of global innovation within your organization?
2. Have you found obstacles to global or local innovation on any of the following organizational levels?
   - Individual
   - Team
   - Management practices
   - Organizational systems
   - Corporate culture
   - Customer relations
3. Are your company's employees most skillful at invention, product development, or the commercialization of new technologies and services? How could performance be improved across all three of these areas on a global scale?
4. Are the requirements of customers abroad incorporated into new products and services? When push comes to shove, do home-country customer needs always carry the day, or are employees abroad able to make a convincing case for their own customer priorities?
5. Which of the five steps to innovation—"bridge," "association," "reversal," "stimulation," or "combination"—have you seen successfully demonstrated in cross-cultural settings? Are there ways to bring into play your global contacts to increase innovation via these methods?

6. Does each subsidiary within your organization innovate in a way that best fits its particular capabilities? Are subsidiaries encouraged and supported in building their capacity to innovate?

7. Is your company able to grow ideas both by using globalization to spur innovative thinking and by leveraging innovative products and services across global markets?

8. Has your organization learned to make innovative social contributions that enable it to become a welcome participant in any country's economy?

CHAPTER TWELVE

Managing Change

Global companies must embrace change in order to build and sustain competitive advantages that satisfy customers around the world. But attempts to transport change initiatives across borders face numerous barriers due to differences in business and management practices.

Tremendous momentum is required to move new changes forward. Organizations need to develop a shared repertoire of global change management skills along with a positive track record of past transformations that engender goodwill among key stakeholders. This means building partnerships with colleagues abroad who can help to see an initiative through from conception to implementation.

Skill #12: Managing Change

There are many reasons why businesspeople in different countries may welcome change or initiate it themselves. Unfortunately, one of the most frequent scenarios in global business settings is the initiative driven from corporate headquarters that meets with stiff local resistance elsewhere. In the absence of a solid change process, a new strategic direction, manufacturing technology, IT system, or human resources policy is likely to face a long gauntlet of blows from the forces of ingrained habit, suspicion of foreign ways, and culturally based preferences for existing procedures. It is useful to be able to recognize and anticipate common obstacles to change.

Obstacles to Change

The first form of resistance that many global initiatives meet is simply inaction. Overseas operations are insulated by the same barriers that make communication with them so challenging. Distant subsidiaries, affiliates, or partners are less immediately visible to top executives at headquarters, who naturally tend to give them less attention than the pressing demands of home-market customers or employees. Moreover, control mechanisms that companies normally use to reinforce change—budget allocations, hiring or firing of staff, compensation packages—cannot always be exercised abroad in the same way or with the same impact that they would have in the home country.

Employees overseas may, of course, have their own ideas about the best way to run their business. The Chinese saying cited before, "Heaven is high, and the Emperor is far away," applies to many corporations. Expatriates enjoy the relative freedom of action they have abroad, but at the same time they are frustrated by the lack of visibility or attention. Local employees frequently take matters into their own hands, implementing, modifying, or ignoring headquarters initiatives as they see fit. In the case of the newly appointed head of International first mentioned in chapter 1, for instance, the country managers chose to disregard his initial set of directives.

Reasons for not implementing a change agenda are myriad. One is the global version of the "flavor of the month" phenomenon that occurs in companies whose transformation efforts lack consistency. Frequent turnover among key corporate leaders or expatriates often results in flip-flops between different global market strategies, leaving overseas employees weary because they must educate yet another aggressive crop of executives regarding what does or does not work in their country environments. Veteran subsidiary employees will say things like, "The first six months it is best to ignore them because they don't know what they are doing yet." In the meantime they will also study new executives closely for cues that will help determine just how seriously to take them: likely tenure in the position, general competence, clout with top management, consistency of direction, and commitment to learn about the local market. Only when a series of contacts has provided positive indications in response to these silent queries does patient inaction give way to a fresh willingness to risk critical local resources and customer relationships.

Besides inaction, obstacles encountered by change initiatives include determined local resistance or, worse, amusement and derision. Yet another brand of failed change efforts falls under the rubric of the "Living Dead," those multiple layers of half-hearted, overlapping, and contradictory initiatives that employees make a show of doing whenever their foreign bosses appear. Overt compliance for a time with changes imposed from abroad can mask stored-up resentment that finally explodes in emotional conflicts, employee departures, and so on.

My Mistake: Managing Change

I was asked to help with a company president's efforts to achieve greater alignment and teamwork within the organization, starting with his global executive team. The manager who initially contacted me, also a member of that team, noted that business divisions and overseas subsidiaries were frequently going their own way and even competing with each other while neglecting corporate-wide priorities, and that there was too much turnover among the top managers themselves.

The firm was a hi-tech enterprise based in Silicon Valley that had grown quickly, and the president was known for his snap personnel decisions. While his choices of U.S. managers for key positions were often brilliant, when it came to overseas subsidiaries he sometimes either brought in local nationals or dispatched expatriates who were not a good fit. The local nationals were in many cases managers with prior international background who caught his eye and talked a good game but who did not have the necessary experience to build up local operations or to have much credibility with employees from their own country. Expatriates included people who had impressive professional credentials but little or no knowledge of the countries or markets they were supposed to serve.

As I began to speak with members of the executive team, it became evident that there was a good deal of fear—this was directed not only toward the president, but also to the manager who was my contact. Both the president and his assistant were ultra–type A personalities who were highly demanding and verbally harsh with subordinates. There was, I heard, a tendency to bring in new people, build them up as the solution to the organization's global business challenges, and then eventually blame these former heroes and cast them out of the organization when issues remained unresolved. As a result, the company was at a standstill in a number of country markets, with executive turnover making it difficult to execute a consistent strategy, while those who remained were afraid to seize the initiative. One person I spoke with pointed out sardonically, "You have been brought in with the same type of fanfare as those other guys!"

I did not grasp quickly enough that the tendency of unhealthy organizations to create scapegoats for their problems had been recast here on a global scale against a backdrop of real global business and personnel challenges. Ultimately I failed to get either the president or his chief aide to reflect on this lethal and originally homegrown pattern, instead becoming more fodder for it myself. Meanwhile, local employees around the world continued to suffer from lack of steady direction, and business outside the U.S. remained stalled.

The "Foreign Capital Company Syndrome."

Perhaps the most common pitfall for cross-border change efforts could be labeled the "Foreign Capital Company Syndrome," a negative cycle of misunderstanding and misguided efforts.

- Well-intentioned "global" initiatives are rolled out from company headquarters, only to encounter limited local capabilities within smaller and less mature subsidiary operations
- Headquarters or its expatriate representatives exert strong verbal pressure to cooperate and to get in step with the global program
- Opposing views from subsidiary employees often appear irrational due to the lack of language skills or an inability to make what headquarters would regard as a strong business case
- These local views are therefore ultimately brushed aside in favor of forceful directives to go ahead as planned
- Under such circumstances, even those local employees who struggle to comply act without gusto, and many harbor the quiet hope that the headquarters initiative will fall on its face because their own views have been disregarded and overridden; some might take actions they view as appropriate that are nonetheless at cross-purposes with headquarters' strategic intent
- Frustrated headquarters representatives ultimately sniff out this lack of wholehearted commitment or compliance and confront local employees
- These employees, who are in no position to offer effective resistance, resign themselves to following instructions, and are less inclined to offer their own frank views next time around (there may be those who literally resign from the organization as well)
- This unproductive stalemate naturally leads to poor business results, which can become the impetus for the next major initiative from headquarters, and the cycle is repeated

Figure 22. **The Foreign Capital Company Syndrome**

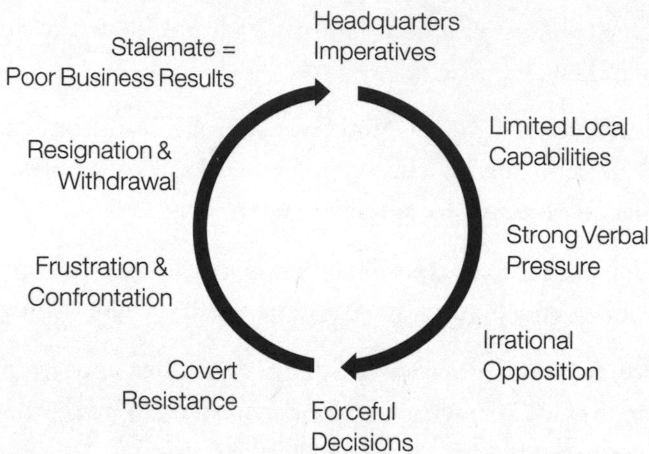

Figure 22 provides a visual representation of the cycle—these are the standard symptoms of a dysfunctional partnership.

It is possible to arrest the cycle at any point, but this is particularly difficult in the case of cross-border transactions. The overlapping obstacles of time, distance, unfamiliar business practices, wishful thinking, and organizational inertia all contribute. Companies must make a concerted effort to develop the full menu of global people skills that will enable them to reverse the descent into this hellish and costly cycle. The shift is a bit like getting all the swimmers in a pool to reverse direction and move the current in the opposite way, although not nearly as easy to accomplish. The alternative, however, is a destructive whirlpool that ultimately drowns corporate resources, individual careers, and once-promising business prospects. Problems can begin innocently enough with someone who is just trying to get an important job done, as demonstrated in the following example.

The Software Rollout (A)

Michael is managing the worldwide rollout of a new software product from the west coast of the U.S. He's speaking via conference call with several colleagues from the European region: Paulette in Paris, Manfred in Stüttgart, and Giulio in Milan. We join the conversation about ten minutes into the call...

Michael: *So we'll begin the upgrade rollout by September 1, right...? Paulette, you'll introduce it to the European partners. And Manfred and Giulio, you'll work with her on that?*

Paulette: *Well, Michael, honestly I don't know how well this is going to work. We have a few other commitments between now and then...*

Michael: *You know that top management has agreed on this and has given us a two-months deadline, right?*

Paulette: *Yes, I know that, but I'm not sure that everyone here thinks that this should be the top priority at this time.*

Michael: *Paulette, you know we have to deliver this on time. I'm counting on your group to do this... Giulio, what do you think?*

Giulio: *Well, yes, it may be possible, but we don't really know the people in the Paris office well, and many of our people are already committed to other projects...*

Michael: *Okay...okay, but you understand what we're up against, right? My group has five main business objectives for this year, and this one is a top priority for us to be able to increase our customer service marks. Our target is to increase customer satisfaction rates by 10 percent within the next three quarters, and this project is a key component of that plan.*

Giulio: *But here it may be difficult to get the necessary buy-in from our local management.*

Michael: [Showing a little frustration.] *Look guys, this is one of our top global priorities.*

[After a pause in the conversation...]

Manfred: *Michael, I think we understand you are saying this is a top priority for you. But we have limited staff here and it won't be easy to* *get our management to agree to allocate resources to do this in the time frame you want.*

Michael: [Getting exasperated.] *Look, this has nothing to do with me! This is a mandate from senior management.*

Manfred: *Has it been discussed with the European Operating Committee?*

Michael: [Trying to calm down a bit.] *This priority was established by top management, and it was announced last month. I know you all got that message, and your management got the same message. My boss is pushing me to deliver within the two-month time frame that's been established. So, has it been discussed? Well, I don't know, but at some level, there's not a whole lot to talk about. It needs to be done, we've decided to do it, and I've been asked to get it done. So, now I'm asking you to help me take the ball and get moving.*

Paulette: [After another pause in the conversation.] *Well, Michael, we'll check with our people here and get back to you.*

Michael: *It's fine to check with your people, but you need to find a way to do this soon. I don't see that we have a choice.*

Comments

Michael interprets the somewhat indirect objections of his European counterparts in this conference call to mean that there is room for his personal persuasive powers to make a difference. In fact, from their point of view, the project is not feasible within the allotted time frame given current resource commitments and lack of sufficient buy-in from their local management. They are trying to get this point across to him without having to spell it out too bluntly, and Michael's escalation of the issue in this forum is not helpful.

Michael is attempting to launch the project over the telephone, but for many people this is not likely to be the best approach (see pp. 102–5 for more on virtual communication). When project participants do not know each other well, and if there are different levels of hierarchy on the call and thus differing expectations for the degree of allowable "push-back," a phone call often does not allow sufficient latitude to ensure open and clear discussion of relevant issues.

It also appears that the European side feels that there has not yet been sufficient communication of the priority of this task by the appropriate people at headquarters to the appropriate management personnel in Europe. As an "empowered" individual, Michael does not understand why this should be a stumbling block. He does not place the same value on introducing ideas through proper channels as do his European colleagues.

The Software Rollout (B)

Following are four follow-up e-mails sent after the conference call.

1. E-mail from Michael to Paulette (cc: Manfred and Giulio)

Paulette: As we discussed, I'm sending you the rollout plan with milestones and deadlines attached. I know it's going to be tight but I'm sure we can do this. Please review the attachment and get back to me to confirm the action items and time frame.

2. Response by Paulette to Michael

Michael: I think we can do part 1, although it will take 2–3 weeks longer than you suggest. Part 2 will be more of a problem. We think that the tasks that you lay out are difficult for us to do without more resources. In addition to other commitments, several of our people will be away over the next few weeks...

3. Response by Michael to Paulette (cc: Manfred and Giulio)

Paulette: I'm glad you'll be proceeding with part 1, but I don't understand why you say part 2 is not doable in the specified time frame. We've got to keep on track in order to get all this done in two months.

4. Auto-response from Paulette

Paulette is out of the office until August 31. If this is urgent, please contact Christophe at....

Michael's *headquarters imperatives* are met with *limited local capabilities* due to resource constraints and previous commitments of the European team. He uses *strong verbal pressure* to get the European team to agree to his timetable and encounters what he perceives to be *irrational opposition.* He tries making *forceful decisions* but runs into *covert resistance* from the Europeans. Over time this will certainly lead to increased *frustration* and ultimately *confrontation.* If European team members are finally coerced into full compliance, the next step would likely be an attitude of *resignation and withdrawal* on their part, which, of course, will produce a slow-moving *stalemate* and failure to meet the original project deadlines (*poor business results*). Table 27 reiterates this nine-step progression in chart form.

Cross-Border Change Management: Recommendations

Change management is a complex skill that is very much based on all the other people skills covered in this volume. Some of the most spectacular failures of cross-border change efforts can be traced to the failure of would-be change agents to establish credibility, obtain accurate information from distant locations, select the right people to drive the project, or lay the proper foundations for productive team interactions.

The problems that the project leader experiences in the software rollout case above, for example, could be examined at the group level, applying the analytical framework for global team issues introduced in chapter 5. Michael, the project leader, and other team members need to adjust their communication styles during virtual meetings to convey important messages to each other more accurately. The team could explore modes of communication other than teleconferences and e-mail. Discussing team systems such as how decisions are made or the roles and responsibilities of each team member might help team members to achieve greater clarity about who ought to be doing what and why. If the team were able to engage in a constructive discussion of competing

Table 27. **The Foreign Capital Company Syndrome: An Example**

Headquarters imperatives	The cycle begins when headquarters gives a mandate to a "global manager" without fully considering local or regional circumstances
Limited local capabilities	Local offices respond that technical capabilities, staff, training, and/or budget are limited
Strong verbal pressure	Headquarters responds with pressure and insists the goals be met (often using the expression "Just get it done")
"Irrational" opposition	Local offices present arguments that headquarters perceives as irrational or inappropriate
Forceful decisions	Headquarters responds with more pressure to get going (often using statements like "Stop being irrational")
Covert resistance	Local offices begin to resist, sometimes ignoring calls or by avoiding e-mail messages
Frustration and confrontation	Headquarters becomes more confrontational with the local office to force them to meet the goals that have been set
Resignation and withdrawal	The local offices reluctantly agree to do the work, but complete it poorly or past deadlines
Stalemate: poor business results	Objectives are not achieved, and the team dynamic becomes still more fractured. Employees carry negative feelings over into future dealings with headquarters

national interests and priorities, this would also assist them in better understanding their situation.

However, improved team practices or other people skills of the kind discussed thus far would not be enough by themselves in this case. The fundamental problem here is that the software rollout process is being rammed down the throats of employees in other countries without their buy-in. The negative "syndrome" of fruitless discussions, imposed change, and covert resistance is beginning to take shape. Michael, the project leader, is set up to fail because he has been given a two-months deadline and told to accomplish the rollout together with other people who have competing priorities. Without real agreement between headquarters and local management at each site, even the most well-intentioned global team members will be hard-pressed to remain on friendly terms for very long. Conflicting management pressures will become a wedge that drives them apart.

In this case, the company has to manage change at a level that goes beyond the project leader or the team. A major new product introduction brings with it far-reaching consequences: repositioning of people and financial investments, higher skill requirements, and delicate transitions with customers. At the same time, it also renders previous products, activities, and even employees themselves obsolete. All of these are significant changes that can give rise to resistance and misaligned management directives, especially when they occur across different languages, nationalities, and time zones. What is required for the software rollout to succeed is a change process that starts with at least some degree of input and informed consent from top management at every location where the software is being introduced. Such initial agreement is just one step along the way to building a true partnership for change that makes it possible for executives and employees at each global location to finally assume ownership.

Ten steps for handling change.

Change initiatives come in many shapes and sizes. Here is a general set of steps for introducing change across borders that has worked well in various settings:

1. **Create a project team that includes strong local leadership.** This builds a sense of accountability from the start of the project. Too many change initiatives founder because they are already partly or fully formed before overseas employees even hear about them. In the optimal situation, leaders from sites where the project will be implemented should have a role in shaping the original content and direction of the change effort.

2. **Review the current systems that are in place in the host-country organization and identify positive elements that can and should be preserved.** Another goal is to acknowledge and preserve local strengths. If these are ignored, defensive mechanisms kick in as employees try to preserve aspects of their current operation that they value and have worked hard to create. On the other hand, when a local practice that is a point of pride can be incorporated and perhaps expanded upon, it becomes a powerful source of support and enthusiasm among participants.

3. **Carry out a needs assessment among key local stakeholders; include internal and external customer groups in the planning process.** Broadening the number of people involved makes the change process more complicated, but it is the best way to create a base of support that goes beyond the planning team, as well as greater long-run commitment to implementing the new system.

4. **Benchmark local and overseas models, including parent company systems.** Taking the team outside the company to look at what other organizations are doing helps to give employees new points of reference. It is as valuable for engendering more flexible thinking on the part of planning team members as it is for obtaining specific "best practices" or implementation ideas. Often, other local firms are implementing a surprising number of changes that employees will regard as a more meaningful precedent than anything that is happening abroad. Having such information also enables them to go back and convince their peers that change is indeed warranted. Depending on the nature of the initiative, positioning headquarters practices as a point of reference rather than an obligatory template often makes the change process easier to swallow.

5. **Analyze related organizational systems to identify opportunities to reinforce primary objectives.** This is a good organization development principle that applies in global contexts as well as domestic ones. If a new process or system can be integrated with, or supported by, other systems—for example, objective setting, budget planning, measuring business results, hiring, job rotation, compen-

sation—the chances are better that it will not be rejected by the immune system of the receiving organization.

6. **Plan the new process or system together.** Changes must be planned in a way that includes both knowledge of new practices and knowledge of the local business setting. However attractive the best practices of other firms might be, program elements must be combined in such a way that a real fit with the existing subsidiary environment is achieved. Involvement in the planning process brings other benefits as well. Employees may willingly adopt more from the parent company and be more determined to implement it if they feel they have a choice in the matter.

7. **Hold periodic meetings with the local executive team and other stakeholders to report progress and to gain support for next steps.** Keeping important stakeholders informed continues to broaden the base of support and ensures that there are no negative surprises. Along the way this can create a wave of support for the change effort so that it becomes a familiar and inevitable part of the local landscape rather than an imposition from abroad.

8. **Use pilot programs to introduce the change; review and revise based on pilot program results.** It is wise to inoculate everyone involved from the beginning with the idea that there will be problems and temporary setbacks along the way. Pilot programs engage local talent in improving and adapting rather than criticizing and resisting; they also reduce the risk of failure by containing initial problems within the boundaries of the experiment.

9. **Hand off responsibilities through a step-by-step process to a local team for ongoing implementation.** Some continuing involvement from overseas personnel may be necessary, but real change is more likely when committed local employees assume the tasks involved in driving it home. A new level of responsibility and capability comes from figuring out what to do and carrying it out rather than doing what we are told. Transferring tasks step by step ensures that the employees who are taking on different roles have the confidence and skills to fulfill them.

10. **Utilize people and lessons learned from previous change efforts to jump-start new projects.** Turning members of a previous planning team into change agents for the next initiative enables people to complete the journey from skeptic to advocate. A local employee who can point to a track record of success and ask his or her counterparts to cooperate in the next change initiative will usually be far more convincing than anyone from headquarters.

This list represents an ideal process, and not all the steps are necessary or advisable with every change effort. Frequently there are limitations—real or imagined—of time, resources, or personnel. In the software example, where none of these steps were taken, the first one would have been the most important. Subsidiary leadership was not consulted or brought on board from the beginning. When local representatives finally became part of the rollout team, their roles were compromised due to their own managers' lack of support for the project, and they were not positioned hierarchically to make decisions about the reallocation of subsidiary resources.

The dictum "slow start, fast finish" applies to most global change initiatives, with "fast start, slow and agonizing failure" being a common alternative. The software project leader, who is off to a fast start, appears doomed to spend many long hours spinning his wheels, generating unnecessary resentment among his counterparts and failing to accomplish his goals. He needs to back up and work with his own management to put the right fundamentals in place instead of lunging eagerly ahead. It is instructive to consider a case where the proper steps were taken from the beginning.

A Success Story: Transforming Human Resources at Sumitomo 3M

Tak Kaneko is a veteran 3M employee who works at the company's joint venture operation in Japan, Sumitomo 3M. About six years ago, after serving as the head of the finance department at Sumitomo 3M, Kaneko-san was asked to come to St. Paul in the U.S. as an expatriate. He was selected to be groomed for even greater responsibilities based on his years of experience, broad thinking, and clout with the Japan management team. During his time in St. Paul, he held the top finance position for 3M's Asia-Pacific region. This job took him on long trips through the region together with top 3M executives, giving them plenty of opportunities to get to know each other well and to exchange views on a variety of subjects.

After several years based in St. Paul, Kaneko-san was asked to consider an assignment as the new head of Sumitomo 3M's human resources function. This was a job he had expressed interest in during prior conversations, so the prospective assignment was not a surprise. Indeed, he was excited about it because he felt it offered an opportunity to transform the corporate culture of the organization into a more dynamic work setting. The existing environment in Sumitomo 3M at that time was still structured along traditional Japanese lines, complete with the usual elements of lifetime employment, promotion by seniority, and a company union. Sumitomo 3M as a whole, while consistently profitable, was trying to better leverage its talented R&D force of more than five hundred scientists to accelerate the pace of innovation and business growth. It was also seeking to achieve greater operating efficiencies to offset cost disadvantages relative to other Asian countries, particularly China.

Once Kaneko-san had accepted the challenge of taking on the HR role, his last six months in St. Paul went by quickly. He was sent to an executive program for human resources professionals and also invited to participate in a series of programs put on by a local university for the 3M human resources community. Colleagues in St. Paul rapidly introduced him to a rich network of internal 3M HR contacts that he could draw upon for deeper, more specialized conversations. Some of them he already knew based on his many years of experience with the company. He spoke not only with people in the U.S. but also with veteran European HR personnel who had experience trying to blend elements of the European and U.S. systems.

In the meantime, Kaneko-san began to map out a transformation of the Japan HR function. This process took place through an intense series of consultations with stakeholders in both Japan and the U.S. Kaneko-san's planning process incorporated ideas gathered from in-depth interviews with more than 120 key Sumitomo 3M employees from all levels of the company over the previous five years, advice from executive peers, change management principles gleaned from his crash course in the U.S., and his own aspirations for the organization. Each new draft of the plan involved more back and forth between colleagues in Japan and the U.S.

Kaneko-san soon started to discuss and lobby various possibilities with a broader set of senior managers in Japan as well as top management in the U.S. He was given remarkable freedom and latitude in most areas by 3M's top executives, nearly all of whom had previously lived overseas themselves and appreciated the differences in human resources systems between Japan and the U.S. Another part of the planning process was a series of benchmarking meetings with HR professionals from leading companies in Japan, including both Japanese-owned and foreign capital firms. These visits led to more plan revisions, more mutual consultation between colleagues, and increasing confidence on Kaneko-san's part regarding external best practices in areas where Sumitomo 3M could make improvements.

The twenty-one elements that were eventually listed in his plan together constituted a huge change agenda for Sumitomo 3M. At the same time, however, they were palatable because most represented a sensible evolution from existing Japanese practices and had emanated originally from employees themselves. Among the proposed changes were the following:

- Revisions in the promotion system to accelerate the advancement of young, high-potential employees
- More frequent and systematic employee rotation
- The introduction of a new compensation system that would place greater emphasis on performance
- A dual-ladder system to provide wider career options for the company's strong technical community
- Job posting of open positions to enable employees to change jobs more freely
- New development programs for high-potential employees and managers

- A voluntary early retirement program coupled with more disciplined performance management and feedback
- Increased opportunities for women
- Changes in travel policies to make it easier and less expensive for junior employees to travel abroad
- An agreement with the company labor union to eliminate the annual spring "strike" in favor of a pre-set formula for wage and bonus increases based on company profits

After completing his stay in St. Paul and returning to Japan as HR director, Kaneko-san began to work on creating broader organizational understanding and support for the change effort. He created an HR reform steering committee composed of key company opinion makers, and another advisory group of employees representing different functions, ages, and genders. He also prodded the local HR department itself into action by bringing in managers with strong business experience and appointing a rare female manager to serve as a role model for women in other departments. Some early, tangible victories were achieved through policy changes that did not require extensive lobbying: the introduction of a more casual dress code just in time for the scorching Japanese summer heat and installation of employee art on the previously barren cafeteria walls. Although minor, these moves increased the scope of employee choice and participation, which symbolized the intent of the entire change package and offered visible signs of progress.

Some elements of Kaneko-san's initial plan required further modification; for example, it was necessary to hold more intensive discussions with the company labor union than originally anticipated in order to win their support. And some senior factory workers were not pleased with changes in the compensation system. As the Japanese economy slipped further into the doldrums, it became necessary to increase the target numbers for early retirements and to manage performance even more strictly.

Over the last two years, however, more changes have taken place in human resources practices at Sumitomo 3M than anyone would have previously thought possible—all aligned with the corporate goals of accelerating the pace of growth while increasing operating efficiency. In total, nineteen of twenty-one changes proposed in Kaneko-san's initial plan have been implemented or are under way. At the present time he is continuing to press ahead with a fresh round of reforms. The effects of the change effort have perceptibly affected the company's atmosphere and, in spite of the tough economic climate, Sumitomo 3M has become the most profitable location for the company worldwide.[1]

Comments

The Sumitomo 3M example is interesting because it not only incorporates key elements of the ideal change sequence, but it also goes beyond them in several ways. As for the ten change management steps for handling change recommended above,

1. Kaneko-san himself certainly plays the role of strong local leadership; other Japanese human resources managers and executive colleagues were involved from the project's early stages as well.

2. The existing HR system in Japan was well known at headquarters and valued for its strengths—if anything, the company erred on the side of being too cautious about respecting local practices.

3. Employees and executives, core stakeholders for the human resources function, were consulted early and often; both employee views and the strategic intent of top management were incorporated into the change effort from the beginning.

4. Another important part of the planning process was benchmarking of Japanese companies and foreign capital firms in Japan.

5. Changes were designed to be complementary, with new training and development opportunities, for example, designed to support accelerated promotion, or voluntary movement through job posting designed to supplement greater rotation.

6. Joint planning resulted in a good balance of old and new, domestic and foreign. Proposals included a balance of better use of traditional Japanese employment practices (e.g., employee rotation),

modifications of existing practices (e.g., annual labor negotiations), and the introduction of timely ideas from abroad (e.g., job posting).

7. Periodic meetings with executives, the union, and other employee representatives kept a widening circle of people informed and on board.

8. Several of the biggest shifts, such as the move toward a more achievement-based compensation system, were piloted with a limited number of managers before rolling them out to the entire employee population.

9. There was no need to hand off responsibilities to a local team because the team was predominantly local from the start.

10. The track record of success to date is being leveraged to jump-start the next wave of change; Kaneko-san and his HR colleagues are already moving on to new projects at their own initiative.

In addition to these sensible measures, other people skills applied at the interpersonal, group, and organizational levels contributed to a successful outcome. 3M executives invested the time and developed the interpersonal contacts to assess Kaneko-san thoroughly prior to his new appointment, and accurately evaluated him as a capable and highly motivated change agent. The company set up an effective training and development environment that enabled him to rapidly ingest up-to-date knowledge about the HR profession, both independently and as part of the larger 3M HR community. It was assumed from the beginning that he was not obliged to import any headquarters practice as is—he had the freedom to select from the U.S. what he found useful and adapt that to the local environment in Japan as he and his colleagues saw fit. On the organizational level, he engaged in a strategic-planning process that brought together the right people, examined relevant local and global data, and allowed many different voices to be heard. Finally, he had access to tested change concepts and best practices, the authority to use them, and close long-standing relationships with other Japanese executives who could help to make the changes happen. Kaneko-san and his 3M colleagues provide an example of effective global leadership through the consistent and persistent application of people skills over time.

Figure 23. **The Virtuous Cycle**

The "Virtuous Cycle."

The mirror opposite to the Foreign Capital Company Syndrome described earlier is a virtuous cycle that generates positive momentum in the same way that the "syndrome" creates a downward vicious cycle. It consists of the components shown in figure 23 and described in table 28.

Clarity About Change

Many change efforts start out as "happy hybrids. " There is an enormous temptation with dicey cross-border business relationships to say, "We'll take some of your way and a little bit of our way and combine them to have the best of both worlds." More often than not, however, the promise that different approaches can be brought together is illusory.

With a corporate merger or acquisition, for instance, there may be short-term tactical value in downplaying the impact of the transaction in the face of potential employee unrest or even local government opposition. But taking the path of least resistance in this kind of situation often produces bigger headaches in the long run. Employees eventually smell out the real story, and when it turns out to be at odds with what they were

Table 28. **The Virtuous Cycle: Core Elements**

Trust and friendship	Shared objectives, commitment to the organization, and strong personal relationships form the backdrop for change.
Effective communication	Company employees in various locations are aware of communication style differences between themselves and their counterparts in other countries. They are dedicated to finding ways to communicate in spite of such differences and know how to make necessary adjustments.
Commitment to subsidiary maturation	Everyone is willing to invest time and energy into increasing subsidiary capabilities in a way that meets market demands. The capabilities of the home-office personnel themselves become more mature through contacts with overseas operations.
Accurate assessment of capabilities	Managers and top executives have a realistic sense of current subsidiary capabilities. They know about the strengths and deficiencies of current personnel, budgetary constraints, competitive pressures, and levels of customer satisfaction.
Local input	Because there is trust and effective communication between different sites, company decision makers, regardless of their location, receive complete and accurate input from employees and/or customers who would be directly affected by a change.
Joint development	Changes are accomplished through mutual consultation and joint development. Whether the project is the creation of a new product, the transformation of IT infrastructure, or the introduction of a revised compensation system, the recommendations of employees in the locations to be affected are naturally solicited and exchanged.
Flexible leadership	With collaboration, trust, and good communication, headquarters becomes increasingly willing to share control. Local employees take on leadership roles in planning and implementing changes.

Table 28. **The Virtuous Cycle: Core Elements (continued)**

Constructive debate	All sides feel their input is relevant. Deeper assessment and discussion of differences is now possible. Constructive debate leads to better ideas and solutions.
Local ownership and enthusiasm	Subsidiary employees who are involved throughout the process of formulating changes are fully committed to making the project a success; headquarters personnel are equally ready to commit themselves to good ideas that come from elsewhere.
Organizational support systems	Organizational systems such as decision making, performance management, compensation, and management of the expatriation cycle are aligned to enhance contributions from around the world.
Mutual learning and transmission of best practices	Growing mutual respect and appreciation encourages all sides to listen and learn from each other. People eagerly seek out best practices from their counterparts around the world. Participants in past efforts approach future change projects equipped with greater knowledge along with a sense of positive momentum.

told initially, the company's credibility is diminished and precious trust is lost. A statement such as, "We're going to retain existing management personnel in this country," may comfort people at first, but the abrupt departure of key local managers after six months or a year will lead to higher levels of uncertainty and more serious consequences than if the acquiring party had been straightforward about its intentions to begin with: "We intend to evaluate existing management personnel and retain those who deliver strong business results."

"Happy hybrids" can also degenerate into "worst of both worlds" combinations. For instance, when the global premium pricing strategy of a foreign partner is applied to locally manufactured products with quality issues that remain unresolved, the results may be high prices and poor quality, accompanied by plummeting sales and defections of key distributors. Or, employees abroad cheerfully accept more generous compensation packages provided by their parent company but still expect to keep the job security and ambiguous performance standards that are common in their country's employment market—now the firm has a higher cost structure without any greater ability to deal with poor performers.

Such ill-fated hybrids tend to occur when management abdicates its responsibility to make tough choices and attempts to please everyone. Employees, too, learn to "game" the system, taking advantage of imported corporate policies or benefits that they find attractive while resisting accompanying demands for greater effort or sacrifices on the grounds that these would violate established cultural norms.

A broader menu of change options beyond superficial hybrid solutions is best faced squarely by those in charge of any corporate makeover. It includes the following choices:

- **Standardize.** Establish a single policy at corporate headquarters that is applied uniformly worldwide.
- **Select.** Work with local managers in each country to choose and apply the elements of a corporate-wide change initiative that have the most relevance for their operations.
- **Adapt.** Alter the form or packaging of a particular change to make it more readily acceptable to local employees or customers.
- **Combine.** Seek out a felicitous combination of ideas from headquarters and local sources that will work better than a one-sided approach.
- **Integrate.** Fuse different-country contributions with a synergistic result that exceeds the sum of the parts.
- **Adopt.** Identify an idea from a nonheadquarters location and apply it in other markets where it offers benefits.[2]

Among these change options, integration has the most seductive appeal. "Happy hybrid" is another way of describing naïve attempts to integrate conflicting approaches that are shaped by different cultural forces. Reconciling the horns of a dilemma to create a synergistic solution can indeed be a powerful process when the reconciliation achieved is a lasting one. Writers on cultural issues gravitate toward this approach because it offers something for everybody and becomes a mutually gratifying way to leverage cultural differences for the benefit of a global organization.[3] Nonetheless, with integration—as with any of the other options—there is a danger that it will do more harm than good if applied to the wrong problem. Not all cross-border business problems are conducive to tidy mutual reconciliation. Integrative approaches are sometimes exploited beyond any practical value for their ideological appeal, producing a false reconciliation that masks either a subtle imposition of authority or an underlying refusal to face up to difficult issues.

Companies should keep in mind the full range of change options and use the approach or combination of approaches most appropriate for a given situation. The various alternatives are best understood in relation to a particular example. Here is the case of a recent acquisition in which the new owner wants to introduce a set of performance management practices.

Performance Management in Italy

You are a member of the management team in charge of integrating and running the operations of a large firm that your company has just acquired. Your job is to ensure that the integration takes place smoothly and to manage the combined European region operations of the two firms from regional headquarters in Brussels. The regional management team is composed of one-third expatriates from your firm, one-third local nationals from the acquired firm, and one-third new executives who have been brought in to help run the company.

The foreign partner that your company has acquired is a manufacturing operation that was formerly based in Italy, and it now provides your firm with a much larger presence in Europe. It still holds a valuable set of real estate assets, and your firm is assured of short-term profitability by packaging and selling off these properties. However, longer-term you are concerned that the operation has no clear path to profitability in its main lines of business unless you are able to introduce new products developed in your home market and alter the company's cost structure. Although the acquired company was effectively bankrupt when your firm purchased it, as far as you can determine, the employees feel that they were victims of Italy's turbulent economic environment rather than any major missteps of their own.

A condition of the acquisition was that your company agrees to make no layoffs anywhere in Europe during the first year. It is also your understanding that this would be very difficult to do in most European labor markets, particularly in Italy. But, you do face a strict directive from your parent company to turn the money-losing parts of the operation around and to start building new and profitable lines of business as soon as possible. You believe that the potential for a turnaround does exist so long as the bureaucratic habits and the entitlement mentality you have observed in the acquired-company employees can be changed.

One of the first topics that came up in consultation with your parent company was the introduction of a new performance management system. Your own corporate management wants to see a new system in place by the beginning of the second half of this year. It seems important to install some metrics to measure performance more accurately and figure out who is actually contributing and who is not. You believe that the compensation system should also be modified to reflect a greater emphasis on performance-based rewards.

Others on the management team—particularly those from the acquired firm—have protested that a U.S.-style performance management system would undermine employee teamwork, pit managers against subordinates, and damage long-standing personal relationships. They have also raised numerous questions about how to determine and implement the right metrics. In your view, the acquired company's employee evaluation system is far too subjective and based on the whims of individual managers.

Specific features of your company's existing performance management system include regular objective setting, biannual reviews, and employee ratings based on performance in achieving key business and professional development goals. Your firm has also adopted the vaunted practice of cutting the bottom 10 percent of employees who are "underperforming."

Corporate headquarters has told you that the new performance management system needs to be implemented throughout Europe beginning in Italy, because that is where the major operating losses are currently occurring. What approach will you take in introducing the new system?

Comments

Full-scale *standardization* based on headquarters practices is clearly not an option here—at least initially—because of the new parent firm's no-layoff guarantee. Even over the longer term, implementing the policy of cutting the bottom 10 percent of employees may also be problematic in countries such as Italy, where restrictive laws require employers to justify firings in court. As one Italian employer remarks, "It is easier to get a divorce than to fire people."[4]

It would probably be wisest to *select* certain aspects of the new parent company's performance management system and introduce only these at the beginning. *Adaptation* to the local business environment can be facilitated through translating forms, training managers in objective-setting and evaluation procedures, and involving both foreign and local management in establishing organizational objectives that become the basis for setting business unit and individual goals. Some degree of *combination* or possibly even *integration* of foreign and local performance management practices could be achieved, for example, through making contributions to teamwork a criterion for judging individual performance or allowing teams to set performance standards. However, this kind of fusion of foreign and local elements may constitute only a relatively minor part of the larger system. The main thrust in this case is to implement a set of practices that measures individual contributions to the accomplishment of corporate objectives, and adaptation of headquarters procedures is likely to be the dominant activity, not integration. Placing too much emphasis on the topic of integration could ultimately come to be seen by employees as deceptive or misleading. While at this time there unfortunately appears to be little in the area of performance management that the parent company can *adopt* from the acquisition and introduce elsewhere within its global network, it should nonetheless stay alert for such features and avoid the automatic assumption that the acquired firm has little to offer.

The ten steps for handling change cited previously are relevant in some way to each of these possible change options. Even a policy that becomes standard across the globe can be developed through discussion and consultation with the people that it is going to affect. The other change options of selection, adaptation, combination, integration, and adoption require successively larger degrees of involvement on the part of local personnel if they are to be successful. The more employees around the world can have a voice in discussing and choosing among these alternatives, the readier they will be to support whatever change process ultimately takes place.

When the virtuous cycle that includes trust, local input, and mutual learning has been established, employees in various locations understand and expect that their leaders will utilize the full range of change options. There is sufficient goodwill to engender support even for the occasional top-down directive during difficult times, in part because employees know that a good idea generated anywhere in the world has the chance to become corporate policy. Combining an inclusive approach with real clarity about the nature of the company's change strategy brings substantial benefits, including credible, consistent decision making and well-coordinated action across the global organization.

Managing Change

SUMMARY AND REVIEW QUESTIONS

1. Resistance to change initiatives from headquarters may take different forms in different settings. What are several of these forms of resistance based on your own experience with overseas operations?

2. Have you encountered any elements of the vicious circle described as the "Foreign Capital Company Syndrome"?

3. Would any of the ten steps for handling change introduced in this chapter (pp. 308–11) be useful in your work? Are there other measures that are important as well? How does your company go about gaining buy-in from local leaders with respect to change initiatives that originate elsewhere?

4. Can you cite successful examples from your own organization of managing change across borders through building successful partnerships? Did these entail elements of the "virtuous cycle" outlined in this chapter?

5. Is there a tendency among people in your company to seek "happy hybrid" solutions without being clear about the type of change that is actually taking place? If you are currently involved in a change effort, which of the alternatives below most accurately describes the real nature of that process?

    - **Standardize:** establish a single policy at corporate headquarters that is applied uniformly worldwide

    - **Select:** work with local managers in each country to choose and apply the elements of a corporate-wide change initiative that have the most relevance for their operations

- **Adapt:** alter the form or packaging of a particular change to make it more readily acceptable to local employees or customers
- **Combine:** seek out a felicitous combination of ideas from headquarters and local sources that will work better than a one-sided approach
- **Integrate:** fuse different-country contributions with a synergistic result that exceeds the sum of the parts
- **Adopt:** identify an idea from a nonheadquarters location and apply it in other markets where it offers benefits

Synthesis: People Skills and Global Citizenship

The global people skills model described in the preceding chapters can be a tremendously effective guide to success in marketplaces around the world. Global competitiveness is ultimately achieved not only through providing superior products and/or services, but also through the sustained cultivation and application of people skills at the interpersonal, group, and organizational levels. Corporate leaders who fully comprehend this model and leverage its value are indeed "GlobeSmart." Figure 24 displays again the model first presented in chapter 1 and described at every level through subsequent chapters.

There is always a danger, however, of getting carried away with the mechanics of learning skills and applying the model while forgetting that it requires a special kind of connection between real people. People skills should be infused with one's own personal approach and introduced into business relationships in a way that acknowledges the distinctive identity and background of others who are involved as well. Acquired skills com-

Figure 24. **Global People Skills**

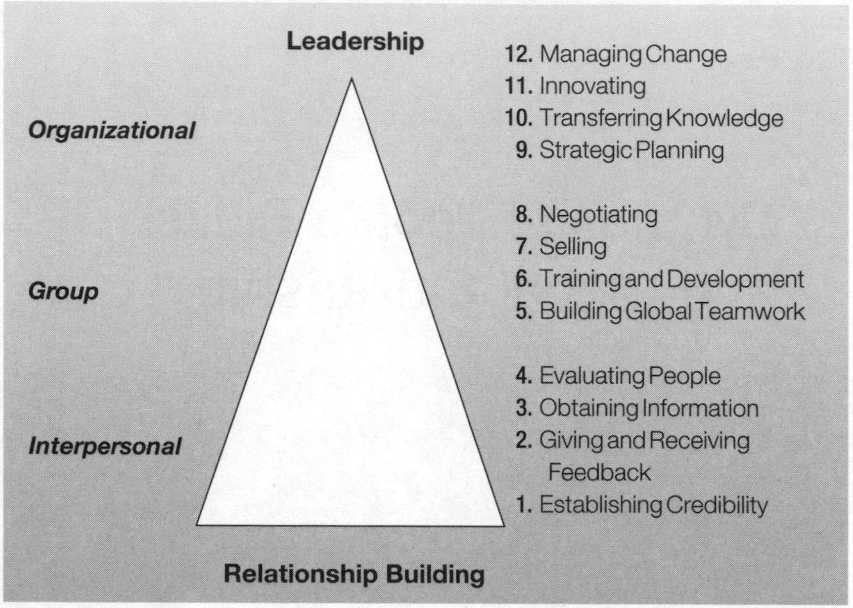

plement a personal touch but are no substitute for it. Everyone who participates in a cross-border transaction must avoid hasty stereotyping of "self" or "other" and leave some flexibility for all to learn and develop.

Changing Values: The Missionary Impulse

Using the skills discussed in this book entails not only practical considerations, but also deeper moral dilemmas, particularly when it comes to changing established ways of doing things. Nearly everyone who has lived abroad experiences aspects of the host environment that he or she would like to somehow "fix": inefficiency, shoddy product quality, political oppression, corruption, environmental degradation, wasteful consumption by a well-to-do elite, stunning gaps between rich and poor. But how much can or should be changed, and how much should be left the same?

Corporate change efforts typically include a values dimension that is crucial although seldom articulated. When expatriates or business travelers are sent off on assignment with a mandate to introduce new technologies, sales techniques, or management practices, they are frequently involved in "educating" customers or employees to accept different forms of doing business. Local counterparts are being asked to adopt new commercial standards and work processes replete with values that may be unfamiliar. "Six Sigma" practices, financial transparency, contractual obligations, 360-degree feedback, and demands for individual initiative and accountability, for instance, embody values such as a task focus driven by facts and data, universalistic legal standards, egalitarianism, or individualism.

Thoughtful people trying to bring change to a foreign environment struggle with the question of when, and to what degree, it is right to alter long-standing customs. Some local practices may appear to be impractical or even illegal within the policy framework of the corporate parent. Yet, the more ambitious the change agenda, the greater the chances are of encountering determined resistance. And the longer one stays in a particular location and comes to understand its business context, the more traditional ways of doing things tend to seem either more sensible or more frustrating.

In spite of such concerns, it is sometimes acceptable and necessary to try to reinterpret existing values or introduce new ones that will enhance customer relations and support continued business growth. Full-scale cultural relativism, which holds that one country's way of getting things done is not inherently better than any other, is not a viable option for companies that need to meet deadlines and generate profits or cease to exist. Economic enterprises must determine what works best in the short term—whether it be, for example, more efficient factory management practices, streamlined supplier relationships, or demanding performance standards. In addition, they have to predict what activities will be viable over a longer span of years. Will it make sense, for instance, for every Chinese to drive a gas-guzzling SUV? No single culture, including those that are most prosperous today, has a monopoly on organizational effectiveness or sustainable products and services.

The best general approach for promoting value change and yet avoiding unwelcome imposition or unproductive clashes is to follow the principles of reciprocity and asking for local input. A change agent who is open to being changed in turn has a better chance of gaining a positive reception. Believing in and developing local talent sometimes has the beneficial result that the foreign manager experiences significant development as well.

Changing Values: Possible Contexts

The safest place to initiate value change is usually where local customers and employees themselves actually desire change or are at least open to it. This could include, for example, the introduction of improved customer service procedures, or hiring and promotion practices that focus on merit and not personal connections or nepotism. The problem here of course is that the points of greatest local receptivity may not be fully aligned with the visitor's change agenda. Critical choices have to be made about whether to alter one's agenda, to attempt to force it through, or to make a tactical detour by emphasizing items on which there is agreement while postponing those that seem controversial.

The receptivity of one's counterparts to change is also not a fixed state of mind, but rather depends on the bearer of the message. A foreign visitor who is seen as arrogant or uncaring will accomplish little. On the other hand, someone who is willing to live and work closely with people, sharing their interests and concerns while building trusting relationships, can be the catalyst for major transformations, including the adoption of new values. One project team member in Latin America who invested his break time playing soccer with local employees—and was initially seen by other foreign project participants as not sufficiently dedicated to the project—turned out to be the most effective change agent on the team. A top executive of a consumer products firm had a high reputation in the countries he visited due to his insistence on staying in local residences and learning about their life-style rather than confining himself to the safe and sanitary confines of luxury hotels.

The desire for change is seldom unanimous, and we must often begin by seeking out, and working with, supporters of change while trying to win over, or perhaps ease out, those who are opposed. This can land a would-be change agent smack in the middle of an awkward political crossfire. Another peril derives from apparent allies who verbally support change but who divert it for their own purposes. Foreigners can easily fall into the trap of having their presence become a symbol of organizational transformation when little or no real change is actually taking place. The presence of a shiny new technology or a management guru sometimes provides local elites with a way to burnish their aura of authority. Meanwhile, they preserve established infrastructure and hierarchy that ultimately reject foreign practices or allow them to wither.

There may even be widespread local opposition to proposed changes because they are perceived as being inimical to cherished values. Foreign ownership of local companies, exploitation of national resources, fast-food establishments, imported movies or theme parks, biotechnology, and modifications to national labor laws have all become flash points of controversy because of the view—sometimes fomented by entrenched local interests—that traditional values are being threatened.

The Global Citizen

Effective cross-border change is most likely to be sparked by people who combine personal values and behaviors that translate well between cultures. While much of this book has been focused on contrasts between business practices in the U.S. and other countries, there is a growing need for "global citizens"—that is, leaders or ordinary employees who can think and act in a way that transcends the limitations of a particular cultural perspective. "Global citizenship" means having the will and the ability to work together effectively with other people anywhere in the world. For many of us this may be a fleeting set of moments rather than a full passport to the world. It is not easy to maintain a perspective that brackets our upbringing, questions our most basic assumptions, and exposes us to an unremitting shower of unfamiliar ideas and behaviors.

Global citizen values certainly include the core items of trust, respect, listening, and so on as discussed in chapter 2. Further basic global citizen values that travel well include

- **Meaningful work:** participation in peaceful transactions across borders that are personally satisfying and actually improve the lives of others
- **Profit:** recognition that there must be a positive result from the equation that compares the worth customers assign to our products with the overall costs of our operations

- **Integrity:** profit through legitimate means; a dedication to fair and honest dealings and relationships of trust with business partners, defined in terms acceptable to them as well as to us

- **Social justice:** a willingness to challenge extremes of poverty and economic inequality, tyrannical governments that do not have the support of their people, and administrative systems that deny equal opportunities while benefiting a privileged few

- **Environmental sustainability:** dedication to the long-term health of our planet and the ecosystems that sustain us

- **Mutual learning:** a constant openness to new ideas and information and a willingness to adopt good ideas from any source

- **Personal and professional growth:** a willingness to accept challenges and to change through encounters with values and ideas that are fundamentally different from our own

A global citizen is first and foremost a citizen of the world. Affiliation to humankind and to the world as a whole is balanced with national allegiance. When there is a choice between what is best for humankind and a narrower nationalistic agenda, the former must finally take precedence. In the corporate environment, this means the ability to keep simultaneously in mind what is of greatest benefit to the global organization and what is good for local customers. Corporate values must be consonant with broader human values—and come before local protectionism.

Global citizen values are contagious because workers in every country can aspire to them—they are not the exclusive possession of headquarters or top management. The word *citizen* recalls the ancient concept of the "freeman," a person who is no one's slave but rather is invested with the rights and responsibilities of full membership in society. No global organization will ultimately benefit from local employees who are more enslaved than free. Indeed, the global organizational systems that support global citizens must integrate and leverage the contributions of every employee for the benefit of customers around the world. The political connotations of citizenship are appropriate. As corporations increasingly transcend national boundaries, they must take on ever-greater responsibility and liability for so-called externalities: their effects on the environment, political structures, living conditions, and differences between rich and poor.

Global Citizens: Synergists at the Center

Janet and Milton Bennett, two seminal figures in the intercultural field, have created a useful development model of cultural awareness that moves from the denial of differences and its accompanying "ethnic encapsulation" toward more advanced stages of adaptation and integration. Figure 25 displays the stages defined by the Bennetts.

For all the utility of their intercultural development model, however, the Bennetts' description of the final stage of integration is oddly truncated. They coin the term *constructive marginality* to refer to a person who can move effectively between cultures, making careful and conscious choices of how to act based on different contexts. But such persons, by virtue of their foreign experience, are forever confined to the margins of their home culture and the stimulating society of fellow marginals; they are constructive critics and valuable linkage points to other realities, yet not central players in the vortex of power.[1] This is an apt description for many academics and consultants, including most of the founders of the intercultural field. Beginning with the unabashed idealism of the Peace Corps, interculturalism has been a movement in which people have volunteered for marginality in order to build new, two-way contacts with the far (from a U.S. perspective) corners of the globe.

However, major corporations today do not require constructive marginality so much as they need global citizens. In our work we have begun to encounter a new breed of leader, a global citizen who does not reside at the margins of his or her organization but rather at the center. This person is a synergist and creator of new institutional values, an integrator who knows the company's past culture and capabilities and who can skillfully draw in new voices and create a broader vision. Global citizens may live abroad for some time and help to transfer knowledge and

Figure 25. **Development of Cultural Awareness**

capabilities around the globe, but at the core they are builders who are equally comfortable and effective at the center and the margins.

The global citizen who acts as a synergist at the center can weave together diverse elements—national differences, center and periphery, local market imperatives and corporate capabilities—to help create a new organizational culture before our eyes. Dynamic global corporate cultures will increasingly reshape and even rival the cultures of nation states. And, they have grown to a scale that matters just as much: fifty-one of the largest one hundred economies in the world are not countries, but corporations.[2]

Global Citizenship: Other Characteristics

Global citizenship is important because it transcends the dichotomies of parent and subsidiary, home and host countries, providing common ground and hope for people who are located anywhere. Positive change occurs when employees and customers can find new ways to join in building innovative solutions based on shared values.

How do global citizens compare with the old image of the international manager? The characteristics listed in table 29 are highly demanding, and few individuals in senior management positions today could claim that they meet every criterion. However, there is a new generation of young people who have grown up with multiculturalism rather than having to learn it later on, and it may be that they will come much closer to combining these kinds of characteristics over the span of their careers.

The Business Case for Global Citizenship

There is a business case for global citizenship that is clear and compelling. Global citizens will be best equipped to perceive the unexpected risks and opportunities that flow from rapid transformation of the commercial and

Table 29. **Global Citizen Characteristics**

	International Manager	Global Citizen
Adaptation process	Learns how to cope with "culture shock" the hard way; initially unprepared to deal with differences	Has steady core values and the versatility to both question these and to adapt to different circumstances
Professional context	Specializes in international business; may or may not be competent in other areas	Is highly competent in a technical discipline
Professional expertise	Focuses on a particular product or market	Has solid general business training and is conversant with other specialized disciplines
Overseas assignment goals	Sent abroad for long periods to work on low-priority assignments without strong home-office focus or backing	Has been assigned to key global markets to grow the business and to develop leadership skills
Language skills	Can do business in a foreign language	Is comfortable working in several languages
Intercultural business skills	Is familiar with the business practices in another country or region	Can move easily between different countries or regions with no drop in performance
Interests	Is interested primarily in home-culture and host-culture events	Cares about, and is conversant with, major events on every continent
Application of cross-border skills	Uses international skills when visiting or living in a subsidiary location or hosting guests	Exercises global skills on a daily basis regardless of location

Table 29. **Global Citizen Characteristics (continued)**

	International Manager	**Global Citizen**
Team affiliation	Works primarily with a set group of foreign colleagues from one country	Serves on several global teams, each with multiple representatives from other cultures
Relationship with headquarters	Is seen as a marginal contributor to the home organization; sometimes inclined toward extremes of "headquarters' way" or "gone native"	Knows headquarters well and is a high-potential "player"; is fluent with central organizational systems and processes and can adapt these skillfully to new environments
Organizational focus	Focuses on transactions between headquarters and subsidiary	Looks for and builds connections between different regional organizations and markets
Contribution	Brings headquarters values, practices, and technical skills into the subsidiary environment	Seeks out best practices from locations around the world and integrates these into existing systems and structures
Image within the company	Is regarded by local employees as a respected headquarters representative	Is regarded by other company employees as a credible global role model
Perspectives on others	Sees foreign colleagues as subsidiary employees	Views foreign colleagues as fellow global citizens

Source: Several of the items in this chart are adapted from a comparison of "traditional international managers" with "transnationally competent managers," in Nancy J. Adler and Susan Bartholomew, "Managing Globally Competent People," *Academy of Management Executive,* 6,3 (1992).

social environment and to implement the changes that are necessary for a company to survive and generate profits. The broad appeal of global citizen values creates a common rallying point for "boundaryless" cooperation across organizational lines between nations, ethnic groups, customers and suppliers, and different business units.

Global citizens are also essential to today's companies because they can recognize important local customer needs, weigh them against the organization's strategic priorities, and invest valuable resources in the best interests of the company as a whole. Global/local balance is the holy grail of management for transnational enterprises, and no one is better equipped to achieve this than the global citizen.

Many North American companies are planning for a future world in which the ratio of overseas to domestic revenues moves from 50/50 to 80/20. It is the global citizens among their employees who will champion this movement, serving the needs of global customers, innovating across borders, and building up operations in prime growth markets. The economic map of the world now features North America, Europe, and Japan, each swollen out of proportion to geographical reality. Global citizens will see a different map of possibilities and gradually transform the economic landscape in the direction of greater regional balance.

Some global citizen values may look overly idealistic at the present time, but changes in the business environment will make them appear increasingly practical as time goes on. With respect to social justice, for example, is it sensible to run the advanced economies of the world as gated communities, where one must have a special pass to enter and the majority of the world's population is shut out? One grotesque statistic documented in a recent U.N. development report is that the assets of the world's *two hundred* richest people exceed the combined income of *two billion* of its poorest. While the U.S. has enjoyed an era of unprecedented prosperity, eighty countries reportedly have lower per capita incomes today than they did a decade ago.[3] Such trends, if unaltered, will inevitably produce major social upheavals.

Global corporations find that they are increasingly held responsible for problems that occur continents away from their headquarters. Several years ago Shell suffered a blow to its reputation because of its reported association with a corrupt Nigerian military dictatorship, the suppression and murder of democratic political activists, and serious environmental pollution. At the same time, less well-publicized examples of good corporate citizenship have become sources of strategic advantage. Ford has received kudos on Thailand's eastern seaboard for its efforts to raise the standards of local educational institutions and to cultivate domestic sources of supply, meanwhile both ensuring itself a better pool of qualified workers and winning important economic and political allies.

Global companies that consider solutions for social issues, poverty, and environmental degradation as part of their strategic agenda in the places where they do business stand a much better chance of being welcomed by national governments and local communities. In countries where local elites monopolize resources and perpetuate inequality, however, these companies face difficult choices about whether, or to what extent, to collaborate with them to be able to do business. Some firms will make a cynical show of values such as social activism or environmental responsibility for their public relations value, meanwhile carrying on with destructive practices and reinforcing the ultimately fatal status quo. Others are quietly experimenting with the application of exemplary values beyond the usual plaque on the wall or cozy management retreat.[4]

The Global Citizen vs. Corporate Blind Spots

The awesome drive and forward momentum of our economy produces significant blind spots that can only be addressed effectively by the global citizen. What lies in the penumbra, outside our strategic plans and quarterly reports, is a host of dark creatures that swell with our neglect and which can emerge from their shadows to directly assault corporate bottom lines.

Indonesia is one example of a flash point between old and new realities. Until a few years ago, all the numbers were up. Western firms, attracted by the country's natural resources, its infrastructure needs, and its status as the world's fourth most populous nation, began to invest. But beyond the rosy figures reported in the economic growth tables, myriad issues have surfaced that investors can only ignore at their peril: rife corruption, social injustice, religious strife, mass poverty, and wanton environmental destruction. Indonesia still teeters on the brink, facing a choice between chastised participation in the world economy and withdrawal into isolation.

Pakistan was hardly on the corporate radar screen several years ago. Although it borders on India, a country with impressive technological capabilities and an increasingly prosperous urban middle class, Pakistan has been so hobbled by political instability, corruption, and the ongoing struggle to control well-armed militant fundamentalists that its legitimate economy is relatively small. Yet, a single terrorist with a backpack who makes the journey from Pakistan to a major U.S. city could not only wreak havoc on thousands of innocent civilians but also completely change the economic calculus for any number of companies.

While Indonesia and Pakistan still seem far away, it is easy to neglect the quiet immigrants who not only toil away in white-collar jobs but also tend the yards, drive the taxis, and staff the factories of any major Western city. "Fortress America" or "Fortress Europe" are illusions, with walls made of Swiss cheese manned by appallingly inept bureaucracies. Well-connected immigrant families can bring another family member or friend across the border and have that person in any U.S. city within two days. Such inexpensive labor is convenient for employers who shut their eyes to questionable documents and the social consequences for schools and hospitals. But, it links us inexorably with the swelling national ghettos abroad that contain hundreds of millions of poor people. The vast majority of immigrants are grateful just for the chance to work and support their families. A few would like to wreak vengeance for the poverty and oppression that they blame on rich, powerful countries and corporations.

As the power of our technologies magnifies the impact of global population growth toward the projected mark of eight to ten billion, other issues now regarded by companies as peripheral or philanthropic will move toward the center of our agenda. Deforestation, air and water pollution, the extinction of species, resistant microbes, ozone depletion, climate change—what commercial enterprise would not be affected if any of these toxic trend lines continued unabated? They could mean opportunities for some (makers of sun block and new antibiotics) and devastation or decline for others (flood insurance providers, farmers in drought-prone regions).

Table 30. **Assumptions for Business in the New Millennium**

Economic Era	Standard Assumptions
Old definition of "business"	• Personal and work life separation • Division of labor between business and government: business complies with regulations; government offsets social impacts of business
Current trends	• Corporate responsibility for creating a vision and mission • Social responsibility, valuing diversity, environmental ethics, stewardship
Business in the new millennium	• Global citizenship as an element of corporate vision and mission • Proactive cross-border social activism and environmental entrepreneurship

Businesses may point to other institutions as bearing the primary responsibility for curing society's ills, but can they afford to wait for government warnings or solutions while this formidable set of problems comes careening into our future? The poverty and powerlessness of other institutions create wider responsibilities for companies that have the wherewithal and the foresight to act in their own long-term interests. Global citizens, with their core values and breadth of perspective, can lead this sea change in the corporate charter, as suggested in table 30.

Laboratories for Global Citizenship

Many of our economic institutions are living laboratories of the future with their forceful confluence of high technology, raw capitalist energy, and democratic impulses toward opportunity, empowerment, and embracing diversity. Workplaces today offer the unprecedented spectacle of every conceivable race and culture striving together toward common goals under the same roof. We may not always cooperate because we want to or because it is easy to find common ground, but such cooperation is essential for our organizations to survive and grow.

However, there are many potential hazards along the path to the future, and only time will tell whether U.S. companies make the choices that nurture continued success. Elsewhere, for example, the collusive, conflict-averse bent of Japan's industrial policies and the ideological poverty of its economic nationalism have been exposed as significant weaknesses in recent years. China's geopolitical future, too, will ultimately hinge on whether China can develop a vision that extends beyond its own regional or global hegemony.

Two glaring weaknesses of U.S.-style globalism are myopic centralization and premature self-congratulation. It is too easy to assume that the U.S. formula is already global and that the rest of the world will, in time, come around and adjust, both linguistically and culturally. The sheer size of prosperous domestic markets can still serve as a shield from the harsh winds of change in other market environments. But, global customers and competitors may not agree to do things the American way, and U.S. domestic markets are not necessarily a good training ground for success in emerging-market countries.

Too many Americans feel that there is little new to learn about other lands beyond that handful of superficial do's and don'ts. Too many live in cozy expatriate ghettos abroad without venturing out to discover how ordinary people live. This type of cruise ship globalism is a dangerous and deceptive pretense. When we are ready to have our deepest values challenged at their roots by radically different life-styles and assumptions, when we take other worldviews seriously and still seek common ground—then and only then are we eligible for the gut-wrenching transformation to true global citizenship.

Global Citizenship: Lowest Common Denominator?

One complaint about the widening reach of global enterprises is that it will eradicate local cultural variety, replacing it with a bland dollar-, yen-, or Euro-worshiping sameness. Wherever we go on the planet, we will have the same limited choices between McDonald's and Burger King, Volkswagen and Toyota. Traditional legends will be replaced by Disneyland's animated dramas, and the rich tapestries of local food, clothing, and customs that have been built up over the ages to fit the circumstances of particular places and groups of people will vanish under a downpour of consumer culture. Even noble local attempts to promote decent labor conditions or environmental protection could be swept away by global trade laws that institutionalize exploitation and the extinction of animal and plant as well as cultural species.

This complaint, too, can be addressed by the values and practices of global citizenship. Corporate cultures with deep-rooted values that extend beyond the worship of quarterly profits will themselves develop a complexity and a commitment to respect important local practices that enrich their own repertoire of knowledge and behavior. Global citizens are humanists with a deep appreciation for differences even as they seek to bring people together and a willingness to adopt practices from others. Rather than sterile monoculture, their activities hold the potential for global learning and shared wisdom on an unprecedented scale. At the same time that major corporations bring new values to previously isolated sites in Latin America or Africa, global citizens can bring traditional values, products, insights, and bonds of friendship from these locales back to their own homes. Greater appreciation of the world's astonishing but fragile variety could be an essential step toward the collective determination to preserve it.

The Global Citizen As a "Bridge Person"

The notion of global citizenship represents an ambitious goal that some may find overly lofty or abstract. However, the path toward this goal is created by mundane, everyday interactions with business and personal contacts from other cultures. Each of the twelve global people skills presented here—beginning, for instance, with establishing credibility, giving and receiving feedback, or building global teamwork—provides ample opportunities for putting the values of the global citizen to work. People skills and global citizenship are complementary forces that deepen each other's impact. An instrumental application of people skills without an underlying framework of global citizen values will only provoke suspicion and mistrust; likewise, advocating the principles of global citizenship without acting on them will produce more skepticism than commitment. But when people skills are coupled with a sincere attempt to act as a *global citizen,* almost anything is possible.

One basic and easily accessible way of combining people skills and global citizenship is to serve as a "bridge person." The act of bridging cultures starts with the premise of mutual respect and an effort to understand before judging or seeking to be understood. It identifies assumptions held by people with different backgrounds, along with core sources of pride and joy. The bridge person interprets one world to another, explains why things are done in a certain way, and builds practical, shared interests. Acknowledging differences and yet focusing on common human goals enables diverse parties to seek solutions to challenges or disputes in a flexible way, looking for the best means to use shared talents and resources while dealing with the issues at hand.

Recent research conducted through interviews with Muslims working in major Western corporations, for example, suggests that even sincere attempts at understanding—the very first step of any bridge person—can have a positive impact, especially when accompanied by gestures of respect and kindness.

- "Sincere questions are fine. I don't hold lack of knowledge against anyone."
- "Devout Muslims pray five times a day. It is sometimes awkward to find a good place to do this, and it is helpful when colleagues understand why we turn our heads to one side to pray when we can't find a room."
- "My boss is very understanding about Friday prayers. I take off for about an hour and it is no problem."
- "Head coverings are seen by some in the West as a form of oppression of women. But, it is important to recognize that many Muslim women feel that the head scarf is a form of modesty that shifts the focus from their physical appearance to their capabilities in the workplace."

- "An Indian colleague who knew about our customs told me 'Happy Ramadan' at the beginning of the Ramadan season. I also appreciate it when colleagues understand why I don't eat during the Ramadan fasting period and are not offended."[5]

Global Citizenship and the Future

Corporations, as a class of all-too-human institutions, do both evil and good. They sometimes meddle in local politics, pawn off shoddy or dangerous products on unsuspecting buyers, contribute to the decline of cherished traditional values, recklessly exploit natural resources, ignore abusive labor practices, and cut and run when profits decrease. On the other hand, they introduce new ideas, undermine corrupt and entrenched elites, increase local wages, promote merit over nepotism, provide higher-quality products, and raise educational and environmental standards. Global citizens employing the full array of people skills can make a powerful difference by helping the companies they work for to make the right choices from one day to the next and into the future.

It has been just a few decades since we were exposed to the astronauts' view of planet earth: a deep blue sphere with islands of green and brown partly shrouded under a delicate mantle of white. This view from space, something that science fiction imagined but which only our generation has been privileged to see, is the definitive metaphor for global citizenship: one planet, one humanity, service to life and to the earth that sustains us.

In the world's advanced economies, we have been privileged to grow up amid a cornucopia of material goods, able to learn and to contemplate better futures without being stunted or misshapen by material wants. We can choose to gorge ourselves on the transient fruits of this abundance, ignoring troubling reports of poverty and degradation that trickle in from outside our increasingly well-defended national and community borders. Or, we can shoulder the responsibilities, both corporate and individual, of the global citizen—to see the world both with and without borders and other human beings as our co-workers, friends, or close cousins. Just as we cherish the light of young life in our own children's eyes, we can find that same light in the eyes of children from other, formerly distant, lands.

In the immediate future we must find ways to spread peace and prosperity and avoid the scourges of despair, fanaticism, hate, and mass destruction. From a longer-term perspective—actually short-term from the standpoint of geology or even the history of our species—a fundamental mission we share is to prepare for the days when we send our ships hurtling off to distant stars. Will the primary product of our generation be an irreconcilable, mad cycle of violence and revenge, or a wise and careful stewardship of the planet earth? No doubt our progeny, too, will be flawed beings who will carry the seeds of mutually assured destruction along with those of love and generous service. But which will have the edge? How can we keep our vision of future human possibilities just ahead of our failings?

The computer chips, the rockets, and the terrible weapons already exist or will soon be available. The single most vital challenge we face is to shape the values and deeds of the beings who have such Promethean technologies in their grasp. We hold a critical key to both past and future, and it is up to each of us to learn, model, and spread the message of people skills and global citizenship.

Appendixes

Appendix A: The Peterson Cultural Style Indicator™

This profile test asks the respondent to complete twenty-four items regarding business-related cultural values and attitudes. A profile can be created on the basis of the test results and compared with the average profile of a person from another country. Sample items are listed below. See www.globesmart.net to create a personal profile online.

Instructions

For each question, you are asked to select the number along the scale that you think best reflects where you would position your views between the two statements. For example, if you strongly agree with the statement on the left, select "0." If you strongly agree with the statement on the right, select "10." Select "5" if you agree equally with the left and right statements. Note: Your responses should reflect *your own views* when you are in *your own country.*

1. You are a new employee in a large organization. After a few days on the job you have an idea for increasing the overall profit of the organization. Will you tell your manager about this idea?

0 — 1 — 2 — 3 — 4 — 5 — 6 — 7 — 8 — 9 — 10

Probably not—because it's a manager's job to think about these things.	Probably yes—because any employee who has a good idea should be listened to.

2. During a discussion in a team meeting, a young member of the team has a viewpoint that is very different from what the older director is saying. In your opinion, what should the young team member do?

0 — 1 — 2 — 3 — 4 — 5 — 6 — 7 — 8 — 9 — 10

He or she should respect the director's authority and not challenge the director's viewpoint.	He or she should confront the director by offering a different viewpoint.

3. A plant manager calls a meeting and makes a brief presentation to the workers on the need to increase productivity. How will you interpret this message from the plant manager?

0 — 1 — 2 — 3 — 4 — 5 — 6 — 7 — 8 — 9 — 10

Based on how it was said—the manager's manner and style, tone of voice, level of dress, formality, etc.	Based on what was said—for example, the main points the plant manager communicated.

4. You will be meeting someone from another company to discuss issues and potential problems relating to an upcoming technology exchange program between your two companies. How will you prefer to proceed in the talks?

0 — 1 — 2 — 3 — 4 — 5 — 6 — 7 — 8 — 9 — 10

Remain respectful and diplomatic, avoiding disagreement when possible.	Have open, frank discussions of concerns and any issues that may arise.

5. You are in a group of employees who must carry out a project together. Given the choice, how will you, personally, want the group to work?

0 — 1 — 2 — 3 — 4 — 5 — 6 — 7 — 8 — 9 — 10

Harmony of the group is the key. A focus on the goals of the group will enable us to achieve more than if we emphasize our individual efforts.	Individual initiative is key. Each person needs to take initiative and work to achieve something unique and useful that will help the group.

6. How do you prefer to define yourself in the community where you live and work?

0 — 1 — 2 — 3 — 4 — 5 — 6 — 7 — 8 — 9 — 10

My identity is based on my family and friends, and on my belonging to various groups.	My identity is based on my own personal characteristics, style, and individual preferences.

7. A business colleague is arriving for a weeklong visit to your headquarters. On his first day at headquarters, what will you, as the host, do together with him?

0 — 1 — 2 — 3 — 4 — 5 — 6 — 7 — 8 — 9 — 10

Pleasure before business: welcome him, spend time making him feel comfortable and getting to know him, and later discuss business with him.	Business before pleasure: after the introductions, cover some basic business objectives first, then move on to more personal issues.

8. You are in a group of people your age (a mix of men and women) at a small company gathering and you have never met some of the people before. As you introduce yourself and get to know the others, what would you prefer to talk about more?

0 — 1 — 2 — 3 — 4 — 5 — 6 — 7 — 8 — 9 — 10

What people do: where they work, what their job is, what hobbies or activities they enjoy, etc.	Who people are: what issues interest them, how they describe themselves, what they feel is important, etc.

This survey was created by Brooks Peterson, Ph.D., founder of Across Cultures, Inc.

Appendix B: Tools for Teams

The tables in this appendix supplement the resources for global team development provided in chapter 5.

Table B-1. **Multicultural Meetings: Techniques for Participants**

- **Clarifying.** Make sure that everyone in the group understands the conversation. It may be necessary to ask speakers to slow down, repeat, give examples, or summarize. All meeting participants, including non-native speakers of English, are responsible for clarifying when they do not understand.
- **Holding native-language discussions.** Often short side conversations are needed for participants from one cultural group to clarify what has been said, and to confirm agreement among themselves. It is wise for everyone to support this process.
- **Advance planning.** Participants who are working in a second language or are accustomed to a slower-paced communication style still need to find ways that they can add value to the meeting rather than sitting back and saying nothing. If they anticipate that they will have trouble joining into the meeting dialogue, they are responsible for thinking through in advance the ideas that they want to contribute and for creating an opportunity to express them. Another option is to speak with the facilitator beforehand to ensure that the meeting format will provide a chance for them to explain their views.
- **Checking for agreement.** Some participants may walk away from a meeting thinking they have agreement when they do not. All sides have a responsibility to confirm what "yes" means. Beware of the yes that means, "I'm here. I'm listening, but not necessarily understanding or agreeing."
- **Reading nonverbal messages.** Important information is often conveyed in nonverbal behavior. In some cultures it may not be necessary to say, "I disagree," because this is already obvious from the nonverbal context. Explicit voicing of disagreement under such circumstances may cause unnecessary strife or be interpreted as a sign of cultural insensitivity.*
- **Acting as cultural guide.** Meeting participants should function as cultural guides for one another whenever necessary. This means explaining how and why things are done in your own country in a manner that is constructive and easy for people from other countries to understand. Everyone must be ready to learn and try new ideas, as well as to instruct others. The ideal situation in a multicultural group is for each participant to be able to play the role of learner or guide as circumstances dictate.
- **Serving as note taker.** For most topics, a visual outline of key points helps to ensure that everyone is following the discussion. The note taker can ask questions, as necessary, to confirm what has been said. He or she is also responsible for producing and circulating a written summary of the meeting results that includes action items and invites further input. Not only words, but also pictures, diagrams, or graphs may be helpful in confirming team understanding.

*Albert Sui, vice president of education and training, AI&I, made this point in an interview in *Face-to-Face*, vol. 1 of the video series *Globally Speaking*, prod. Shelley Lieberman, Aperian Global, San Francisco, 1997.

Table B-2. **Conference Call Guidelines**

1. Solicit agenda items from participants in all locations and distribute agenda prior to meeting.
2. Ensure that technical tools are set up prior to the meeting. Work with contacts at each location to make sure all sites are able to join the call without difficulty.
3. Briefly mention the names of everyone who is present at the start of a teleconference, and introduce anyone who is new to the group.
4. Identify yourself when you speak on a teleconference call that involves a large number of people. This will help to ensure that participants know who is talking even if they are not able to recognize the speaker's voice.
5. Note when anyone new enters the teleconference, or when a participant departs.
6. Remember that it is more difficult for non-native speakers to understand voices over the phone than in person; modify speech to make listening comprehension easier for them.
7. Refrain from long monologues; pause at regular intervals and ask for other views and/or questions.
8. During videoconferences, look into the camera when you are speaking; do not look only at people who are with you in the same room.
9. Avoid extended conversations with people in your own teleconference or videoconference room that fail to engage people in other locations.
10. If there is a lag between the time a statement is made and the time it is heard in another videoconference location, be patient and do not jump in with fresh statements that will confuse listeners—this is particularly essential when there are translators present as well.
11. Try to supplement conversation with graphics during a videoconference to facilitate understanding.
12. Deliberately provide "air time" to people who have not been able to get into the conversation.
13. Close the meeting by asking participants to confirm action items.
14. Follow up after the meeting by writing a summary of main points and action items and circulate it to each participant in a timely manner.

Table B-3. **Decision-Making Strategies**

Directive
- Leader makes decision based on his/her view of the issue
- Leader announces decision to team

Consultative
- Leader asks for opinions from all members
- Leader acknowledges and confirms opinions
- Leader makes decision
- Leader explains rationale for decision with reference to members' input

Democratic
- Leader guides discussion
- Leader ensures that all voices are heard
- Leader states question and calls for a vote
- All votes carry equal weight
- Vote determines outcome
- Threshold is usually 50 percent for decision to carry; percentages may vary, and must be agreed on prior to the vote

Consensus
- Leader guides discussion
- Leader periodically summarizes status of discussion
- Discussion continues until all are in agreement
- Even one dissenter precludes decision

Defer to Expert
- Leader guides discussion
- Leader suggests deferring decision to expert on team
- Leader must have either consensus or majority support to defer
- Once deferred, expert makes decision
- Expert explains rationale for decision

Table B-4. **Multicultural Teamwork: Mutual Listening Exercise**

Purpose

Meeting participants from different cultures will interview each other to gain a deeper understanding of critical issues.

Instructions

Take three *priority* items—those prioritized highest by the group—and interview your counterparts on what business actions are most helpful, actions that are least helpful, and recommendations for the future.

Guidelines for Interviewers

- Remain in a deep listening mode and draw out deeper meanings
- Don't talk about your opinions; seek the opinions and insights of the interviewees
- Use the three interview questions listed below to guide the interview
- Use an "interview guide" for taking notes on each of the three issues

Guidelines for Interviewees

- Give concrete examples to illustrate your responses to the interviewer
- Provide historical background and explain local circumstances when possible
- Don't hold back your valuable ideas and expertise; make sure that the interviewer clearly understands your perspective on the priority issues

Interview Questions

- What kinds of actions are most helpful?
- What kinds of actions are least helpful?
- What recommendations do you have for future action steps?

Appendix C: Western Assumptions and Possible Alternative Perspectives

Following is a set of alternative assumptions derived from various major overseas markets: China, Russia, Saudi Arabia, and Southeast Asia.

Table C-1. **Western Assumptions and Possible Alternative Perspectives**

Western Assumptions	**Possible Alternative Perspectives**
Serving customer needs is the foundation of our business.	"Unless you can get government approval, your business project is dead."
The product with the best quality and price will win out.	"We have no relationship. We don't trust you. You don't take time to talk to us. Why should we buy your product?"
Time is money. We must get things done quickly and efficiently.	"We have been living like this for two thousand years. We can wait a little longer."
Alternative viewpoints are good.	"You are the boss. *You* decide."
Each country has an official government to deal with.	"Those are national regulations. I'm talking about the local government's policy. And of course the mayor has his own interpretation of that policy."
This is a win-win situation, an expanding pie.	"*Nyet.* What is pie? You are always trying to change the subject to put us at a disadvantage."
The written contract is the final word.	"But the situation has changed! You must be flexible or we cannot continue to do business together. Bringing in your lawyers is an insult."
We have come to be helpful, to teach. Business is a positive, democratic force.	"You have come to plunder our resources, make quick money, and move on, leaving us to pick up the pieces. We don't need your corrupt Western values."

Notes

Preface

1. See, e.g., Robert Rosen, *Global Literacies: Lessons on Business Leadership and National Cultures* (New York: Simon and Schuster, 2000); Morgan McCall, *Developing Global Executives: The Lessons of International Experience* (Boston: Harvard University Press, 2002); and J. Stewart Black, Allen Morrison, and Hal Gregersen, *Global Explorers: The Next Generation of Leaders* (New York: Routledge, 1999).
2. See, e.g., Fons Trompenaars and Charles Hampden-Turner, *Riding the Waves of Culture: Understanding Diversity in Global Business* (New York: McGraw-Hill, 1998); and Geert Hofstede, *Culture's Consequences: International Differences in Work-Related Values* (Beverly Hills, CA: Sage, 1980).

Chapter 1

1. There is considerable confusion in the management literature around the question of what is a skill and what is a competency. I will use the two terms interchangeably here. One trendy practice is to define a *competency* as a more specific and concrete performance factor—particularly with reference to one's own

model—while relegating *skills* to a more general category used sometimes to refer pejoratively to the models of others. The word *competency* sounds reassuringly technical. In the end, however, there seems to be little substantive difference between the two terms aside from marketing panache.

2. See, e.g., Jeffrey Pfeffer, *The Human Equation: Building Profits by Putting People First* (Boston: Harvard Business School Press, 1998).

3. See, e.g., Tom Peters and Robert Waterman, *In Search of Excellence: Lessons from America's Best-Run Companies* (New York: Warner Books, 1982), 10. The other four elements of the McKinsey system are staffing, styles, shared values, and skills.

4. See, e.g., Nancy J. Adler, *International Dimensions of Organizational Behavior* (Cincinnati: South-Western Publishing, 2002), 89–90.

5. George Renwick, interview in *Face-to-Face,* vol. 1 of the video series *Globally Speaking: Skills and Strategies for Working with Asia,* prod. Shelley Lieberman, Aperian Global, San Francisco, 1997.

6. These comments were contributed by GlobeSmart online users in reference to various countries. Slight modifications have been made to the original remarks to enhance readability; see www.globesmart.com, Aperian Global, San Francisco.

Chapter 2

1. See, e.g., Trompenaars and Hampden-Turner, *Riding the Waves of Culture,* 23–24.

2. Clifford Geertz, *The Interpretation of Cultures* (New York: Basic Books, 1973), 89. Trompenaars et al. also cite Geertz.

3. Steven Rhinesmith makes a similar point in his book *A Manager's Guide to Globalization: Six Keys to Success in a Changing World* (Homewood, IL: Business One Irwin, 1993), 131–32. It has been argued that culture is an overriding variable or an envelope that shapes all the other factors (Fons Trompenaars, personal conversation, February 2002). There is certainly some truth to the idea that national culture shapes corporate cultures, individual personalities, professional specialties, and so on. However, this is a more indirect form of cultural influence that is harder to analyze, and the impact appears to be mutual. Organizational cultures of major corporations most definitely affect the countries in which they operate, for example, and a powerful individual can put his or her stamp on a culture and shift it in a new direction.

4. Nancy Adler makes a similar distinction using different terminology. She distinguishes between "harmful" and "helpful" stereotypes, describing the latter as consciously held, descriptive rather than evaluative, accurate, the best "first guess" about a group prior to acquiring information, and modified based on further observation and experience with actual people and situations. See Adler, *International Dimensions,* 81.

5. I faced this in my very first overseas experience more than thirty years ago at the age of fifteen—a high school homestay in Mexico City. My introduction to the household included a meeting with three maids from village Native American tribes—several more than I had met during my life up to that point. The entire

time I was there I met just one other young man besides myself who did not smoke. "¿Quieres un cigarrillo?" was a question that I learned to be more than a simple functional query. It was a gesture of friendship and a conversation starter that I awkwardly turned down for months. It seemed like every young man played the guitar and sang; I didn't play the guitar and sang only poorly.

One of the most common activities among my Mexican friends was to drive to coffee shops in the center of town together to talk—"Vamos al centro a platicar"—when I couldn't figure out for the life of me how they found so much to talk about for hours on end. Sometimes they bought drinks in paper cups before going home and then later rolled down the car windows on the way and tossed everything out into the streets; of course I was a budding environmentalist. Several young Mexicans who I met during that time bribed their way out of national military service, describing the act of bribery cheerfully as if it were an art form. I was beginning to struggle with my own conscience about the Vietnam War and did not consider bribing government officials to evade the draft to be a morally acceptable option.

As I have thought back on these experiences over the years, in every single case there was a significant clash of cultural values that made it hard to digest. The fact that I could not adjust gracefully or readily placed the values I had taken for granted—about social status, friendship, style, ethics, politics, sex—into a whole new and not entirely favorable perspective, and set me thinking for a lifetime.

6. For effectiveness in a multicultural environment, see, e.g., Paul Illman, *Selecting and Developing Overseas Managers* (New York: Amacom, 1976); and D. J. Kealey and B. D. Ruben, "Cross-Cultural Personnel Selection: Issues, Criteria, Methods," in *Handbook of Intercultural Training,* vol. 1, ed. R. W. Brislin and D. Landis, 156–75 (New York: Pergamon Press, 1983). For leadership characteristics, see Black, Morrison, and Gregersen, *Global Explorers.* There is overlap, for instance, between Ruben's categories of "tolerating ambiguity" and "empathy" and Black et al.'s descriptions of "perspective" and "character."

7. The descriptions of core values and dimensions of national culture given here were first published in Ernest Gundling, "The Future of Global Management," in *International Focus: In-Depth Articles for the Global HR Professional* (Alexandria, VA: Society for Human Resource Management, 2000), 1–15. Used with permission from SHRM.

Chapter 3

1. George Renwick, interview in *Transforming Leadership,* vol. 6 of *Globally Speaking,* Aperian Global.

2. The following advice from a Western manager who has done business in Turkey highlights the importance of ascription versus achievement in documenting qualifications, and relationships rather than task-focused, direct inquiries in drawing out their meaning:

> Your resume in Turkey should include your educational as well as professional experience and should note all degrees that you hold. In your resume, avoid using the results-oriented style preferred by many U.S. companies. Instead, list your academic and professional experiences factually with a neutral tone. Similarly, if you receive a resume from your Turkish counterpart, it is likely that it will understate his/her accomplishments. Be aware also that you are likely to receive an evasive answer if you directly question a Turkish counterpart about his/her background, at least until you have developed a relationship.

See www.globesmart.com, Aperian Global, San Francisco.
3. Albert Sui, interview in *Face-to-Face,* Aperian Global.
4. George Renwick, interview in *Face-to-Face,* Aperian Global.

Chapter 4

1. For example, a Chinese manager who grew up in the People's Republic of China described how her mother ended up spending time doing hard labor in a work camp. After expressing very mild criticism of the government during her student days, she was denounced by one of her best friends, tried, and convicted. Imagine how cautious this woman and every member of her family will be in the foreseeable future about stating their real opinions! Personal communication.
2. Albert Sui, interview in *Face-to-Face,* Aperian Global.
3. Lee Ting, interview in *Transforming Leadership,* Aperian Global.
4. To my knowledge, these terms were coined by Clifford Clarke.

Chapter 5

1. George Renwick, interview in *Team Systems,* vol. 5 of *Globally Speaking,* Aperian Global. Mr. Renwick contributed this analogy and several of the ideas in the preceding paragraph. He also suggests that one good informal method for improving the team's cohesion is to place it in an unfamiliar environment where team members will have to rely on each other.

> As with individuals, we want to provide many opportunities for the team to spend time together in informal situations. There is nothing so integrating for a multicultural team as for its members to be by themselves in a foreign environment, having to figure out how to take their next step there. This reduces differences, and really puts everybody in a challenging situation and a more interdependent situation if they are foreign together.

2. Albert Siu, vice president of education and training, AT&T, interview in *Team Meetings,* vol. 4 of *Globally Speaking,* Aperian Global.
3. Pat Cross, manager for training and development, KOMAG, suggested this approach in an interview in *Team Meetings,* Aperian Global.

4. Mary O'Hara Devereaux, interview in *Communicating Across Technology,* vol. 2 of *Globally Speaking,* Aperian Global.
5. Paul Jap, Singapore sales manager for Lucent Technologies, interview in *Team Meetings,* Aperian Global.

Chapter 6

1. George Renwick, interview in *Strategies for Training,* from the video series *Managing in China,* prod. Gina Levy, Aperian Global, San Francisco, 1997.
2. Ibid.
3. Two Vietnamese trainees recently flattered me by expressing their eagerness to have their picture taken together with me. In retrospect, however, this eagerness was probably due more to the fact that this was literally their first trip out of the country than any particular virtue of mine. Having their picture taken with a foreign instructor gave them proof to show their friends and colleagues.
4. Klaus Koster, general manager, Tianjin Henkel, interview in *Technology Transfer,* from *Managing in China,* Aperian Global. The original quote has been slightly altered to make it more readable.
5. George Renwick offers this advice:

> Performance appraisal actually increases tension in the supervisor/subordinate relationship which is most critical to the performance of the whole organization. Instead of dealing with this one-on-one, and possibly disrupting this critical relationship, let's take a systems approach. Let's put in place some standards that everybody's very clear about. Let's present...some examples of excellent performance—people doing it in exactly the way we want them to do it. And provide employee development—systematic, in-depth training, careful coaching by the manager of each subordinate. And let's make some commitments to the subordinates, both a manager's commitment and the organization's commitment. What do we receive in return? Their commitment to the manager and to the organization so that, yes, they are performing better because they are committed to the organization.

Interview in *Transforming Leadership,* Aperian Global.
6. Nick Zhang, director of business development, Xian Janssen, interview in *Performance Management and Compensation,* from *Managing in China,* Aperian Global.
7. "I've had instances where an employee got five things good, and one needs improvement, and they want to quit because they've lost face and they feel that their boss doesn't trust them. That's very, very common throughout China." Kathy Hanna, director of human resources, Greater China, Allied Signal, interview in *Performance Management and Compensation,* Aperian Global.
8. Yi Qing, franchise manager, Laboratoires Fournier, interview in *Performance Management and Compensation,* Aperian Global.

Chapter 7

1. These are the classic Wilson Learning types pioneered by Larry Wilson, which have been popular for many years. Although Mr. Wilson has long since left the organization he founded, the Wilson Learning Corporation still bears his name.
2. George Renwick, interview in *Transforming Leadership*, Aperian Global.
3. Ibid.

Chapter 8

1. For a similar list of topics related to diplomatic negotiations, see Richard H. Solomon, *Chinese Negotiating Behavior* (Washington, D.C.: U.S. Institute of Peace Press, 2001).

Chapter 9

1. This model was created at my request by a group of MBA students at the University of California, Berkeley.
2. The "what," "who," and "how" described here are similar to what Nancy Adler defines as scope, representation, and process. See Nancy J. Adler and Susan Bartholomew, "Managing Globally Competent People," *The Academy of Management Executive* 6,3 (1992): 52–65.
3. Michael Porter, "What Is Strategy?" *Harvard Business Review* (November–December 1996): 61–78.
4. Many of these questions are inspired by Michael Porter's definition of strategy.
5. Christopher A. Bartlett and Sumantra Ghoshal, *Managing Across Borders: The Transnational Solution* (Boston: Harvard Business School Press, 1991), chap. 10. The authors recommend building an "integrated network" in which corporate resources are both dispersed and interdependent—national units make their own differentiated contributions while leveraging integration with worldwide operations.
6. See J. Stewart Black, et al., *Globalizing People Through International Assignments* (Menlo Park, CA: Addison-Wesley, 1999), 94. At the extreme end of this spectrum of experience is the expatriate war-horse who says, "They gave me a plane ticket and a check and told me to go start up operations in Chile."
7. A recent count of top 3M executives showed that ten out of the top twelve had completed expatriate assignments and/or were born outside the U.S. See Ernest Gundling, *The 3M Way to Innovation: Balancing People and Profit* (New York: Kodansha International, 2000), 137.

Chapter 10

1. An expanded version of this maquiladora case was originally written by Jim Latimer, an Aperian Global colleague who spent more than a year working in the

two factory locations. I was fortunate enough to be able to visit with Jim in both the U.S. and the Mexican factories and to review early drafts of the article. The case first appeared in "Cross-Border Knowledge Transfer," *Technical Training* (September–October 1999): 49–51. Passages from the article are summarized or paraphrased here with permission from the American Society for Training and Development.

2. Sources for this section include approximately forty interviews conducted in China in preparation for the *Managing in China* video series produced by Aperian Global. Among the titles in this series are *Technology Transfer, Strategies for Training,* and *Localizing Leadership*. Gina Levy was the producer for this series. My colleagues and I at Aperian Global—and prior to that at Clarke Consulting Group—have also been involved directly in projects including a U.S.–Japan joint venture manufacturing plant in Thailand; a U.S.–Russian joint venture in Siberia; a transfer of Japanese manufacturing operations to the U.S.; Korean and European management training projects in Silicon Valley; and a U.S. firm's quality training program in Japan.

3. Helmut Klassen, managing operations director, Shanghai Fu Hua Glass Company, interview in *Technology Transfer,* Aperian Global.

4. Klaus Koster, general manager, Tianjin Henkel, interview in *Technology Transfer,* Aperian Global.

5. George Renwick, interview in *Technology Transfer,* Aperian Global.

6. The bulk of this section is based on information in Gundling, *3M Way to Innovation,* 138–42.

7. This is true not only in developing countries, but also in advanced economies such as Italy, for example, where many residents have a preference for text messages sent to cell phones rather than e-mail. See "The Way to Reach an Italian? Not E-Mail," *Business Week,* April 15, 2002.

8. This anecdote is excerpted with permission from Ernest Gundling, "How to Communicate Globally," *Training and Development* (June 1999): 28–31.

9. Robert Keigher, human resources director, Johnson & Johnson, Shanghai, interview in *Localizing Leadership,* Aperian Global.

10. See www.knowledgebusiness.com for a summary description of the Global Most Admired Knowledge Enterprises research program. It is interesting to note that the award criteria are not focused on information technology, even though this is an important feature of many knowledge transfer projects, including Buckman's. The eight award criteria used are

- Creating a corporate knowledge culture
- Developing knowledge leaders
- Delivering knowledge-based products/services/solutions
- Maximizing enterprise intellectual capital
- Creating an environment for collaborative knowledge sharing

- Creating a learning organization
- Focusing on customer knowledge
- Transforming knowledge into shareholder value

Buckman Laboratories' website, www.buckman.com, outlines the company's environmental programs and awards and contains the most recent annual report.
11. "2001 Buckman Laboratories Annual Report," www.buckman.com.
12. Ibid.
13. Glenn Rifken, "Buckman Labs Is Nothing but Net," *Fast Company* (June 1996). Rifkin provides an early, entertaining description of Buckman's knowledge transfer initiative as it was beginning to gather momentum.
14. Ibid. See also Carla O'Dell and C. Jackson Grayson, Jr., *If Only We Knew What We Know* (New York: The Free Press, 1998), 145. This book takes up Buckman Laboratories as a knowledge transfer case study in considerable detail (144–51).
15. William A. Fischer, professor, International Institute for Management Development, Lausanne, Switzerland, interview in *Technology Transfer,* Meridian Resources Associates.
16. Jason Lum, vice president and regional director of human resources, Asia-Pacific, Motorola, interview in *Localizing Leadership,* Aperian Global.

Chapter 11

1. Many of these items are based on research on 3M, outlined in Gundling, *3M Way to Innovation.* See especially the list of competencies for "Nurturing Innovation" on p. 106. As usual, similar issues can appear within a monocultural environment, but the obstacles to innovation become more acute in a cross-border context when the cultural heritage and institutions that shape employee behaviors differ.
2. This was apparently the case in the invention of the "Soapless Washing Machine" by Sanyo Electric, in which a senior sales executive pushed the company's R&D community to invent a product that he was convinced would be a winner in the marketplace. The researchers were skeptical at first and more than once told the executive that his idea was impossible. Ultimately, however, they achieved a genuine breakthrough by incorporating technology from a division located nearby that made ultrasound cleaning systems for swimming pools. They invented a washing machine that offered consumers the option of cleaning clothes with or without soap. (This story was narrated in a speech by a Sanyo Electric R&D manager in May 2002 and received considerable attention in the Japanese press.)
3. See Gundling, *3M Way to Innovation,* chap. 1, esp. 33–34.
4. See ibid., 122–34, for more information and examples on these areas of innovative activity.
5. NHK Group, *Good Mileage: The High-Performance Business Philosophy of Soichiro Honda* (Tokyo, NHK Publishing, 1996), 35.
6. Ibid., 36–37.

7. See Tetsuo Sakiya, *Honda Motor: The Men, the Management, the Machines* (Tokyo: Kodansha International, 1982), 118–25.
8. See ibid., 115, 145–46.
9. See ibid., 120–25, 201–2.
10. See ibid., 182. Soichiro Honda was also reportedly the only Japanese automobile executive willing to meet with consumer crusader Ralph Nader during his visit to Japan in 1971 (165).
11. www.nytimes.com/2002/06/12/business/12HOND.html
12. www.infosys.com/credentials/default.asp
13. www.infosys.com/innovation/default.asp
14. www.rediff.com/news/2000/dec/13spec2.htm
15. www.cnn.com/2001/BUSINESS/asia/10/05/india.infosys.biz
16. The "India's Most Respected Company" ranking was made by *Business World;* the number-one India-based firm ranking comes from the *Far Eastern Economic Review.* See www.infosys.com/awards/company.asp. See also www.infosys.com/social/default.asp.
17. www.rediff.com/news/2000/dec/13spec1.htm

Chapter 12

1. The author worked closely with Kaneko-san and 3M in launching this organizational change project.
2. Nancy Adler outlines a related set of options for dealing with problems based on divergent cultural practices. These include cultural avoidance, cultural dominance, cultural compromise, cultural synergy, and cultural accommodation. See Adler, *International Dimensions,* 122–29.
3. Charles Hampden-Turner and Fons Trompenaars, for example, have developed a well-tuned methodology for dilemma reconciliation, justly receiving considerable attention for their efforts. See, e.g., Fons Trompenaars and Charles Hampden-Turner, *Twenty-One Leaders for the Twenty-First Century: How Innovative Leaders Manage in the Digital Age* (New York: McGraw-Hill, 2002). Sincere practitioners of this art find that the greatest challenge lies in moving from reconciliation between different ideas and values to reconciliation at the level of everyday organizational systems and practice.
4. An economist who helped to draft proposed changes to existing laws was recently assassinated outside his home in Bologna. See "European Economies: Italian Labor Law Fuels Strikes, Murders," quote.Bloomberg.com, March 22, 2002.

Synthesis

1. See Janet M. Bennett, "Cultural Marginality," in *Education for the Intercultural Experience,* ed. Michael R. Paige (Yarmouth, ME: Intercultural Press, 1993).
2. See Jay Mazur, "Labor's New Internationalism," *Foreign Affairs* (January–February 2000): 80.

3. See ibid., 80–81.

4. A positive illustration of global citizenship is the new set of products known as hydrofluoroethers (HFEs) that have been developed by 3M's Specialty Chemicals Division. HFEs are designed to replace the chlorofluorocarbons (CFCs) and other ozone-depleting substances that have had such a devastating impact on the earth's ozone layer. The 3M HFEs have zero ozone depletion potential and have generated a great deal of excitement within the global specialty chemicals market. This new family of products shows every sign of being a great success in the rapidly growing worldwide market for CFC replacements. It is targeted at specific customer needs, has outstanding performance and safety features, is actively promoted by government regulatory bodies, and is fully disposable when it has reached the end of its life cycle. 3M can justifiably take both pride in, and profits from, this achievement.

5. The author conducted these interviews with employees of several different firms in the financial and electronics industries in the fall of 2001.

Bibliography

Books and Publications

Abegglen, James. *Sea Change: Pacific Asia As the New World Industrial Center.* New York: The Free Press, 1994.

Adler, Gordon. "The Case of the Floundering Expatriate." *Harvard Business Review* (July–August 1995): 24–40.

Adler, Nancy J. *Managing International Transitions.* Montreal: Alcan, 1980.

———. "Managing Cross-Cultural Transitions." *Group and Organization Studies* 6,3 (1981): 341–56.

———. *International Dimensions of Organizational Behavior.* 4th ed. Cincinnati: South-Western Publishing, 2002.

Adler, Nancy J., and Susan Bartholomew. "Managing Globally Competent People." *Academy of Management Executives* 6,3 (1992): 52–65.

Adler, Nancy J., and Fariborz Ghadar. "Strategic Human Resource Management: A Global Perspective." In *Human Resource Management in International Comparison*, ed. Rudiger Pieper, 235–60. Berlin: De Gruyter, 1990.

Adler, Nancy J., and Mariann S. Jelinek. "Is 'Organizational Culture' Culture Bound?" *Human Resource Management* 25,1 (1986): 73–90.

Althen, Gary. *American Ways: A Guide for Foreigners in the United States.* Yarmouth, ME: Intercultural Press, 1988.

Alvi, S. A., and S. W. Ahmed. "Assessing Organizational Commitment in a Developing Country: Pakistan, a Case Study." *Human Relations* 40,5 (1987): 267–80.

Argyris, Chris. *Knowledge for Action.* San Francisco: Jossey-Bass, 1993.

Austin, James E. *Managing in Developing Countries: Strategic Analysis and Operating Techniques.* New York: The Free Press, 1990.

Axtell, Roger E. *The Do's and Taboos of International Trade: A Small Business Primer.* New York: John Wiley and Sons, 1991.

———. *Do's and Taboos of Body Language Around the World.* New York: John Wiley and Sons, 1993.

———. *Gestures: The Do's and Taboos of Body Language Around the World.* New York: John Wiley and Sons, 1998.

Barnathan, Joyce. "Passage Back to India." *Business Week* 17 (July 1995): 44–46.

Barnlund, Dean C. *Communicative Styles of Japanese and Americans: Images and Realities.* Belmont, CA: Wadsworth, 1989.

Bartlett, Christopher A., and Sumantra Ghoshal. "Tap Your Subsidiaries for Global Reach." *Harvard Business Review* (November–December 1986).

———. *Managing Across Borders: The Transnational Solution.* Cambridge, MA: Harvard Business School Press, 1989.

———. "What Is a Global Manager?" *Harvard Business Review* (September–October 1992).

———."Changing the Role of Top Management: Beyond Systems to People." *Harvard Business Review* (May–June 1995): 132–42.

Beal, Tim, and Sallie Yea. "Corruption, Development and Maturity: A Perspective on South Korea." Fifth conference of the Asian Forum on Business Education. Patumtani, Thailand, Rangsit University, June 1997.

Benedict, Ruth. *Patterns of Culture.* New York: Houghton Mifflin, 1934.

———. "Anthropology and Culture Change." *The American Scholar* 11,2 (1942): 243–48.

Bennett, Janet M. "Cultural Marginality." In *Education for the Intercultural Experience*, ed. Michael R. Paige. Yarmouth, ME: Intercultural Press, 1993.

Berenbeim, R. E. *Managing the International Company: Building a Global Perspective.* New York: The Conference Board, 1983.

Birkinshaw, Julia, and Neil Hood. "Unleash Innovation in Foreign Subsidiaries." *Harvard Business Review* (March 2001): 131–37.

Black, J. Stewart, and Hal B. Gregersen. *So You're Going Overseas.* San Diego, CA: Global Business Publishers, 1998.

Black, J. Stewart, Hal B. Gregersen, and Mark E. Mendenhall. *Global Assignments: Successfully Expatriating and Repatriating International Managers.* San Francisco: Jossey-Bass, 1992.

Black, J. Stewart, Hal B. Gregersen, Mark E. Mendenhall, and Linda K. Stroh. *Globalizing People Through International Assignments.* Menlo Park, CA: Addison-Wesley, 1999.

Black, J. Stewart, Allen J. Morrison, and Hal B. Gregersen. *Global Explorers: The Next Generation of Leaders.* New York: Routledge, 1999.

Blackman, Carolyn. *Negotiating China: Case Studies and Strategies.* St. Leonards, Australia: Allen and Unwin, 1997.

Boyacigiller, Nakiye, and Nancy J. Adler. "The Parochial Dinosaur: The Organizational Sciences in a Global Context." *Academy of Management Review* 16,2 (1991): 262–90.

Brake, Terence, Danielle Medira Walker, and Thomas Walker. *Doing Business Internationally.* Burr Ridge, IL: Irwin, 1995.

Brislin, Richard W., and Tomoko Yoshida. *Intercultural Communication Training: An Introduction.* Thousand Oaks, CA: Sage, 1994.

Brown, Clair, and Michael Reich. "Developing Skills and Pay Through Career Ladders: Lessons from Japanese Companies." *California Management Review* (Winter 1997): 124–44.

Burke, W. Warner. *Organization Development: Principles and Practices.* New York: HarperCollins, 1982.

Castaneda, Jorge. "Ferocious Differences." *Atlantic Monthly* (July 1995): 68–76.

Cerny, Keith. "Making Local Knowledge Global." *Harvard Business Review* (May–June 1996): 22–38.

Chaney, Lillian H., and Jeanette S. Martin. *Intercultural Business Communication.* 2d ed. Upper Saddle River, NJ: Prentice Hall, 2000.

Christensen, Clayton M. *The Innovator's Dilemma.* New York: HarperBusiness, 2000.

Church, Peter, ed. *Focus on Southeast Asia: A Country-by-Country Introduction.* Hong Kong: ASEAN Focus Group, 1995.

Contractor, Farok, and Peter Lorange. *Cooperative Strategies in International Business: Joint Ventures and Technology Partnerships Between Firms.* Lexington, MA: Lexington Books, 1988.

Copeland, Lennie, and Lewis Griggs. *Going International: How to Make Friends and Deal Effectively in the International Marketplace.* New York: Random House, 1985.

Cox, Taylor, and S. Blake. "Managing Cultural Diversity: Implications for Organizational Competitiveness." *Academy of Management Executive* 5,3 (1991): 45–56.

Crane, Robert, ed. *European Business Culture.* Harlow, England: Pearson Education, 2000.

Cushner, Kenneth, and Richard W. Brislin. *Intercultural Interactions: A Practical Guide.* 2d ed. Newbury Park, CA: Sage, 1996.

Cutcher-Gershenfeld, Joel, et al. "Japanese Team-Based Systems in North America: Explaining the Diversity." *California Management Review* (fall 1994): 42–64.

Daniels, John D., and Lee H. Radebaugh. *International Business: Environments and Operations.* 9th ed. Upper Saddle River, NJ: Prentice Hall, 2001.

Daniels, John L., and N. Caroline Daniels. *Global Vision: Building New Models for the Corporation of the Future.* New York: McGraw-Hill, 1993.

Davenport, Thomas, and Laurence Prusak. *Working Knowledge: How Organizations Manage What They Know.* Boston: Harvard Business School Press, 1998.

Davis, Stanley M. *Comparative Management: Organizational and Cultural Perspectives.* Englewood Cliffs, NJ: Prentice Hall, 1971.

Deal, Terrence E., and Allan A. Kennedy. *Corporate Cultures: The Rites and Rituals of Corporate Life.* Reading, MA: Addison-Wesley, 1982.

De Mente, Boye Lafayette. *NTC's Dictionary of Mexican Cultural Code Words: The Complete Guide to Key Words That Express How the Mexicans Think, Communicate, and Behave.* Lincolnwood, IL: NTC Publishing Group, 1996.

Denison, Daniel R. *Corporate Culture and Organizational Effectiveness.* Wiley Series on Organizational Assessment and Change. New York: John Wiley and Sons, 1990.

Deresky, Helen. *International Management: Managing Across Borders and Cultures.* 3d ed. Upper Saddle River, NJ: Prentice Hall, 2000.

Donaldson, Thomas. "Values in Tension: Ethics away from Home." *Harvard Business Review* (September–October 1996): 48–62.

Drucker, Peter F. *Managing in a Time of Great Change.* New York: Truman Talley Books/Plume, 1995.

Duarte, Deborah L., and Nancy Tennant Snyder. *Mastering Virtual Teams: Strategies, Tools, and Techniques That Succeed.* San Francisco: Jossey-Bass, 1999.

Evans, Paul, Yves Dox, and Andre Laurent, eds. *Human Resource Management in International Firms: Change, Globalization, Innovation.* New York: St. Martin's Press, 1990.

Fadiman, Jeffrey. "A Traveler's Guide to Gifts and Bribes." *Harvard Business Review* (June–August 1986): 120–27.

Fatehi, Kamal. *International Management: A Cross-Cultural and Functional Perspective.* Upper Saddle River, NJ: Prentice Hall, 1996.

Ferguson, Henry. *Tomorrow's Global Executive.* Homewood, IL: Dow Jones-Irwin, 1988.

Ferraro, Gary P. *The Cultural Dimension of International Business.* 4th ed. Upper Saddle River, NJ: Prentice Hall, 2002.

Filatotchev, Igor, et al. "Corporate Restructuring in Russian Privatizations: Implications for U.S. Investors." *California Management Review* (winter 1996): 87–105.

Fisher, G. *International Negotiation: A Cross-Cultural Perspective.* Chicago: Intercultural Press, 1980.

Francesco, Anne Marie, and Barry Allen Gold. *International Organizational Behavior: Text, Readings, Cases, and Skills.* Upper Saddle River, NJ: Prentice Hall, 1998.

Friedman, Thomas L. *The Lexus and the Olive Tree: Understanding Globalization.* New York: Anchor Books, 2000.

Frost, Peter J., et al., eds. *Organizational Culture.* Beverly Hills, CA: Sage, 1985.

———, eds. *Reframing Organizational Culture.* Newbury Park, CA: Sage, 1991.

Gannon, Martin J. *Understanding Global Cultures: Metaphorical Journeys Through 23 Nations.* 2d ed. Thousand Oaks, CA: Sage, 2001.

Geertz, Clifford. *The Interpretation of Cultures.* New York: Basic Books, 1973.

Gesteland, Richard R. *Cross-Cultural Business Behavior: Marketing, Negotiating, and Managing Across Cultures.* Copenhagen: Copenhagen Business School Press, 1999.

Global Road Warrior: 95-Country Handbook for the International Business Traveler. San Rafael, CA: World Trade Press, 2000.

Goffee, Rob, and Gareth Jones. "What Holds the Modern Company Together?" *Harvard Business Review* (November–December 1996): 133–48.

Greer, Charles, and Gregory Stephens. "Employee Relations Issues for U.S. Companies in Mexico." *California Management Review* (spring 1996): 121–45.

Gundling, Ernest. "Ethics and Working with the Japanese: The Entrepreneur and the Elite Course." *California Management Review* 33,3 (1991): 25–39.

———. "Japan-Bound Training." *Training and Development* (July 1992): 41–44.

———. "How to Communicate Globally." *Training and Development* (June 1999): 28–31.

———. "The Future of Global Management." In *International Focus: In-Depth Articles for the Global HR Professional* (Society for Human Resource Management, 2000): 1–15.

———. *The 3M Way to Innovation: Balancing People and Profit.* Tokyo: Kodansha International, 2000.

Hall, Edward T., and Mildred Reed Hall. *Understanding Cultural Differences: Germans, French, and Americans.* Yarmouth, ME: Intercultural Press, 1990.

Hamada, Tomoko, and Willis E. Sibley, eds. *Anthropological Perspectives on Organizational Culture.* Lanham, MD: University Press of America, 1994.

Hamel, Gary. *Leading the Revolution.* Boston: Harvard Business School Press, 2000.

Hampden-Turner, Charles, and Fons Trompenaars. *Building Cross-Cultural Competence: How to Create Wealth from Conflicting Values.* New Haven, CT: Yale University Press, 2000.

Harris, Philip, and Robert Moran. *Managing Cultural Differences*, 2d ed. Houston: Gulf Publishing, 1987.

Harrison, Lawrence E., and Samuel P. Huntington, eds. *Culture Matters: How Values Shape Human Progress.* New York: Basic Books, 2000.

Heenan, David A., and Howard Permutter. *Multinational Organizational Development.* Reading, MA: Addison-Wesley, 1979.

Hellweg, Susan, Larry A. Samovar, and Lisa Skow. "Cultural Variations in Negotiation Styles." In *Intercultural Communication: A Reader.* 6th ed. Ed. Larry Samovar and Richard Porter. Belmont, CA: Wadsworth, 1991.

Hickman, Craig R., and Michael A. Silva. *Creating Excellence: Managing Corporate Culture, Strategy, and Change in the New Age.* New York: New American Library, 1985.

Hofstede, Geert. *Culture's Consequences: International Differences in Work-Related Values.* Beverly Hills, CA: Sage, 1980.

———. "Motivation, Leadership, and Organization: Do American Theories Apply Abroad?" *Organizational Dynamics* 9,1 (1980): 42–63.

———. *Cultures and Organizations: Software of the Mind.* New York: McGraw-Hill, 1997.

Hori, Shintaro. "Fixing Japan's White-Collar Economy: A Personal View." *Harvard Business Review* (November–December 1993).

Hu, Wenzhong, and Cornelius L. Grove. *Encountering the Chinese: A Guide for Americans.* Yarmouth, ME: Intercultural Press, 1991.

Illman, Paul E. *Selecting and Developing Overseas Managers.* New York: Amacom, 1976.

Inkpen, Andrew. "Creating Knowledge Through Collaboration." *California Management Review* (Fall 1996): 132–48.

Jaeger, Alfred M. "The Transfer of Organizational Culture Overseas: An Approach to Control in the Multinational Corporation." *Journal of International Business Studies* 1,2 (1983): 91–114.

James, David L. *The Executive Guide to Asia-Pacific Communications: Doing Business Across the Pacific.* New York: Kodansha America, 1995.

Johnson, Simon, and Gary Loveman. "Starting Over: Poland After Communism." *Harvard Business Review* (March–April 1995): 44–57.

Joynt, Pat, and Malcolm Warner, eds. *Managing in Different Cultures.* New York: Columbia University Press, 1985.

Kanter, Rosabeth Moss, Barry A. Stein, and Todd D. Jick. *The Challenge of Organizational Change: How Companies Experience It and Leaders Guide It.* New York: The Free Press, 1992.

Katzenbach, Jon R., and Douglas K. Smith. *The Wisdom of Teams: Creating the High-Performance Organization.* New York: HarperBusiness, 1993.

Kealey, D. J., and B. D. Ruben, "Cross-Cultural Personnel Selection: Issues, Criteria, Methods." In *Handbook of Intercultural Training.* Vol. 1, ed. R. W. Brislin and D. Landis, 156–75. New York: Pergamon Press, 1983.

Kelley, Tom, with Jonathan Littman. *The Art of Innovation.* New York: Doubleday, 2001.

Kenna, Peggy, and Sondra Lacy. *Business China: A Practical Guide to Understanding Chinese Business Culture.* Lincolnwood, IL: Passport Books, 1994.

———. *Business Mexico: A Practical Guide to Understanding Mexican Business Culture.* Lincolnwood, IL: Passport Books, 1994.

Kilmann, Ralph H., Mary J. Saxton, and Roy Serpa, eds. *Gaining Control of the Corporate Culture.* San Francisco: Jossey-Bass, 1985.

Kim, Linsu. "The Dynamics of Samsung's Technological Learning in Semiconductors." *California Management Review* (spring 1997): 86–100.

Kirkbride, Paul, and Shae Wan Chaw. "The Cross-Cultural Transfer of Organizational Cultures: Two Case Studies of Corporate Mission Statements." *Asia Pacific Journal of Management* 5,1 (1987): 55–66.

Klare, Michael. "The New Geography of Conflict." *Foreign Affairs* 80,3 (2001): 49–61.

Knowledge and the Firm. Special issue of *California Management Review* (Haas School of Business, University of California, Berkeley) 40,3 (spring 1998).

Kohls, L. Robert. *Survival Kit for Overseas Living: For Americans Planning to Live and Work Abroad.* 3d ed. Yarmouth, ME: Intercultural Press, 1996.

Kong, Tat Yan. "Corruption and Its Institutional Foundations: The Experience of South Korea." *IDS Bulletin* 27,2 (1996): 48–55.

Kotter, John P. *Leading Change.* Boston: Harvard Business School Press, 1996.

———. *What Leaders Really Do.* Boston: Harvard Business Review, 1999.

Kras, Eva S. *Management in Two Cultures: Bridging the Gap Between U.S. and Mexican Managers.* Rev. ed. Yarmouth, ME: Intercultural Press, 1995.

Latimer, Jim. "Cross-Border Knowledge Transfer." *Technical Training* (September–October 1999): 49–51.

Leifer, Richard, et al. *Radical Innovation: How Mature Companies Can Outsmart Upstarts.* Boston: Harvard Business School Press, 2000.

Leppert, Paul. *Doing Business with Mexico.* Fremont, CA: Jain Publishing Company, 1996.

Lingle, Christopher. *Singapore's Authoritarian Capitalism: Asian Values, Free Market Illusions, and Political Dependency.* Fairfax, VA: The Locke Institute, 1995.

Lipnack, Jennifer, and Jeffrey Stamps. *Virtual Teams: Reaching Across Space, Time, and Organizations with Technology.* New York: John Wiley and Sons, 1997.

Lovelock, Christopher, and George Yip. "Developing Global Strategies for Service Business." *California Management Review* (winter 1996): 64–86.

Malloy, Ruth Lor. *China Guide.* Columbus Circle Station, NY: Open Road Publishing, 1996.

Marquardt, Michael J., and Nancy O. Berger. *Global Leaders for the 21st Century.* Albany, NY: State University of New York Press, 2000.

Marquardt, Michael J., and Lisa Horvath. *Global Teams: How Top Multinationals Span Boundaries and Cultures with High-Speed Teamwork.* Mountain View, CA: Davies-Black Publishing, 2001.

Marsden, D. "Indigenous Management." *International Journal of Human Resource Management* 2,1 (1991): 21–38.

McCall, Morgan W., Jr., and George P. Hollenbeck. *Developing Global Executives: The Lessons of International Experience.* Boston: Harvard Business School Press, 2002.

Mead, Richard. *International Management: Cross Cultural Dimensions.* Cambridge, MA: Blackwell, 1994.

Mintzberg, Henry, et al. "The 'Honda Effect' Revisited." CMR Forum: A Symposium. *California Management Review* (summer 1996): 78–117.

Mitroff, Ian I. *Business Not As Usual.* San Francisco: Jossey-Bass, 1987.

Moran, Robert, and Philip Harris. *Managing Cultural Synergy.* Houston: Gulf Publishing, 1982.

Morrison, Terri, Wayne A. Conaway, and George A. Borden. *Kiss, Bow, or Shake Hands: How to Do Business in Sixty Countries*. Holbrook, MA: Adams Media Corporation, 1994.

Negandhi, Anant R. "Convergence in Organizational Practices: An Empirical Study of Industrial Enterprise in Developing Countries." In *Organizations Alike and Unlike*, ed. Cornelis J. Lammers and David J. Hickson, 323–45. London: Routledge and Kegan Paul, 1979.

Newman, William H., "Cultural Assumptions Underlying U.S. Management Concepts." In *Management in an International Context*, ed. J. L. Massie and S. Laytie, 327–52. New York: Harper and Row, 1972.

NHK Group. *Good Mileage: The High-Performance Business Philosophy of Soichiro Honda*. Tokyo: NHK Publishing, 1996.

O'Dell, Carla, and C. Jackson Grayson, Jr., with Nilly Essaides. *If Only We Knew What We Know: The Transfer of Internal Knowledge and Best Practices*. New York: The Free Press, 1998.

O'Hara-Devereaux, Mary, and Robert Johansen. *GlobalWork: Bridging Distance, Culture, and Time*. San Francisco: Jossey-Bass, 1994.

Osborne, Milton. *Southeast Asia: An Introductory History*. 7th ed. St. Leonards, Australia: Allen and Unwin, 1997.

Osland, Gregory, and S. Tamer Cavusgil. "Performance Issues in U.S.–China Joint Ventures." *California Management Review* (winter 1996): 106–30.

Paige, Michael R., ed. *Education for the Intercultural Experience*. Yarmouth, ME: Intercultural Press, 1993.

Perera, Audrey. *The Simple Guide to Customs and Etiquette in Singapore*. Kent, England: Global Books Ltd., 1996.

Perlmutter, Howard V., and David A. Heenan. "How Multinational Should Your Top Managers Be?" *Harvard Business Review* 52,6 (1974): 121–32.

———. "Cooperate to Compete Globally." *Harvard Business Review* 64,2 (1986): 136–52.

Peters, Thomas J., and Robert H. Waterman, Jr. *In Search of Excellence: Lessons from America's Best-Run Companies*. New York: Warner Books, 1982.

Peterson, Richard B., ed. *Managers and National Culture: A Global Perspective*. Westport, CT: Quorum Books, 1993.

Pfeffer, Jeffrey. *The Human Equation: Building Profits by Putting People First*. Boston: Harvard Business School Press, 1998.

Porter, Michael. "What Is Strategy?" *Harvard Business Review* (November–December 1996): 61–78.

Pucik, Vladimir, Noel M. Tichy, and Carole K. Barnett, eds. *Globalizing Management: Creating and Leading a Competitive Organization*. New York: John Wiley and Sons, 1992.

Ratiu, I. "Thinking Internationally: A Comparison of How International Executives Learn." *International Studies of Management and Organization* 13,1–2 (1983): 139–50.

Rhinesmith, Stephen H. "An Agenda for Globalization." *Training and Development* (November 1991): 22–29.

———. "Going Global from the Inside Out." *Training and Development* (February 1991): 42–47.

———. *A Manager's Guide to Globalization: Six Keys to Success in a Changing World.* Alexandria, VA: The American Society for Training and Development, 1993.

Rischard, Jean-François. *High Noon: 20 Global Problems, 20 Years to Solve Them.* New York: Basic Books, 2002.

Roces, Alfredo, and Grace Roces. *Culture Shock: Philippines.* Portland, OR: Graphic Arts Center Publishing Company, 1985.

Ronen, Simcha. *Comparative and Multinational Management.* New York: John Wiley and Sons, 1986.

Ronen, Simcha, and Oded Shenkar, "Clustering Countries on Attitudinal Dimensions: A Review and Synthesis." *Academy of Management Review* 10,3 (1985): 435–54.

Rosen, Robert. *Global Literacies: Lessons on Business Leadership and National Cultures.* New York: Simon and Schuster, 2000.

Ross, John. "Treasure of the Costa Grande." *Sierra* (July–August 1996): 22–24.

Rotberg, Robert. "Africa's Mess, Mugabe's Mayhem." *Foreign Affairs* 79,5 (2000): 47–61.

Sackmann, Sonja A. *Cultural Knowledge in Organizations: Exploring the Collective Mind.* Newbury Park, CA: Sage, 1991.

Sakiya, Tetsuo. *Honda Motor: The Men, the Management, the Machines.* Tokyo: Kodansha, 1982.

Samovar, Larry A., and Richard E. Porter. *Intercultural Communication: A Reader.* 6th ed. Belmont, CA: Wadsworth, 1991.

Sanyal, Rajib N. *International Management: A Strategic Perspective.* Upper Saddle River, NJ: Prentice Hall, 2001.

Sathe, Vijay. *Culture and Related Corporate Realities.* Homewood, IL: Richard Irwin, 1985.

Schmitt, Bernd, and Yigang Pan. "Managing Corporate and Brand Identities in the Asia-Pacific Region." *California Management Review* (summer 1994): 32–48.

Schneider, Susan C., and Jean-Louis Barsoux. *Managing Across Cultures.* London: Prentice Hall Europe, 1997.

Scott, Bill. *The Skills of Negotiating.* New York: John Wiley and Sons, 1981.

Shama, Avraham. "Entry Strategies of U.S. Firms to the Newly Independent States, Baltic States, and Eastern European Countries." *California Management Review* (spring 1995): 90–109.

Sheridan, Kyoko, ed. *Emerging Economic Systems in Asia: A Political and Economic Survey.* St. Leonards, Australia: Allen and Unwin, 1998.

Smith, Douglas K. *Taking Charge of Change: 10 Principles for Managing People and Performance.* Reading, MA: Addison-Wesley, 1996.

Soloman, Richard. *Chinese Negotiating Behavior.* Washington, D.C.: Institute of Peace Press, 2001.

Spar, Debora. "Lawyers Abroad: The Internationalization of Legal Practice." *California Management Review* (spring 1997): 8–28.

Stewart, Edward C., and Milton J. Bennett. *American Cultural Patterns: A Cross-Cultural Perspective.* Rev. ed. Yarmouth, ME: Intercultural Press, 1991.

Sullivan, Jeremiah J. *Exploring International Business Environments.* Boston: Pearson Custom Publishing, 1999.

Terpstra, Vern, and Kenneth David. *The Cultural Environment of International Business.* 2d ed. Pelham Manor, NY: South-Western Publishing, 1985.

Tichey, Noel M., with Eli Cohen. *The Leadership Engine: How Winning Companies Build Leaders at Every Level.* New York: HarperBusiness, 1997.

Torbiorn, I. *Living Abroad: Personal Adjustment and Personnel Policy in Overseas Settings.* New York: John Wiley and Sons, 1982.

Trompenaars, Fons, and Charles Hampden-Turner. *Riding the Waves of Culture: Understanding Diversity in Global Business.* 2d ed. New York: McGraw-Hill, 1998.

———. *Twenty-One Leaders for the Twenty-First Century: How Innovative Leaders Manage in the Digital Age.* New York: McGraw-Hill, 2002.

Tung, R. "Selection and Training of Personnel for Overseas Assignments." *Columbia Journal of World Business* 16,1 (1981): 68–78.

Tushman, Michael L., and Charles A. O'Reilly III. *Winning Through Innovation: A Practical Guide to Leading Organizational Change and Renewal.* Boston: Harvard Business School Press, 1997.

Van Maanen, John, and Andre Laurent. "The Flow of Culture: Some Notes on Globalization and the Multinational Corporation." In *Organizational Theory and the Multinational Corporation*, ed. S. Ghoshal and D. E. Westney. New York: St. Martin's Press, 1991.

Varner, Iris I., and Linda Beamer. *Intercultural Communications: The Global Workplace.* Chicago: Irwin, 1995.

Ward, Colleen, Stephen Bochner, and Adrian Furnham. *The Psychology of Culture Shock.* 2d ed. Philadelphia: Routledge, 2001.

Weidenbaum, Murray. "The Chinese Family Business Enterprise." *California Management Review* (summer 1996): 141–56.

Wick, Calhoun W., and Lu Stanton Leon. *The Learning Edge: How Smart Managers and Smart Companies Stay Ahead.* New York: McGraw-Hill, 1993.

Wild, John J., Kenneth L. Wild, and Jerry C. Y. Han. *International Business: An Integrated Approach.* Upper Saddle River, NJ: Prentice Hall, 2000.

Witham, Lynn. *Malaysia: A Foreigners' Guide.* Waterbury Center, VT: Hornbill Books, 1988.

Yip, George S. *Total Global Strategy II.* Upper Saddle River, NJ: Prentice Hall, 2003.

Videos

Globally Speaking: Skills and Strategies for Working with Asia. 6 vols. Prod. Shelley Lieberman, Aperian Global, San Francisco, 1997.

1. *Face-to-Face*
2. *Communicating Across Technology*
3. *Team Formation*
4. *Team Meetings*
5. *Team Systems*
6. *Transforming Leadership*

Managing in China. 6 parts. Prod. Gina Levy, Aperian Global, San Francisco, 1997.

1. *Localizing Leadership*
2. *Performance Management and Compensation*
3. *Recruiting & Retaining Employees*
4. *Recruiting & Retaining Senior Management*
5. *Strategies for Training*
6. *Technology Transfer*

Index